LEADERS OF RELIGION

General Editor
Reverend Professor C. W. Dugmore D.D.

John William Colenso

BISHOP OF NATAL

1864.

FROM A PHOTOGRAPH BY J. E. MAYALL.

JOHN WILLIAM COLENSO

BISHOP OF NATAL

by

PETER HINCHLIFF D.D.

Professor of Ecclesiastical History
Rhodes University, Grahamstown, South Africa

NELSON

THOMAS NELSON AND SONS LTD

36 Park Street London W1
Parkside Edinburgh 9
10 Warehouse Road Apapa Lagos
P.O. Box 25012 Nairobi

THOMAS NELSON (AUSTRALIA) LTD
117 Latrobe Street Melbourne C1

THOMAS NELSON AND SONS (AFRICA) (Pty) LTD
P.O. Box 9881 Johannesburg

THOMAS NELSON AND SONS (CANADA) LTD
81 Curlew Drive Don Mills Ontario

THOMAS NELSON AND SONS
Copewood and Davis Streets Camden 3, N.J.

SOCIÉTÉ FRANÇAISE D'ÉDITIONS NELSON
97 rue Monge Paris 5

———

First Published 1964

Printed in Great Britain by
Thomas Nelson (Printers) Ltd, London and Edinburgh

FOR
ROBERT COLLIER
WHO STARTED
IT ALL

Contents

Contents

Author's Note

Colenso may be considered as important in Church History in two ways: as one of the protagonists in the constitutional struggle which took place in South Africa; or as representative of 'liberal' Anglican theology in the mid-nineteenth century. It is with the second of these two themes that I have been chiefly concerned. The South African part of the story is, for the most part, dealt with only in outline. Further detail on the constitutional issue can be found in my *Anglican Church in South Africa,* which contains a full bibliography on Colenso.

Acknowledgments

I wish to acknowledge my indebtedness to the Most Reverend the Lord Archbishop of Cape Town for permission to make use of the archives at Bishopscourt; the staff of the libraries and archives which I have used, and particularly Miss Killie Campbell of the Campbell Library in Durban; the authors and publishers of the works from which I have quoted. I should also like to thank all those who have helped me to obtain information which would not otherwise have been available to me—Canon Broomfield, Professor F. E. Vokes, the Lord Bishop of Southwell, the Reverend C. Linnell, Mr W. G. Winckler, Mr J. R. de S. Honey, Miss M. B. Armstrong, Dr C. F. Goodfellow and, most particularly, the Reverend F. P. Law, by whose kindness I was allowed to examine the minutes of the Depwade Clerical Society. My thanks are also due to Dr E. W. Kemp and Professor C. W. Dugmore who both gave me much helpful advice, and Mrs M. Hoyle who typed the manuscript and reduced its chaos to order.

CHAPTER I

The Background

THE pattern of Colenso's life is a little unusual. The period of his greatest fame does not come towards the end of his life, but in the middle of it. The great climax, when he was condemned for heresy and the echoes of that condemnation made his name a household word, came when he was fifty—and Colenso was some eight thousand miles away from the place where the trial was held. Thereafter he began to sink into obscurity. His concerns became more local. Circumstances compelled him to confine himself to a small and remote colony. For one brief moment he reappeared on the English scene towards the end of his life and then he went back to live out his last ten years in Natal. If a graph of his life were to be drawn, in terms of his importance for English Church history, it would rise in a long slow curve for the first forty years, then begin to climb more steeply as his various theological and biblical writings became known, coming to a sharp point at his conviction for heresy, and then decline slowly through the long controversy about Church and State relations, flattening out at the last fifteen years as he became buried in Natal. The chapters of this book reflect such an imaginary graph. The first and the last of them each cover a period of Colenso's life greater than all the rest put together.

In these days when Colenso's story is dealt with at all, and there has recently been something of a revival of interest in the bishop and his doings,[1] it is usually misrepresented in one of three ways. It is portrayed as a personal struggle between Colenso and Bishop Robert Gray of Cape Town, or as a clash between catholic and protestant parties within the Anglican Church in South Africa, or as a witch-hunt directed against an early Old Testament critic who happened, by chance, to be a missionary. Each one of these conventional pictures is very misleading. Colenso was not an Evan-

[1] See W. Rees, *Colenso Letters from Natal*, 1958; A. O. J. Cockshut, *Anglican Attitudes*, 1959; P. O. G. White, 'The Colenso Controversy', *Theology*, LXV, pp. 402 ff; and P. Hinchliff, 'John William Colenso: A Fresh Appraisal', *Journal of Ecclesiastical History*, XIII, pp. 203 ff

gelical, but a member of the old 'Low' or 'Broad' Church tradition.
He was not a great Old Testament scholar, nor a profound theologian, but he was much influenced by F. D. Maurice in England
and by the early liberal protestant biblical scholars on the Continent. He cannot be regarded as a great figure in the history of
English theology, if original thought, the founding of a new
'school', or massive scholarship, are to be the criteria. Colenso was
not an initiator so much as a mirror. He regarded himself as an
'ordinary', a 'common sense' man—almost a 'man in the street'.
He was deeply affected by current ideas and events. It was his
ambition to translate these into terms which the 'ordinary' man
could understand and accept. It was his purpose to make modern
scientific learning a help rather than a stumbling-block to the
educated layman who desired to be a Christian. If he made no
great original contribution to theology this was partly because he
desired rather to reflect the ideas of others as he understood them.
His life consists largely of his reaction, favourable or unfavourable,
to the ideas and movements of the Church of his time, and it is
therefore absolutely essential to see him first and foremost against
the setting of early nineteenth-century Church history.

Colenso was born in January 1814. This was the year in which
Napoleon was sent into exile in Elba. The British government,
having twice occupied the Cape of Good Hope in the course of
the wars with France, kept possession of the colony when hostili-
ties ceased. Two bills to grant relief to Roman Catholics in England
had just been narrowly defeated in Parliament, but the Unitarian
Relief Act had been passed. The first bishop for India was consecrated, in spite of bitter opposition. Missions were a subject for
violent debate, and a vigorous controversy over the policy of the
British and Foreign Bible Society had only just died down. Social
and political disturbances were to be characteristic of the half-
century following the Napoleonic war: the Church also, it was
clear, was about to pass through a period of bitter quarrel and
debate.

When the nineteenth century opened the Church of England
found its establishment attacked on every side. The middle classes,
who were very largely Dissenters in religion, pressed hard for the
removal of religious tests and barriers which kept them from certain political offices and from the universities. The Toleration Act
of the reign of William and Mary had given them a certain status.
Annual indemnity acts from 1727 onwards gave them some further

relief, but only if they were willing to conform occasionally to the rites and ceremonies of the Established Church. They were, therefore, conscious of being second-class citizens, required to compromise with their own conscience if they were ever to hold office in the state. But this does not mean that they were entirely without a voice in political affairs or powerless to make their wishes known and even obeyed. A man like William Wilberforce represented an organised body of opinion, dissenting as well as Anglican, which was capable of acting as an effective political pressure group. The Evangelicals within the Church were associated with Dissenters in bodies like the London Missionary Society and the British and Foreign Bible Society. The Baptist, Presbyterian and Congregational churches in the London area elected deputies each year who in turn elected a committee to act as spokesmen for Dissenters, to see that such political rights as Dissenters possessed were defended by the courts, and to ensure that members of Parliament were made aware of dissenting opinion when religious crises arose. Organised Dissent compelled even the Tories to pass the Toleration Act of 1812 which gave the Dissenters more freedom in religious affairs, and a rising tide of expressed opinion at last forced Parliament to repeal the Test and Corporation Acts in 1828. John Wilks,[1] who was Radical member of Parliament for Boston from 1830, was also secretary of the 'Protestant Society' which he had founded in 1811; and the fact that he was the representative of organised dissenting opinion made him a powerful parliamentary figure. It ought to have been obvious that such a state of affairs could not continue for long. A large body of well-to-do, well-organised Dissenters could not be allowed *some* right to express their opinions without their inevitably demanding full political privileges.

In all this the Established Church was inevitably thrown on to the defensive. Some historians represent the events as the struggle of the privileged to maintain their privileges;[2] some, as the result of unwise zeal on the part of the Church's supporters in Parliament, anxious only for the mission of the Church.[3] Quite clearly, though, the French Revolution had made the dissenting, liberal, group unpopular and rallied mob support round 'Church and King'. Once the Napoleonic wars were over and some of the fever had died away the Church of England, or at least the Tory and

---

[1] Not to be confused with the more famous Radical, John Wilkes
[2] R. Cowherd, *The Politics of English Religious Dissent*, 1959, pp. 22ff
[3] E. W. Watson, *The Church of England*, 3rd ed., 1961, p. 144

High-Church party, felt that the Establishment was threatened by the rising power of Whigs and Dissenters alike. The repeal of the Test Acts and the Reform Bill were two aspects of the same process.

It has been recently very clearly shown[1] how the meaning of 'establish' changed between the reformation and the nineteenth century. The Elizabethan settlement established the Church of England in the sense that it sought to impose a single authority and a uniform practice upon the Church. It may be doubted whether Elizabeth ever achieved any considerable uniformity even in externals. The bewildering succession of liturgical changes between 1548 and 1559—six in ten years—must have meant that a great many people continued to use a prayer book already long out of date. Nevertheless, uniformity, or at least conformity, was the keynote of Elizabeth's 'establishment'. At the Restoration it proved no longer possible to equate establishment, conformity, and comprehension. Opinions had hardened. Laudian bishops, although they had inherited Laud's tradition of tolerance,[2] could no longer subscribe to the same prayer book as Puritan divines. Dissent in England really begins when Puritan clergy were forced to leave their livings rather than subscribe to the new settlement. Restrictions were imposed upon Dissent, whether Roman Catholic or Puritan, perhaps to make them return to the Established Church, perhaps to prevent any possibility of a recurrence of the Civil War.

When dissenters supported the Whig revolution of 1688 new efforts were made to return to a policy of establishment by comprehension and conformity, but this was found to be impossible. Instead, some recognition of dissenting clergy and churches was provided for by the Toleration Act. But legal recognition of dissenting bodies meant that 'establishment' could no longer mean 'the only religion recognised by law'. Establishment came to mean the 'official or the public or the privileged religion', as opposed to the religion of private persons—the religion of the State. From this it was an easy step to argue that the Church was not so much recognised by the State, but a creation of the State owing its existence to State favour. After 1829 when Roman Catholics had been emancipated, too, it was no longer possible for the Church

---

[1] O. J. Brose, *Church and Parliament*, 1959, pp. 11ff

[2] W. Haller, *The Rise of Puritanism* (Harper Torchbooks reprint); cf pp. 233ff & 242f

to be viewed as the religious aspect of the nation, for the nation now consisted, in its public affairs, of Dissenters and Roman Catholics as well as of Anglicans.

Attacks upon the privileges of the Established Church continued with unabated vigour after 1829—and the Church's opponents completely lost sight of the disadvantages which went with the privileges of establishment. Since the silencing of Convocation in 1717 the Church had been in no position to speak with a single voice in anything like the effective manner of the dissenting deputies. So soon as non-Anglicans became members of Parliament even the fiction that Parliament was the champion of the Church could no longer be maintained. The Reform Bill of 1832 brought the crisis to a head. Secular critics of the Church, like John Stuart Mill, pointed to the vast sums of money which they believed to be wasted on Church endowment. Tory bishops, voting against reform, found that mob violence could be directed against *them* as easily as it had been against Unitarian ministers in the first years of the war against revolutionary France. Bishop Robert Gray of Bristol had his palace burnt by the mob and obstinately persisted in attending services in his cathedral even when his attendants warned him that his life might be threatened. The bishop's son, also called Robert Gray, was doing the grand tour of Europe at the time, but he always believed that his father had been something of a confessor, one who suffered for the faith and to maintain the Church. Eighteen years later the younger Robert Gray became a bishop himself and went off to Cape Town to establish an Anglican Church in South Africa.

By the time the see of Cape Town was created in 1848 the Church of England had confounded the expectations of those critics who had foreseen its imminent dissolution. Bishop Blomfield and the Ecclesiastical Commission had done much to set the Church's house in order. Machinery had been created whereby new parishes could be made in industrial areas by a method less cumbersome than that which had been used since the days of Henry VIII.[1] Church finances and endowments were overhauled and the money more evenly and 'usefully' distributed than before. There was no sign of the Establishment's being brought to an end, but nothing had been done to resolve or define the uneasy relationship between the Church and the State. The Church was still 'privileged' and still expected to obey a Parliament whose

[1] W. Macmorran, *Handbook for Churchwardens,* 22nd ed., 1957, pp. 6ff

members need no longer be members of the Church. Convocation was not allowed to legislate for the Church. The Crown appointed bishops and other dignitaries. But the Church was not expected to control the actions of the State in any way. Establishment might guarantee that England remained officially a Christian country, but whether a handful of bishops in the House of Lords could, or would want to, ensure that England *behaved* like a Christian country, was a very different matter. This 'inequality' in the Church and State relationship was to become a great burden on the conscience of some churchmen. 'The reciprocity', the younger Gray later said, 'is all on one side'.[1]

A further modification of the nexus of establishment which was to cause a great deal of controversy in the nineteenth century, to prove a further 'burden' on the consciences of churchmen, and to be a great boon to Colenso himself, was the abolition of the Court of Delegates in 1832. The Privy Council became the final court of appeal in ecclesiastical causes.[2] In 1833 the Judicial Committee of the Privy Council took over this jurisdiction. Sir Robert Phillimore, the great canon lawyer, protested against this transfer, not because it was substituting a secular for an ecclesiastical court, but because it was substituting a court of amateurs for a court of experts. There was nothing to guarantee that any single member of the Judicial Committee would have any knowledge of the principles of canon law or of formal theology. Much later, and just before Colenso's own case became a controversial issue, the Gorham judgment made it plain that the Judicial Committee would use the principles of common law, and not canon law, to arrive at its decisions.

At this particular stage in the history of the Church of England it was particularly tragic that there was no ecclesiastical court which could command the respect and obedience of every churchman, for there were within the Church distinct schools of thought whose opinions differed so radically in so many important respects that sooner or later there was bound to be open conflict. When such conflict finally came to a head, it was felt that some public and official declaration must be made as to what the Church of England did or did not believe. Since Convocation had been muzzled in the eighteenth century, because it had presumed to

---

[1] C. N. Gray, *Life of Robert Gray*, 1876, I, p. 125
[2] See E. W. Kemp, *Introduction to Canon Law in the Church of England*, 1957, p. 74.

exercise this very function, there was no body other than the ecclesiastical courts to pronounce on the matter.

Within the Church the dominant party, in the sense that it commanded the largest number of positions of dignity, was the High Church group, closely linked with the Tories, and benefiting from the enthusiastic wave of 'Church and King' sentiment produced by the Revolutionary and Napoleonic Wars. The Evangelicals were declining somewhat from their first vigour. They had originated in the previous century, in the same period and with many of the same principles as the Methodists. Evangelicals within the Church of England were usually Calvinist in sympathy and had originally stood primarily for a revival in real personal religion, the belief in justification by faith, and a high standard of clerical life, morals and education. Not many of them held high office in the Church, but the 'Simeon Trust' owned the gift of a number of livings and was able to ensure that Evangelicals controlled these parishes. Evangelicals were also influential in missionary, philanthropic, and humanitarian societies[1] and through their connection with the Dissenters.

The Dissenters themselves fell into two groups. Firstly there were the 'Old Dissenters' or 'Three Denominations'—Presbyterian, Baptist and Congregationalist. These were solidly middleclass. The Presbyterians in particular had been much affected by Unitarianism in the eighteenth and early nineteenth centuries. And these denominations were now largely concerned, as we have seen, with the struggle for the extension of the franchise. Secondly, quite distinct from them was the Methodist group of dissenters, the descendants of the movements started by Wesley and Whitefield, and the off-shoots of those movements. The Methodists were the largest group of Dissenters in England. On the whole they were conservative in temper and represented a lower class than the Old Dissenters. Like the Tory bishops they tended to oppose the Reform Bill.

Within the Church, in addition to the High Church and Evangelical groups, there was a third principal 'party', whose ancestry was rather more complicated. In the seventeenth century a group of scholars, known as the Cambridge Platonists, sought to restate the Christian Faith, through an Idealist philosophy, in such a way as to make the faith both intellectually defensible and at the same time spiritually satisfying. They aimed at a Christianity which

---

[1] See *infra*, pp. 21ff.

would both use man's reason and inspire him to a life of virtue. From them developed the Latitudinarians of the eighteenth century, the 'Low Church' party, Whig in sympathies. Less imaginative than the Cambridge Platonists, less concerned with the spiritual, the Latitudinarians set a high value on a religion which could be discovered and proved by reason. They tended to deprecate revelation, but emphasised ethics.

But Samuel Taylor Coleridge was just as much a product of Cambridge Platonist influence. There was a pantheistic and Unitarian phase in his thinking. He has been called 'the Father of the Broad Church Movement'. Yet he stood outside the normal Latitudinarian pattern, since he rejected any attempt to prove the truth of Christianity, reacting against both rationalism and formalism. Coleridge sought a religion of the heart, with a strong emphasis upon morality. 'Liberals' of the mid-nineteenth century were therefore a group containing a wide variety of opinions. Some were like the old Latitudinarians, preaching a religion of common sense and ethics. Some were like Maurice, in whom the influence of Coleridge was strong. Some sought to reinterpret Christianity in terms of the new intellectual climate. Hampden and Maurice and Arnold and Stanley were all regarded as 'liberals', yet it is sometimes extremely difficult to find common ground between any two of them.

And in the meantime the Oxford Movement had begun to make itself felt. If Newman was right in dating the beginning of the Oxford Movement from Keble's famous sermon on national apostasy, then the Movement started as a counter-attack on those who threatened the position of the Established Church. The sermon was provoked by the proposal to suppress some of the Irish bishoprics. Keble interpreted the proposal as a deliberate attempt on the part of the nation to disown or deny 'that, as a Christian nation, she is also part of Christ's Church, and bound, in all her legislation and policy, by the fundamental rules of the Church'.[1] Keble believed that 'toleration' is merely another word for 'indifference'; and that a willingness to grant toleration was an alarming omen of the nation's apostasy.

One of the greatest problems in the history of the Oxford Movement is the fact that neither of the conventional dates for the beginning of the Movement seems to have any direct connection with the later history of Newman, Keble and Pusey and the ideas

[1] J. Keble, *Sermons Academical and Occasional*, No. 6

for which they stood. The famous meeting at Hadleigh Rectory included neither Newman nor Keble. Froude belonged to the same world as the Oriel common room men, but Perceval, Palmer and Rose were of a rather different stamp, never quite at home with later developments in the Movement.

It may be, as has been lately suggested,[1] that the assize sermon was only the beginning of the Movement *in Newman's mind*. It may be that the Hadleigh group was formed, 'not by [Newman's] means, but in God's providence for him'.[2] But surely the real link between Hadleigh, the assize sermon, and the tracts is the old High Church party, stronger, more firmly rooted in country rectories than has often been supposed? The meeting at Hadleigh was first intended to lead to the formation of an Association of Friends of the Church against the attacks of secularists, Roman Catholics and Dissenters. *Afterwards* Keble and Newman introduced an emphasis on the sacraments and the apostolic succession.[3] The assize sermon was concerned simply with the typical High Church platform—defence of the Establishment against attacks from without—though it is also true that the sermon does stress the nature of the Church as a divine institution. The addresses to the archbishop of Canterbury in 1834 took as their theme loyalty to the established Church.

When Newman's *Tracts for the Times* began to appear in 1833 they again struck the kind of note likely to appeal to old-fashioned High Churchmen. The first tract is unemotional, unexciting, aimed at preserving the Church of England, by raising the tone of its clergy, against attacks from those who would disestablish it or throw its gates open to every loose form of Christianity. The appeal of the early tracts would be largely to the very people whom the leading Tractarians would later describe as 'high and dry'.

In 1834 and 1835 there was renewed agitation to abolish subscription to the XXXIX Articles in the universities. A bill to make it possible for Dissenters to take degrees was passed by the Commons, but defeated in the Lords in 1834. It was proposed that a general declaration should be substituted for a formal subscription to the Articles, and this was not acceptable to Tractarians at this stage (Tract XC had not yet been written). They

---

[1] O. Chadwick, *The Mind of the Oxford Movement*, 1960, p. 34
[2] Warre Cornish, *History of the English Church in the Nineteenth Century*, 1910, I, p. 230
[3] *Ibid.*, p. 233

viewed such moves as but another attack on the established religion. The younger Robert Gray was not a Tractarian. He had gone down from Oxford in 1831, before the Oriel College group began to influence their wide circle of young men. By 1835 he was a parish priest in a country living in the diocese of Durham. But he wrote to Keble, whom he scarcely knew:

> I do not require any arguments to convince me of the inexpediency of abolishing subscription to the XXXIX articles at matriculation, by the publication of the proposed declarations, and of the manifest injury to established religion which must attend such a measure.[1]

There must have been many men like Gray, not very old nor very dry (Gray was seventeen years younger than Keble), to whom the views of the Tracts made an obvious appeal. They 'did not require any arguments' in order to appreciate 'the manifest injury to established religion'.[2] Later on it was rather different. Some, like the Tractarian leaders themselves, moved away from a blind support of Establishment and began to think, like Gladstone, for instance, that it was better to have the true faith without the State connection than to retain the establishment and lose the faith.[3] As the Oxford Movement drifted towards the crisis of 1845, of Newman's secession and the cloud of suspicion that gathered around the Tractarians, some of the support in the country vicarages melted away. Many men preferred the old patterns to the dangers of new experiment. The old alliance of Tractarian and High Churchman broke down, or was at least altered out of all recognition.

There is nothing particularly new in suggesting that the Tractarian tendency to be condescending about old-fashioned High Churchmen was the product of events after 1840. Professor Sykes has shown how the Tractarians, like the Methodists, minimised what they owed to earlier generations and so came to label the eighteenth century as the 'dead period'.[4] The Tractarian leaders

---

[1] Keble College, Oxford; Keble Papers (91), Robert Gray to John Keble, 14 April 1835

[2] Colenso was twenty in 1834, in his first year at Cambridge. There seems to be no surviving comment from him on the principle of subscription from this period.

[3] D. C. Lathbury, *William Ewart Gladstone: Correspondence on Church and Religion*, 1910, I, p. 127

[4] N. Sykes, *Church and State in England in the XVIIIth Century*, 1934; see especially pp. 3ff.

began by adopting what was simply the traditional High Church position. They were naturally, then, supported by all the hundreds of clergymen already established in country vicarages all over England who had grown up in that tradition. It was precisely the difference between Newman on the one hand and Keble and Pusey on the other, that they had been part and parcel of that tradition while he had not. But Tractarian theology developed. The press of events made it imperative for them to alter some of their attitudes. They were labelled as Romanists and Ritualists. And they, in turn, began to speak of the 'high and dry'.

The principal events of the story of the Movement are, of course, well known. Even before the addresses to the archbishop had been finally dispatched, Newman had begun to issue his tracts. Pusey was drawn into the Movement, giving it the weight of his scholarship and his assured position. Pusey was humourless and pedestrian, compared with Newman, but he gave the movement a solidity, a stability that the emotional Newman could never give it. And very soon the 'Tractarians' were engaged in much more solid work than the production of tracts. Translations of the Fathers began to appear. By the late 1830s, however, a great many people had begun to suspect that the movement was a Romeward one. When one of the tracts advocated reserve in communicating religious knowledge men began to feel that Tractarians might be crypto-papists, dribbling out their teaching as they felt their public were able to bear it, but all the time working to persuade men to accept the full Roman position.

It was, indeed, true that some of the younger adherents of the Movement, particularly some of Newman's young friends, were already inclined to look on the Church of Rome as, at least in some respects, the ideal Church. In 1836 Dr Hampden was appointed Regius Professor at Oxford. Tractarians and Evangelicals joined in opposing the appointment on the ground that Hampden was too 'liberal', but very soon after this date Evangelicals became so suspicious of the Romish tendencies of the Movement that there could be no further hope of alliance between the two. Not until the publication of *Essays & Reviews* in 1860 was there anything approaching a renewal of the anti-liberal alliance. By 1838 it was already clear to some that the Movement was splitting into a group headed but not led by Newman and a group led by Keble and Pusey.[1] In the same year the plan to erect a monument to the

[1] Warre Cornish, *op. cit.*, I, p. 249

Reformers, Cranmer, Latimer and Ridley, in Oxford was used as a means of rallying Evangelical opposition to the Tractarians. And at about the same time Keble and Newman published Hurrell Froude's *Remains*, the intimate reflections of an early associate of the Movement. Unfortunately the book contained unfavourable comparisons of the Church of England with the Roman Church, and neither Keble nor Newman would deny an old friendship by specifically dissociating themselves from the ideas expressed in the *Remains*.

In 1841 the proposal that the English and Prussian (Lutheran) Churches should combine to provide a bishop for Jerusalem brought most Tractarians out in violent opposition to any such tampering with the 'apostolic succession'. Pusey seems at first to have favoured the scheme, but to Newman it was one of the early indications that the Church of England could not really claim to be 'catholic'. In the same year as the foundation of the Jerusalem bishopric he wrote Tract XC, an attempt to reconcile the XXXIX Articles with post-Tridentine Roman doctrine. It was a desperate attempt to prove the 'catholicity' of the Church of England and so is itself proof of the fact that Newman was beginning to accept Rome as the standard of catholicity. There was a storm of protest, in Oxford and in the country in general. Golightly, a former friend of Newman's, acted as chief whip to the opposition.[1] Newman was censured by the Hebdomadal Council of the university. The bishop of Oxford asked that publication of the Tracts be stopped and several members of the movement met with petty persecution within the university. Pusey himself was suspended from preaching within the university on the ground that he held and expounded heretical doctrines of the Eucharist.

Newman began to lose heart. He withdrew from Oxford to live in semi-monastic seclusion at Littlemore. In 1845 the Convocation of the university stripped W. G. Ward of his university degrees for expressing views like those of Tract XC and would have censured the Tract itself if the proctors had not vetoed the motion. Ward became a Roman Catholic. Others amongst Newman's younger and more radical followers did the same, and Newman himself, always particularly susceptible to the emotional pressure of his friendships, eventually submitted later in the same year. He felt himself disowned and condemned by his Church and university and he found that the logic of his arguments would not allow

[1] R. W. Greaves in *Journal of Ecclesiastical History*, IX, No. 2, pp. 209ff

him to remain in the position outlined in Tract XC. For a time it seemed as though the whole Movement must end. If Newman had really been the personal creator and leader of the 'Puseyite' party, as he is sometimes made out to be, that must have happened. But Pusey and Keble never wavered in their allegiance both to the Church of England and to the catholic revival.

In the meantime, though, Tractarians were desperately un-popular. Bishop Blomfield of London was compelled to withdraw the regulations issued for his diocese requiring very moderate and modest 'ritual'—like the wearing of the surplice. Bishop Stanley of Norwich denounced the doctrine of the apostolic succession in a charge to his diocese. Colenso had just been appointed rector of a parish in the diocese of Norwich and he found Stanley a bishop after his own heart.[1] Hampden was appointed bishop of Hereford. It looked as though the Tractarians were lost for good. And finally in 1850 the papacy began to revive a hierarchy for England, appointing Wiseman as archbishop of Westminster. The 'papal aggression' roused all sorts of hysterical emotions and, amongst other things, made life even more difficult for Tractarians who were now regarded as the papacy's fifth column. By the middle of the century the Oxford Movement was at its lowest ebb, dis-credited, suspect, and shaken by Newman's defection.

The appointment of Hampden to Hereford seemed a disaster to Tractarians because they had all along regarded liberalism as the great enemy—liberalism which Newman later defined as treating one religion as as good as another.[2] One of the interesting by-ways of the Tractarian story is Pusey's contact with the new German biblical scholarship, and his brush with Hugh James Rose, hitherto regarded as the English expert on German theology.[3]

Pusey had spent some time in Germany; he had studied under Eichhorn, the Old Testament scholar, whose lecture on Balaam's ass was a recognised annual exercise in satire, and who had arrived at the conclusion that the 'Books of Moses' could not all have been written by one person. He also attended the lectures of Freytag, the orientalist. A fellow-pupil of his was Heinrich Ewald whose *History of Israel* was to be one of the great landmarks of future biblical criticism. It would seem that Pusey was appalled by the 'rationalism' he found rampant in Germany. 'Neither the strict

[1] W. Rees, *Colenso Letters from Natal*, 1958, p. 32
[2] W. Ward, *Life of John Henry Cardinal Newman*, 1912, II, p. 460
[3] See H. P. Liddon, *Life of Edward Bouverie Pusey*, ch. VIII

traditional school of Luther, nor the Pietists . . . had been able to stand against unbelief'.[1] Pusey believed that the English Church was as ill-equipped to combat the new scepticism as German Lutheranism had been and hoped that some such revival as that of Schleiermacher might be set on foot in England before it was too late. Rose, on the other hand, was convinced that the weakness of Lutheranism lay in the absence of episcopacy and a proper church order and discipline. When Pusey published his *Historical Enquiry into the Probable Causes of the Rationalist Character lately predominant in the Theology of Germany* in 1828, Rose condemned it as too sympathetic to the German critics and Newman said it was 'sadly deformed with Germanisms'.[2] In fact Pusey was in no way inclined to accept the conclusions of Eichhorn, though he was perhaps willing to turn a blind eye toward Schleiermacher's unorthodoxy, but he was determined to amass such learning in the field of Old Testament studies as to be able to refute the 'rationalist' position. Indeed as he became older, Pusey became less and less willing to entertain critical opinions.

But Pusey could not prevent 'higher criticism' from doing its work. His fear that the English Church would not be equipped to meet it was a much more valid attitude than his obstinate belief that yet more learning could completely defeat it. The collapse of fundamentalism was really inherent in the unrecognised tension of the post-Reformation approach to the Scriptures. The reformers, by and large, combined an insistence on the sole authority of the Bible, individually interpreted, with a belief that of the four traditional modes of interpretation (the literal, the allegorical, the moral and the anagogical) only the literal was proper to an understanding of the Scriptures. From this it was a natural and logical course of events which led to Hooker's assertion that reason, in asking what is God's will, should seek not proof texts but the sum total of revelation. Hobbes's argument for a critical study of the Old Testament and Locke's view that it is reason which ought to dictate how much of the supernatural one may accept in interpreting the Scriptures develop quite naturally from Hooker.

In Germany, however, critical and rationalist theology had gone much further than in England. J. G. Eichhorn of Göttingen arrived at the conclusion, in 1783, that there were at least two written sources behind the Pentateuch, which could not therefore

[1] *Ibid.*, I, p. 175
[2] *The Letters & Correspondence of J. H. Newman*, I, p. 186

be the sole work of Moses himself. Eichhorn's analysis, based on the fact that two different names for God, Jahweh and Elohim, are used in the 'Books of Moses' had been anticipated by Jean Astruc thirty years earlier, but Eichhorn's conclusions seem to have been independently arrived at.[1] In 1806 Wilhelm de Wette, soon to be professor at Heidelberg, worked out a theory that Deuteronomy was the law book discovered in the Temple in Josiah's reign[2]—reaching a conclusion already advanced by Jerome in the fifth century! In 1853 Hupfeld made the now generally accepted distinction between the two sources of the Pentateuch which use the name 'Elohim'—now called 'P' & 'E'. Hupfeld argued that P was the earliest of the sources, J & E next, and D the latest; although other scholars had already begun to suggest that P was a late source. Ewald produced his *History of Israel* between 1843 and 1852, using critical methods to reconstruct the historical account from the Biblical narrative. Ewald was not a radical critic. He maintained, for instance, that there was a unity of design and of authorship in Genesis, and a similar position was adopted by Friedrich Bleek. Bleek maintained that Genesis had a basically Mosaic core which had subsequently passed through two redactions. Ewald, De Wette and Bleek all adopted this rather conservative approach to criticism, De Wette, in his time, having been regarded by the rationalists as a reactionary and by the bulk of Christian theologians as a radical. It was these scholars with whom Colenso was to have most in common.

In the field of New Testament D. F. Strauss's *Leben Jesu*, published in 1835, seems to have disturbed conservative Christians more than any other work. Otto Pfleiderer, in the introduction to the sixth edition of George Eliot's translation of Strauss, said that though De Wette had treated the birth narratives of the Gospels as myth and explained away some of the miracles, Strauss's work was so uncompromising as to shock even the milder rationalists.

The novelty in the work of Strauss was not the application of the principle of 'myth' to Biblical narratives; others had already made use of it in the case of the Old Testament and to some extent in the case of the New Testament; the originality lay in the uncompromising thoroughness with which the principle was applied to

---

[1] See A. S. Peake, *Recent Developments in Old Testament Criticism*, lecture delivered at Manchester University, 1928; and R. H. Pfeiffer, *Introduction to the Old Testament*, 1941, pp. 47ff.

[2] 2 Kings, 22:8

every section of the gospel story; the originality lay in the merci-
less acumen and clearness with which the discrepancies between
the gospels and the difficulties presented to the critical understanding by their narratives were laid bare, and with which all
the subterfuges of supernaturalist apologists, as well as the forced
and artificial interpretations of semi-critical Rationalists, were ex-
posed, thereby cutting off all ways of escape from the final
consequences of criticism.[1]

The position in Germany, then, was that by the middle of the
nineteenth century there was a large number of more conservative
critics who would apply the full method of the rationalists to a
study of the Old Testament but would tend to be far more chary
of applying the same methods in full when dealing with the New
Testament. They might question and explain away some of the
elements of the miraculous in the gospels, but they remained conservative. Some, like Bleek, continued to affirm the traditional
authorship of the Fourth Gospel. But these were regarded by men
like Strauss as lacking the courage of their convictions.

The position in England was very different. It is true that in the
seventeenth century men like Sir Thomas Browne combined a
deep and sincere religion with an attitude to the Bible which was
not literalist. It is true that the eighteenth century saw an attack
on the miraculous element in the gospels by the Deists. Thomas
Woolston attempted to show that the miracles were not to be
taken literally, but were to be treated as parables. But, even
amongst theologians, this was regarded as a dangerous and
disastrous attitude.

Biblical criticism was deprecated. Marsh's translation of
Michaelis' *Introduction to the New Testament* 1793, his own book
on the *Origin & Composition of the first three Canonical Gospels*
1801, and Thirlwall's translation of Schleiermacher's *Essay on St.
Luke's Gospel* 1825 were received with a good deal of suspicion.
. . . Milman's *History of the Jews* 1829 was thought secular, because he offered human, psychological explanations of the actions
of Bible characters, and applied what might be called mildly
critical and rationalising methods to the narrative.[2]

Much more typical of the kind of Biblical scholarship admired
by English orthodoxy was Bengel's *Gnomon of the New Testament*,

[1] D. F. Strauss, *Life of Jesus* (translated from 4th German ed.), p. xii
[2] S. C. Carpenter, *Church & People, 1789-1889* (Seraph Book reprint, 1959),
p. 21

first published in 1742, used a great deal by Wesley, and brought
out in an English edition in 1858. Bengel's exegesis includes
textual criticism, but hardly acknowledges 'higher' criticism at all.
He calculated the date of Creation as 3940 B.C., and reckoned the
period between man's creation and the fall as lasting from autumn
to the tenth day of the seventh month (i.e. the day kept by the
Jews as the Day of Atonement).[1] His handling of New Testament
material may best be illustrated by an actual quotation.

On Mark 12:29, Bengel's comment is:

πρώτη πασῶν ἐντολη—This is a reading midway between extremes,
and answers to ver. 28. The editions read πρώτη πασῶν των ἐντολων
and so the Syr. Vers. as also Greek MSS: however, for πασῶν, Al.
Byz. Gehl Mosc. Wo 1, 2, and many others, have πάντων, though
some of them retain πασῶν at ver. 28. παντῶν has originated by
alliteration to πρωτή and ἐντολή . . .

There follows a good deal more textual criticism, but no consideration at all of the relationship of this passage in Mark with
Matthew 22 and Luke 10. On Mark 8:25 Bengel makes the
delightful comment:

Boys are also capable of being subjects of demoniacal possession,
ch. ix, 21, 24: as also heathens.

Biblical criticism was not the only liberal force with which
conservative orthodoxy had to reckon. New scientific methods
and discoveries were presenting a challenge to the literalist view
of the Scriptures. Lyell's *Principles of Geology* was published in
1830, Darwin's *Origin of Species* in 1859. It was obvious that an
acceptance of the new discoveries in natural science could not easily
be combined with a belief in the literal inerrancy of Genesis. Moreover there was something of a spirit of 'liberalism' invading
theology itself. The case of F. D. Maurice illustrates very well
both the impact of new ideas and the horrified reaction they provoked. Maurice is, moreover, of particular importance in Colenso's
story, for his theology was probably the strongest single factor in
the development of the bishop's ideas.

Maurice was born in 1805 and was therefore nine years older
than Colenso. His father was a Unitarian minister and a colleague
of Joseph Priestly, the scientist, whose house was burnt by the
mob in 1791 because he was believed to sympathise with the

[1] J. A. Bengel, *Gnomon of the New Testament* (English translation, 1858),
p. xx

principles of the French Revolution.[1] Some of the members of
the family ceased to be Unitarians, including eventually Maurice's
mother, and the household was distressed and disturbed by constant friction over religious matters—while continuing to be a
deeply affectionate and united family. Maurice himself remained
a Unitarian. He was an undergraduate at Trinity College, Cambridge, where he learnt philosophy from Julius Hare, who taught
his pupils to grapple with and understand Plato's thought. Hare
was also considerably influenced by the new German trends in
theology.

Maurice was unable to take a degree at Cambridge because, as
a Unitarian, he was not able to subscribe to the XXXIX Articles,
still a necessary pre-condition for graduation. The young man
then went to London where he became involved in social and
political questions, criticising the prevailing utilitarian philosophy
of Bentham. By 1829 he had gradually come to accept a Trini-
tarian belief and became an Anglican. He now went up to Oxford
to prepare for ordination. He was baptised in 1831 and ordained
in 1834. By this time the *Tracts* were well under way, and the
Oxford Movement was gathering momentum. Newman's conception of the Church as a divine society was not quite Maurice's,
but both agreed in regarding it as more than an organisation
created and approved by the State. Maurice mistrusted the hero-
worship and the party organisation of the Movement.

> If they err and stumble in their sincere endeavours after the
> recovery of old and forgotten truths, if they even are tempted to
> forget that the Church is Catholic while they are in the act of
> pleading for its Catholicity, if they do anything unwillingly to
> hurt that unity which they so earnestly contend for, may their
> oversights be all forgiven, all corrected, and may they daily
> advance more themselves and lead others further in the know-
> ledge of all truth.[2]

In 1835 Maurice was involved in the controversy over subscription to the XXXIX Articles as a requirement in the
universities. He wrote *Subscription no Bondage* in which he made
it clear that he was no Latitudinarian. Theology must have a firm
and stable basis, otherwise one was left not with liberty, but with
anarchy, a watery creed and a rootless faith. The Articles were 'a

---

[1] Cf *supra*, p. 3
[2] F. Maurice, *Life of Frederick Denison Maurice*, 4th ed., 1885, I, pp. 161f

declaration of the terms on which the university proposed to teach its pupils, upon which terms they must agree to learn' and they are 'warnings to [the undergraduate] against hindrances and obstructions which past experience shows that he will encounter . . .'[1] Liberals in the normal sense, Maurice despaired of. He thought Dr Hampden 'utterly unfit for the Divinity Chair'.[2] But his own theology was suspected by almost every Christian group in England. When *The Kingdom of Christ* was published in 1836 the Tractarians disapproved of it because Maurice did not follow Pusey's line on Baptismal Regeneration. Free Churchmen disliked it because Maurice assumed that the Established Church was *the* Church in England and because he emphasised the commission of the priesthood and the reality of the sacraments. Evangelicals and Latitudinarians disapproved of his high view of the Church.

In 1840 Maurice became professor of English Literature at King's College, London. During the next decade he attempted to harness Christian ethics to solve the social problems of England. Economic distress and working class agitation in the 1830s had produced the Chartist movement. William Lovett, founder of the London Working Men's Association, and Francis Place drew up the 'Peoples' Charter' in 1838, asking for universal male suffrage, the secret ballot, and annual parliamentary general elections. Three times the House of Commons rejected petitions from the Chartists. After the third occasion, in 1848, the fiery Irish demagogue O'Connor threatened the possibility of violence. Maurice began to advance his own solution to the problem. With J. M. F. Ludlow and Charles Kingsley he formed the Christian Socialist movement to appeal to the Christian conscience against sweated labour, poor working conditions and other social evils. The rise of the Trades Unions was influenced by his work, but he became intensely unpopular in certain quarters as a result.

His theology also made him increasingly unpopular. In 1853 Maurice's *Theological Essays* were published. In this book he criticised the conventional view of hell and eternal punishment, his platonism leading him to the belief that eternity was perfection not infinitely prolonged time.

> Punishment, I believe, seems to most men less dreadful than death, because they cannot separate it from a punisher, because

---

[1] *Ibid.*, p. 180   [2] *Ibid.*, p. 191

they believe, however faintly, that He who is punishing them is a Father. The thought of His ceasing to punish them, of His letting them alone, of His leaving them to themselves, is the real, the unutterable horror.[1]

His supposedly unorthodox opinion on the endlessness of future punishment led to Maurice's being compelled to resign his chair. From 1854 onwards he was chiefly concerned with the fatherhood of God in its practical aspects, in Christian Socialism, in the founding of Working Men's Colleges. In 1870 he became, for the last two years of his life, professor of Moral Philosophy at Cambridge, but his greatest and most influential work was already done. Amongst those he had influenced most was Colenso.

In the social aspects of his teaching Maurice stands midway between two groups of men. In subsequent generations his Christian Socialism was to influence the Anglo-Catholics as they attacked the slums of the East End of London. Before his time the great exponents of the duty of man towards his neighbour had been the Evangelicals—men like Wilberforce, who fought all his life for the emancipation of slaves until at last Parliament passed the Act in the very year that Wilberforce died. Shaftesbury, who carried on the Evangelical struggle for better working conditions in factories, better treatment of child labour, was a contemporary of Maurice's, but a man with a completely different, much less personal approach. Samuel Taylor Coleridge, a pioneer preacher of social righteousness,[2] influenced Maurice's thought and Maurice is really more like Coleridge, the odd man out, than like either the earlier Evangelical humanitarians or the later Anglo-Catholic socialists.

It was not for England alone that the nineteenth-century Christians sought better social conditions. Exeter Hall was founded in 1831 to provide a central meeting place and a focus for Evangelical interest, Anglican and Dissenting, in missions at home and abroad. 'Exeter Hall' came to stand for the uncomfortable Evangelical conscience, awkward for both Church and State, always insisting that the fatherhood of God implied the brotherhood of men. In particular 'Exeter Hall' was hated in South Africa, where Colenso was to spend most of his working life. Lord Glenelg, Secretary of State for the Colonies in the 1830s, was the son of Charles Grant, one of the original members of the Evangelical

---

[1] F. D. Maurice, *Theological Essays*, ed. E. F. Carpenter, 1957, p. 321
[2] S. C. Carpenter, *op. cit.*, p. 303

and humanitarian Clapham Sect. The London Missionary Society in South Africa was believed to be working hand-in-glove with Glenelg and Exeter Hall to denigrate the white settlers and favour the Hottentots and the African population of the colony. When the Evangelical and humanitarian group had succeeded, in 1807, in obtaining an Act of Parliament abolishing the slave trade, they proceeded to take all the coloured population of the British colonies under their metaphorical wing. A Royal Commission was appointed to investigate conditions in the colonies and a Society for the Protection of Aboriginees was formed, one of the plethora of missionary, humanitarian and philanthropic societies that sprang up in the first half of the nineteenth century.

Missionary societies, to spread the Christian gospel at home and abroad, were extremely popular. The Society for Promoting Christian Knowledge had been founded by Bray in the seventeenth century. The Society for Diffusing Religious Knowledge among the Poor followed fifty years later; and the Society for Propagating the Gospel was also formed as an off-shoot of the S.P.C.K. to undertake more specifically missionary work rather than the dissemination of religious literature. The Religious Tract Society came in 1799, another body concerned with publishing and distribution. It also was a non-denominational body, one of the examples of co-operation between Anglican Evangelicals and Dissenters.[1] Out of the Religious Tract Society there came eventually the British and Foreign Bible Society in 1804. Charles Grant and William Wilberforce were amongst its early supporters, though the original idea seems to have been put forward by Joseph Hughes, secretary of the Religious Tract Society. English bishops encouraged the work, but the committee contained clergymen and laymen of a great many denominations. Within the next decade there was a sharp controversy over the Society's policy. Were Bibles to be placed indiscriminately in the hands of the most uneducated people? Did religious freedom mean the right of every individual to read and interpret the Scriptures as he wished? There were those, notably Marsh—later famous for his 'Trap to catch Calvinists'[2]—who believed that the S.P.C.K. alone ought to have the support of Anglicans. But there were also Churchmen willing to come forward in defence of the Bible Society and it continued to be supported by the Established Church.

[1] R. G. Cowherd, *op. cit.*, pp. 17ff
[2] Cf A. Pollard in *Church Quarterly Review*, CLXIII, No. 345

In 1795 there had been formed a more specifically missionary body, the London Missionary Society—again undenominational, and finding a good deal of Anglican support. After some prodding by Evangelicals—Simeon, Wilberforce, Grant and Venn—the Church Missionary Society, a specifically Anglican body, was formed to take the gospel to India and Africa. The S.P.C.K. and S.P.G. had undertaken some missionary work in America, but the other British colonies were sadly neglected. The C.M.S.[1] was actually formed in 1799. The influence of laymen and Evangelicals on the C.M.S. was much stronger than on the S.P.G. The archbishop of Canterbury has always been president of the latter; a prominent layman has usually filled the same office in the former.

Africa and India were the two fields about which the Evangelicals were most concerned. Henry Martyn, a disciple of Charles Simeon, was one of the first missionaries to go to India. The Chartered Company, which controlled British possessions in India, was never anxious to encourage missionaries. Warren Hastings, the great servant and embodiment of the Company, made it his declared policy to discourage and inhibit missionaries lest the Indians themselves feel that the government was likely to compel conversion to Christianity among Hindus. But men like Wilberforce and Simeon felt it a terrible burden on their conscience that the British influence was not a specifically Christian influence in India. Wilberforce pressed, towards the end of the eighteenth century, for definite provision for missionaries in the India Company's charter, but it was not until 1813 that such clauses were inserted. In the following year a bishopric of Calcutta was established, with oversight of India, and all places between the Cape of Good Hope and Magellan's Straits. In the same year (1814) the C.M.S. sent four official missionaries to India.

Once the see of Calcutta had been established, other colonial dioceses followed. In 1834 bishops were sent to Jamaica and Barbados, and there were soon other sees in India and the Americas. In 1836 the first bishop was consecrated for Australia. Officially and theoretically the bishop of London was responsible for the episcopal oversight of all colonies where there was no bishop. When Blomfield was bishop of London, with his zeal for overhauling ecclesiastical administration and the practical reform of

[1] See E. Stock, *History of the Church Missionary Society*, 3 vols., 1899, especially chs. V-IX; cf R. Lovett, *History of the London Missionary Society*, 1899, chs. I & II.

abuses, he began to press for some more effective method of supervising and expanding the colonial Church. In 1841 the Colonial Bishoprics Fund was founded[1] to raise money to endow sees in the colonies. High Churchmen naturally supported an organisation designed to propagate episcopacy. W. E. Gladstone became one of the treasurers of the Fund.

During the next ten years the number of colonial bishoprics increased rapidly. In 1847 the Fund was given a very large sum of money by Miss Angela Burdett-Coutts, heiress of a wealthy banking family. Half the money was to be used to endow a new see in Australia, the other half for the creation of the see of Cape Town. In the following year Robert Gray arrived in his new diocese to find that he was to control a vast geographical area (all British possessions in southern Africa together with the island of St Helena) and that Anglicans in the colony did not particularly want to be controlled by him. The Church was organised in what has been called 'Erastian Congregationalism'[2]—separate white congregations, each established by government ordinance, and each regarded as separately in communion with the Church of England. There was no missionary work. The colonists had had to finance their own churches. They saw no particular need to spread their faith. They resented the fact that the Crown had wished a bishop on to them, when they had managed very well without one for nearly half a century.

Gray found that it was as ridiculous to expect a bishop in Cape Town to control the Church throughout the sub-continent, as it was to expect the bishop of London to control the Church in every British colony. He was soon pressing the authorities in England to allow him to divide his diocese. In 1853 letters patent were issued by the Crown creating two new sees of Grahamstown and Natal. Gray invited Colenso to go to Natal and the two new bishops were consecrated in the same year.[3] Bishop Wilberforce of Oxford preached at the ceremony on the text from Acts 13:2— 'Separate unto me Barnabas and Saul'. At the nomination of a High Church bishop, with the sermon of another High Church bishop to encourage him, John William Colenso became first bishop of Natal.

[1] See F. W. France, *The Overseas Episcopate*, 1941; and E. Hawkins, *Documents relative to the Erection and Endowment of Additional Bishoprics in the Colonies*, 1885.
[2] A. T. Wirgman, *English Church and People in South Africa*, 1895, p. 123
[3] P. Hinchliff, *The Anglican Church in South Africa*, 1963, chs. I & II

CHAPTER 2

The Young Colenso

THERE is very little information available about Colenso's boy-hood, little more indeed than is printed in Cox's biography,[1] written in 1888, and most of the story has to be read between the lines. In a sense, perhaps, this does not greatly matter. The real interest in Colenso's life lies in ideas rather than action. In the early years the important thing is the development of the deeply religious but conventional boy into the young man who learnt so many novel and disturbing ideas from F. D. Maurice. Maurice provided Colenso with a foundation on which he was able to con-struct both his 'heretical' theology and his courageous essays in biblical criticism. The actual events of Colenso's life up to the age of forty are only really of importance in so far as they made him the uncomfortable person he was—courageous, adventurous, prickly, obstinate and kind. We know that his father, a Cornish-man who lived at St Austell, was employed as one of the mineral agents for the Duchy of Cornwall. When John William Colenso was born in 1814 the duke of Cornwall was the future George IV, then Prince of Wales and Regent. The elder Colenso was, there-fore, in a sense a Crown official, one of the many minor employees whose job it was to bring in the revenues of the duchy which supported the heir to the throne. But he also apparently owned some private interest in a Cornish tin mine, on which the family depended for most of its income. The Colensos also owned a place called Pentuan. Presumably the family was originally tolerably well-to-do. The letters they wrote to each other are those of ordinary middle-class folk. They were reasonably well educated and well read. They were comfortably situated. They were prob-ably non-conformists in religion.[2]

---

[1] Sir G. W. Cox, *Life of John William Colenso*, 2 vols., 1888, ch. 1, on which most of the early part of this chapter is based.

[2] I can find no specific authority for suggesting that Colenso was brought up a non-conformist. Yet the letter quoted by Cox, *op. cit.*, vol. I, pp. 2f, and *infra* p. 27, seems quite clearly to be the work of a non-conformist considering the possibility of becoming an Anglican. Note the use of the possessive pronoun in referring to the local Independent congregation—'our poor little Meeting'.

But while John was still a boy, his father lost almost all his money. His mother, whom he adored, died about 1830, and it seems to have fallen to John William, as the eldest son, to take charge of and responsibility for the other children. His father seems virtually to have disappeared from the scene—or at least he seems no longer to have counted for anything. The initial financial disaster which struck the family was caused by the flooding of the tin mines by the sea. But there seems also to be a suggestion that Mr Colenso was held partly to blame. It has recently been pointed out[1] that there is something rather mysterious—'obscure and over-discreet'—in family references to Colenso's father. At all events there was no money to educate the children. It was John William rather than his father who had to raise the money for his own training and that of his brothers. Pentuan, too, was lost and it seems, again reading between the lines, that the property was mortgaged, the mortgage foreclosed, and that the family considered that they had been deprived of some just rights in the matter.[2] For the young Colenso life became a long and desperate battle to gain the very minimum of those advantages which earlier he might reasonably have expected to be given in life. Anxiety about money and something of a sense of being unjustly treated were to be constant factors in his formative years.

What the boy actually did to earn money to educate his young brothers, was to go to work as an usher in a parish school in Dartmouth, the moment his own schooling was completed. There was certainly no lack of courage in Colenso. He was up at five in the morning to call the boys so that the day's work might begin at six. Meals provided teacher and pupils with a break and there was a period of recreation, but the schoolmaster's working day did not end until eight at night. Colenso was just seventeen when he started this job.

Religion seems to have meant a very great deal to him at the earliest age. At sixteen he wrote to an aunt saying that he was aware that faith had taken root in him in the course of the previous two years.[3] He claimed no 'conversion experience'—indeed he spoke harshly of his own reliance upon 'feeling', dismissing it as 'mere enthusiasm'. He accused himself of having used his prayers as a means to 'feel more of his Saviour's love, enjoy more

[1] W. Rees, *Colenso Letters from Natal*, p. 29
[2] Cox, *op. cit.*, I, p. 8   [3] Cox, *op. cit.*, I, p. 2

of his presence', while he ought to have found his greatest joy in active service of God. Presumably John Colenso had little sympathy with Methodist piety with its emphasis upon conversion and enthusiasm.

Evangelical Anglicanism and old-fashioned Dissent seem to have come closer to his own religious attitude than any other type of English Christianity. When the Tractarians began to make their views known, Colenso approved their 'entire devotedness of heart and life' but was appalled at the 'wrong direction' in which the movement was hurrying.[1] He was too introspective, too emotional perhaps, to be attracted by the old High Churchmen; of the unusual churchmanship of men like Coleridge and Maurice he, as yet, knew nothing.[2]

Like most young men who take religion seriously, Colenso was prone to doubt, self-accusation and a questioning of his own motives. When there was the possibility of a cholera epidemic in England it served for Colenso as a *memento mori*, a cause for a thorough examination of the conscience.

> For the last two years instead of (as I thought myself repeatedly) being a humble and hungry follower of Jesus, I have made a god of myself, and an idol of my own soul.[3]

There were, no doubt, a great many more mature men driven to less worthy reflections on their spiritual condition by causes just as remote as a cholera scare.

Colenso's biographer is at great pains to point out that the boy's self-accusations are not to be taken at their face-value, but as evidence of a very sensitive conscience. Such excuses are unnecessary. One does not expect profundity from a boy of seventeen. Colenso was plainly a genuine, sincerely religious youth —sometimes over-sensitive, sometimes morbid, always a little precocious. One surprising political comment from this period suggests that Colenso regarded the passage of the Reform Bill of 1830 as unfortunate, and that he would have approved the actions of those bishops who voted against the bill.[4] One had imagined Colenso on the side of the middle-class non-conformists who were enfranchised by the act. Like Gladstone, Colenso seems to have become more 'Liberal' as he grew older.

As the young man matured he came to believe that his vocation

[1] *Ibid.*, p. 15   [2] *Ibid.*, p. 21   [3] *Ibid* I, p. 4
[4] *Ibid.*, & cf *supra*, p, 5

was to serve God in the ministry of the Church—but which Church? He appears, as a boy, to have had no very high opinion of the sincerity and zeal of the clergymen of the Church of England. A famous, or notorious, and oft-quoted letter of the sixteen-year-old Colenso[1] puts the problem as he saw it:

I am now, since we have had Mr. Hockin here, fully convinced that a Church minister may be a man of God; and his opportunities of being useful must far exceed those of a Dissenting one. The first and a very striking, advantage (so, at least, it appears to me) of the Church minister over the Independent is his actual *Independence*. There are not so many bigots in the Church as there used to be, nor have the bishops the same tyrannical power which they used to have over the body of which they represent the head . . . When once the Church minister is settled in his church, unless guilty of some heinous dereliction of duty, he cannot be expelled . . . Not so, however, with the Independent. He must preach not what he likes, but what his congregation likes: he must obey the voice of his flock, and in too many instances the flock turns out a flock of wolves in sheep's clothing, as for instance in our poor little Meeting, where all is riot and confusion . . . But whatever may be the advantages on the one side or the other, I trust I am prepared to enter whatever situation the Almighty may in his unerring wisdom have designed for me . . . I have as yet abundance of time before me, comparatively speaking, for I am not yet seventeen; but if nothing should occur to realise my wishes with respect to the Church, I am prepared for the Independents. Yet in either case let me pray that the doctrine of the Gospel may be mine, unclouded by party principles, unobscured by the impious intrusion of man's own ignorant wishes and baneful speculations.

It is not necessary to regard all this, as one of Bishop Gray's admiring biographers does,[2] as evidence of a strangely un-youthful eye for expediency. Yet it is a remarkable piece of work for a boy of sixteen. It bears all the marks of that earnestness, the wholehearted if somewhat joyless seriousness, which was characteristic of the generation which was to be known as 'early Victorian'. It is no longer fashionable to poke Stracheyesque fun at Victorians and to regard them as comic, hypocritical characters.[3] It is now

[1] Cox, *op. cit.*, I, pp. 2f; & cf A. Brooke, *Robert Gray*, 1947, p. 91
[2] A. Brooke, *loc. cit.*
[3] See e.g. D. Thompson, *England in the Nineteenth Century*, 1950, ch. v; M. R. Reckitt, *Maurice to Temple*, 1946, p. 15; & Rees, *op. cit.*, p. 23.

generally agreed that earnestness was their hall-mark; not smug-
ness, but a devotion to duty, which was real *devotion* of the whole
personality. So Pusey was honestly and deeply hurt at unbelief.
So Shaftesbury drove himself to care for slaves, while thinking of
them, with unconscious condescension, as 'niggers'.[1] Certainly
John William Colenso had that characteristic, and it developed
early. It makes him appear to modern eyes as a somewhat humourless figure and one wonders whether twentieth-century youth
would have thought that Colenso had had any real childhood and
adolescence at all.

At all events Colenso chose for the Church, honestly believing
that he would best be able to preach the offence of the gospel
with less hindrance there than in the chapels. That which nearly
prevented the realisation of his 'wishes in respect of the Church'
was lack of money to send him to Oxford or Cambridge. Practically speaking there were no theological colleges, in the modern
sense, in the 1830s. St Bees had been started by the bishop of
Chester in 1816 to train non-graduates. The C.M.S. had had perforce to provide an institution to train its missionaries. King's
College, London had been founded in 1828. Durham University
was created, largely from the endowments of the cathedral chapter
and see of Durham, in 1832. It was still true, however, that the
vast majority of men ordained in the Anglican ministry had been
trained in one or other of the ancient universities, and most of
them had had no formal training in theology. At Oxford the
young Robert Gray read for a pass degree and then put himself
through a stiff course in theological reading afterwards.[2] At Cambridge the mathematics degree was regarded as the normal foundation for a liberal education for young men. If the clergy who came
to South Africa are a reliable cross-section of their brethren 'at
home' then a degree in mathematics at Cambridge was the most
usual background. Owen, the first Anglican missionary in Natal,
James Green, Colenso's future dean and antagonist, Frederick
Mackenzie, archdeacon of Natal and first bishop in Central Africa,
and, of course, Colenso himself, all came to the colony with a
brilliant mathematical reputation in the Cambridge schools. But
in 1832 there was no guarantee that Colenso would ever reach
Cambridge. Mr Glubb, incumbent of the parish in whose school
Colenso taught, was convinced that the young man had a brilliant

[1] E. Hodder, *Life & Work of the Earl of Shaftesbury, K.G.*, 1887, p. 476
[2] C. N. Gray, *Life of Robert Gray*, I, pp. 30 ff

career before him and that it would be a fearful waste of talent if he never reached the university. The young schoolmaster began a desperate search for the means to keep himself at Cambridge for three years.

His requirements were pathetic in their modesty—£20 to secure his place in St John's College, and £33 a year for his three years in the university. But his grandmother, to whom he turned first, was utterly unable to help. It is significant that it was his mother's family to whom he turned and, failing his grandmother, Colenso next approached his mother's brother, W. P. Blackmore.

> My object is to enter as a sizar at St John's . . . Mr Glubb, and all I can converse with on the subject, assure me there will be no difficulty in supporting myself by private pupils, and a thousand other aids which a studious man cannot help receiving. . . .[1]

In the end uncle and grandmother seem to have joined to guarantee him the money for the first two years. Colenso left for Cambridge in September 1832. But the struggle to find money was not over. His expenses were heavier than he had expected. By the end of his third term he had been forced into a sort of minor authorship, helping to translate the classics and to annotate St Matthew's Gospel for a firm of publishers. He won exhibitions and at last became a scholar of his college. Nevertheless he was compelled to write again to his relations for money, in spite of the fact that he was still taking pupils of his own, men less brilliant than himself, and had written a small textbook on mathematics. But the examinations of 1836 proved that all this struggle had been worth while. Colenso was placed second wrangler. In the following year he was elected a fellow of his college.

Dr Longley, headmaster of Harrow, was inquiring in Cambridge for a man to teach mathematics. He was advised to try and get Colenso. In the same year Colenso was made deacon by the bishop of Ely in whose diocese Cambridge lay, and he was probably ordained priest three years later when he was twenty-five.[2]

[1] Cox, *op. cit.*, I, p. 5
[2] There is some confusion over the date of Colenso's ordination. Cox (*op. cit.*, I, p. 9) says he was made deacon in 1839, but adds that this was the same year in which he went to Harrow. Since Longley left Harrow in 1836 this cannot be accurate. I am assuming that the dates of his two ordinations have been confused. Fellowship at a Cambridge college and ordination would normally go together, and Colenso would then have just reached the canonical age for the diaconate.

We do not know how much training in theology he received before ordination, nor what it consisted of. We know that Paley's *Evidences of Christianity*, with its emphasis on the reasonableness of the Christian faith, was perhaps the most frequently used book. Candidates were required to satisfy the bishop's examining chaplains that they had a knowledge of the Bible and of the classical languages. Degrees in theology were not normally held by candidates for orders, and how much real training they received depended largely on the bishop and his chaplains. Sometimes it might be very little; sometimes a considerable amount.[1]

Longley did not remain at Harrow long after Colenso arrived there. He was an Oxford man, and had been an undergraduate and then a tutor at Christ Church. At the age of thirty-five he had become headmaster of Harrow and after seven years there began a steady climb up the episcopal ladder, reigning successively over the sees of Ripon, Durham, York and Canterbury. Longley was essentially a conservative Churchman, conscious of the dignity of the Establishment, unwilling to defy any of the provisions of English law, equally mistrustful of the papistry of the Tractarians and of the unbelief of the liberals. It was to fall to Longley, as archbishop of Canterbury, to try to quell Colenso's attempt to popularise biblical criticism and to call the first Lambeth Conference partly in order to remove the 'scandal' caused by Colenso's opinions.[2] But, for the moment, the association between Colenso and Longley seems to have been without friction. Colenso was still an undistinguished young clergyman who happened to be also a good mathematician. His views on theology were as yet not influenced by new-fangled ideas, but were soundly and mildly Evangelical.

But Longley left Harrow very shortly and was succeeded by Christopher Wordsworth, nephew of the poet. Wordsworth was a brilliant scholar, later to be bishop of Lincoln. He was also an old-fashioned High Churchman, an authority in the field of patristics, and famous for his commentary on the Bible. At one time when, twenty years after their period of association at Harrow, Colenso was fumbling after a critical understanding of the Pentateuch, Wordsworth was dismissing source criticism of the Gospels

---

[1] See A. M. G. Stephenson, ' "G.O.E." in 1837', *Church Quarterly Review*, CLXIII, pp. 200 ff. This is the exact period at which Colenso was ordained.
[2] See *infra* p. 181.

and defending the verbal inerrancy of the Scriptures.[1] Wordsworth's conservatism may have prejudiced Colenso's undoubtedly
partisan biographer against him. He describes Harrow as sinking
'very low in general repute under the management of Dr Wordsworth . . .'[2] and attributes some of Colenso's continued financial
difficulties to this fact.

Quite clearly Colenso's situation grew worse rather than better
during the time he was at Harrow. The boarding house which he
ran was burnt down very shortly after it had been built. He hired
the home of the local lord of the manor as a substitute, but the
cost of fitting out two houses in succession crippled him and after
six years at the school he was in a desperate situation, £5000 in
debt and with no assets at all to speak of.[3] He was now nearly
thirty. It was time that his life was settled. In this very year he
first met the girl he wanted to marry.[4] He was obliged to leave
Harrow, return to St John's as a tutor, and resume the struggle
to raise more and more money, to pay the interest on his crushing
debts and to attempt to redeem the capital sum also. When
Colenso was old and outcast one of his least lovable traits was a
grasping attitude to money—a trait that accords oddly with his
undoubted generosity of spirit. But the apparent paradox is to be
explained by his perpetual struggle, from the age of fifteen, to
meet one debt after another.

One of the expedients with which Colenso tried to meet this
crippling debt brought him, almost accidently, some fame. In
1843 he published his *Arithmetic for Schools*. Colenso does not
himself seem to have regarded it as a particularly valuable or important thing in his life.[5] But for a generation of schoolchildren
'Colenso's Arithmetic' was a household word, long before its
author became a notorious heretic. Charlotte Yonge was to make
one of her characters refuse to do her sums because the textbook
was written by that 'dreadful Dr Colenso'.

In a modest way the young Cambridge don was making his
mark in other fields. We are told that already while still at
Harrow he was highly thought of as a preacher, counsellor and
pastor.[6] At Cambridge he was much in demand in the town as

<hr>

[1] See e.g. Wordsworth's attempt to account for the divergences in the various
accounts of the same incident in the Gospels: *The New Testament of Our Lord
and Saviour Jesus Christ in the Original Greek with Introductions and Notes by
Chr. Wordsworth, D.D.*, 2nd ed. 1881, pp. xlviff.
[2] Cox, *op. cit.*, I, p. 8   [3] *Ibid.*, pp. 18f   [4] W. Rees, *op. cit.*, p. 28
[5] Cox, *op. cit.*, I, p. 21   [6] *Ibid* I, p. 9n

a preacher;[1] though an amusing story suggests that the university authorities were less anxious to sit at his feet. When it fell to Colenso to preach the Latin sermon before the university in the Michaelmas term of 1844, the officials 'forgot' that the ceremony was due to take place at all.[2]

Meanwhile Colenso's religious opinions had undergone considerable modification. While he was at Harrow his correspondence reveals that he was still chiefly preoccupied with self-examination, introspection, and the growth in grace that follows from obeying the will of God. Colenso uses language which seems strange coming from the pen of the man who was to go down in history as the iconoclast who tore down the traditional beliefs.

> . . . when our Saviour comes to visit us, will He really find faith upon earth, find us throwing our whole souls upon His work . . . Or will He find us still hampered with the entanglement of earth-love and earth-bound desires.[3]

Then came, when he moved to Cambridge, what he called 'a more complete insight into the utterly lost and helpless condition of our souls'.

> Daily was I labouring . . . in this most unprofitable work of trying to plaster over my faults, and present myself clean and comely in the presence of my God: but it was all in vain. . . . And now, perceiving that the whole work of reparation was utterly out of my own power or comprehension, but that only the Holy Spirit of God . . . could carry on and complete the blessed work in His own time and in His own way. . . . We love Him because He first loved us. . . . I see in it now the secret of all growth in grace and love and holiness—continual, frequent and unfainting prayer.[4]

One is reminded of Luther's development of thought (though Colenso's agonising is milder than that of the reformer) when, under the influence of Staupitz, he came to see that it is dependence upon the love of God rather than the striving for one's own perfection, which is at the heart of the Christian religion. But just as Luther moved beyond the teaching of Staupitz, so Colenso also developed further. He came under the influence of F. D. Maurice.

[1] Rees, *op. cit.*, p. 30
[2] Cox, *op. cit.*, I, p. 39
[3] *Ibid.*, p. 17
[4] *Ibid.*, I, p. 21

The editor of Mrs Colenso's letters maintains that it was his future wife who introduced Colenso to Maurice and Maurice's theology,[1] but Colenso's biographer makes very little mention of Mrs Colenso's part in the relationship which gradually developed between the two men. On 10 April 1843 Colenso writes to a friend that he has never been satisfied by either the Tractarian or the Evangelical theology, and has begun to learn from Coleridge and Maurice.[2] Six months later he writes again to say that he has been reading *The Kingdom of Christ*.

Maurice's *Kingdom of Christ* is a very long and solid piece of work. In form it is an attempt to persuade the Quaker, assaulted by the arguments of the Romanist, the Evangelical, the Dissenter, and the Churchman that there is a Catholic Church as opposed to sectarianism. Maurice states his purpose as being 'to inquire if there be a Church Catholic here or not, and if there be, under what circumstances it exists . . .'.[3] There follows an examination of Quakerism itself, the Protestantism of the Reformation, Unitarianism, and the religious, philosophical and political movements of the eighteenth and nineteenth century. Then Maurice goes on to show how man feels after some sort of universal society wider than the nation and yet more akin to the family. He proceeds to speak of the universal society based on a name—the Kingdom of Christ —and then relates Baptism, the Creeds, the Liturgy, the Eucharist, the Ministry and the Scriptures to the idea of the Kingdom. The heart of the Christian gospel is the proclamation that the ideal society already exists.

> If the Gospel be the revelation or unveiling of a mystery hidden from ages and generations; if this mystery be the true constitution of humanity in Christ, so that a man believes and acts a lie who does not claim for himself union with Christ, we can understand why the deepest writings of the New Testament, instead of being digests of doctrine, are epistles, explaining to those who had been admitted into the Church of Christ their own position, bringing out that side of it which had reference to the circumstances in which they were placed or to their most besetting sins, and shewing what life was in consistency, what life at variance, with it.[4]

[1] Rees *op. cit.*, p. 30   [2] Cox, *op. cit.*, I, p. 23
[3] F. D. Maurice, *The Kingdom of Christ*, 4th ed., p. 21
[4] *Ibid.*, p. 296

Maurice's book stirred the serious Colenso into almost lyrical excitement.

O what glorious missionary principles are there, the only ones, as it seems to me, which can give real life and energy to the messenger of Truth, who comes, not as if from the clouds above, or the deeps beneath, but a fellowman among his brethren, all of whom have the same Heaven above them that he has made, and every daily mercy, rain and sunshine, life and breath and all things, speaking to them as to all as tokens that they have a *Father there*, that they are living in a world from which the cause of disobedience has been removed, that they too may look upward, and fear, and put their trust in the mercy of Him that made them.[1]

Colenso goes on to say that he cannot become a missionary—as yet at any rate. His way is 'effectually barred against it'. It was chiefly barred by two things: his lack of money and his desire to marry Miss Frances Bunyon.

Frances Bunyon was an intelligent girl, serious but with flashes of wit which suddenly show through the earnestness and make one realise what an attractive, vivacious person she must have been. An early photograph, which she herself later described as 'silly and simpering', shows her as not particularly beautiful, but with a sweet gentle expression, widely spaced eyes, rather a long nose, and dark hair dressed down over her ears and caught up in a knot at the back.[2] There seems to be no early picture of Colenso in existence, but he was, particularly in his younger days, a man of great charm. Even later, when he was a notorious heretic and iconoclast, his opponents found themselves obliged to modify their dislike of him and surrender to his ability to win friends.[3] For his wife he was always saint and hero, romance and duty, all rolled into one. They fell in love at first sight, and they seem to have remained lovers for the rest of their lives. Their letters to one another are proof of this. They had five children, who adored them and for whom they made a happy and contented home even when

[1] Cox, *op. cit.*, I, p. 22
[2] See Rees, *op. cit.*, p. 33.
[3] It must be said, however, that not all his opponents thought him good-looking. Sabine Baring Gould (author of 'Onward Christian Soldiers') says, in his *Early Reminiscences, 1834–64*, that Colenso was 'not a pleasing looking man. He had a grey, muddy complexion....'

circumstances were very difficult. The love which existed between Colenso and his wife was real and deep, carrying them
through every crisis, calm yet absorbing and completely satisfying. When Colenso died, Frances referred to the date as the
day when 'our dear Lord left us'.[1]

They met when Frances came to Cambridge in 1842 to see
her brother, Charles. Colenso seems to have been attracted
immediately and deeply. 'For two weeks, he was in constant
attendance. . . .'[2]

Frances came from well-to-do middle-class stock.[3] Her
maternal grandfather was one of the founders of the Norwich
Union: her father was the first secretary of the London board
of the same company. Mr Bunyon died, having lost his for-
tune, about two years after Frances met Colenso. The Bunyons
and the Colensos had the same experience, comparative poverty
following comparative wealth.

Frances had faced the intellectual problems of belief with
the aid of Coleridge's writings, initiating and maintaining a
thoughtful correspondence with Maurice. Colenso was introduced to Maurice at last and the two men became friends. For
a time Colenso helped Maurice with his work at Guy's hos-
pital. But he was looking for something more permanent—
some job that would provide a home and an income on which
he could marry Frances. At one time there was a possibility
that he might become headmaster of a big school at Putney—
'to give a general practical education, in contradistinction from
the exclusively classical [one] of Public Schools. . . . It em-
braces Classics, but more decidedly Mathematics, and Practical Science'.[4] It might have been the ideal job for the
author of 'Colenso's Arithmetic'. But Colenso decided that he
was 'deficient' in some of the necessary qualities.[5] At the same
time Frances' relations used their good offices to obtain for him
one of two livings created by dividing the parish of Forncett in
the Norwich diocese.[6] A new rectory was to be built for the

---

[1] Rees, *op. cit.*, p. 374   [2] *Ibid.*, p. 28
[3] For the early life of Mrs Colenso, see Rees, *op. cit.*, Part I.
[4] Cox, *op. cit.*, I, p. 37
[5] Nevertheless Colenso applied for the post of headmaster of Sherborne
School in 1845 and again in 1850. See A. B. Gourlay, *History of Sherborne
School*, 1952, p. 104.
[6] I am indebted to Professor F. E. Vokes of Trinity College, Dublin, lately
Rector of Forncett for information about the division of the parish and Colenso's
activities there.

Colensos. John planned to take private pupils to augment his income of £500 *per annum* from the living. F. D. Maurice married John and Frances in January 1846. Colenso was thirty-two. His wife was thirty.

Forncett was probably not in any sense an interesting place. The countryside is flat and undulating: not flat enough to provide long and magnificent views; not undulating enough to create real hills and valleys. It lies a few miles south of Norwich, but is rather cut off from the main stream even of Norfolk life. And Norfolk itself a hundred years ago was an isolated and backward part of England, at least as regards the country districts. New ideas took a long time to penetrate. Strangers remained strangers after forty years. The country people were uneducated; schools were few and far between. The churchmanship of most parishes was old-fashioned 'Broad'; even the Evangelicals had made very little headway. Nonconformity was strong and the Established Church was able to do little to meet the challenge. A narrow parochial patriotism, and a good deal of superstition, were to be found in the villages. It was not likely, one would have thought, that a Norfolk village would prove to be the ideal setting for the young 'Maurician' clergyman.

It was during his time at Forncett that Colenso developed what he called his Maurician theology. In 1842 he had regarded himself as in 'almost entire ignorance' of theology,[1] and he was extremely diffident in accepting any pupils in that field. Hardly more than ten years later he felt himself competent to publish commentaries and theological treatises. In that decade the mathematician came to regard himself as a theologian, and he did so largely under the influence of Maurice.

After he had read *The Kingdom of Christ* Colenso's letters become sprinkled with two predominating ideas, and two ideas which might seem to be mutually contradictory. In the first place there is continual assertion of the fatherhood of God—Maurice's universal society, with the 'family' aspect of it stressed. And this assertion has, in Colenso, a universalist sense. The other dominant idea is that of missions, that the heathen might not perish—'I say not eternally—which is in the hands of Infinite Truth and Love,—but temporally, in the

---

[1] Cox, *op. cit.*, I, p. 28

loss of that light and joy and glorious hope, which quicken by the Grace of God our own hearts'.[1]

The strict, logical outcome of combining these two points, Colenso had not yet reached. But during the ten years from 1843 to 1853 he came gradually to adopt the inevitable belief that all the heathen were already redeemed by Christ and that the prime job of the missionary was not to convert but to teach the heathen to enjoy the fruits of their redemption. By the time Colenso came to publish his *Commentary on Romans*, this had become his most cherished theological opinion. The effect of Maurice's teaching on Colenso was, in fact, not always of such a kind as Maurice himself could approve. In the passage already quoted above[2] in which Colenso comments on *The Kingdom of Christ* it is possible to discern the seeds of Colenso's future greatness, the enthusiasm (a word he himself would have despised) and the aching love for those he had come to regard as God's children first and foremost. But there are in the same passage indications of the unsatisfactory tendencies in his thought, his lopsided, over-objectivised view of the atonement, his too great reliance upon natural religion. What he says is not, in itself, an inadequate theology of the atonement, but *by* itself it is theologically inadequate and unbalanced. When its author came to insist that this was the *whole* and only possible statement of the doctrine, he was trying to bind the Church to an impossibly narrow theology. But it is important to realise that Colenso was not playing games with Christian doctrine like the Patriarch Photius who invented a new heresy because his predecessor, Ignatius, had held that theology was unnecessary and Photius wished to see how he would cope. Most heresy has not been a species of parlour game, it has arisen because someone saw a need which the Church did not seem to be meeting, and tried to provide the answer to that need. So for Colenso there was a need, and he tried to meet it.

For too long, it seemed to him, men had regarded God as an abstract principle to be argued about. Coleridge, indeed, had expressed himself weary of 'evidences' of Christianity. Maurice, in commenting on Coleridge in connection with his own *Kingdom of Christ* said that the principal question with which men of his own generation seemed to be faced was whether Christian doctrines ought 'to be taken upon trust from the early ages, or

[1] *Ibid.*, p. 23   [2] *Supra*, p. 34

whether we are to look upon them as matters for our own inquiry, to be acknowledged only so far as they accord with what seems to us either the declaration of Scripture or the verdict of reason'.[1] 'The atheism of Hume' Maurice said, had driven men to discover 'that the highest truths are those which lie beyond the limits of Experience, that the essential principles of Reason are those which cannot be proved by syllogisms . . .'.[2] For Maurice, then, the heart-religion of Coleridge was not irrational. Reason had its part to play in determining how the faith was to be believed, but the question of *whether* man should believe lay beyond the limits of rational inquiry. In Colenso's letters of this period there is little or nothing of metaphysical argument. At the very period in which he was beginning to come to grips with theology, he seems less than ever concerned with questions of whether man ought to believe in God—more and more concerned with the joy of faith, the great privilege which follows from knowing what God has done, and the necessity of expressing that joy in love. Colenso was not concerned with meeting 'the atheism of Hume' directly, but he was concerned with the aridity which the intellectual arguments about faith were imposing upon theology. There is the beginning of an idea, later to become prominent in his thought, that the great heathen, 'Plato, Sophocles, Thucydides', spoke the truth 'from the Divinity itself'. Already in 1843 Colenso interprets the second chapter of Romans as meaning 'that none of God's reasonable creatures are left without sufficient guide of Life'.[3] But what might have been a typical Broad Church attitude—that piety and morality as exhibited in the ancients is itself evidence for the reasonableness of Christianity—is infused for Colenso with a passionate desire to love.

One of the profoundest things Colenso ever said concerns this fact and belongs to this period.

> What I meant in reference to Mr. Maurice's principle was this—that there are *very few* who discern the *very great* distinction between the two endeavours—*to be loved* and *to love*, and therefore very few set themselves to labour for the grace which shall enable them to *love*, as Christians.[4]

[1] In the dedication to Derwent Coleridge in the 4th edition of *The Kingdom of Christ*, 1891, pp. xxivf
[2] *Ibid.*   [3] Cox, *op. cit.*, I, p. 25   [4] *Ibid.*, p. 31

It was this which made Colenso a missionary—'turning to the far-off heathen, dark and benighted as they are, yet not given over as a prey to destruction, but having still tokens around and voices within, which are speaking to *them* of a Father in Heaven, and to us of their connection (we do not presume to analyse or comprehend it) with Him who is the Head of the whole race, the Son of Man, the Saviour of the world'.[1] It was this same sense of the difference between loving and being loved which made him almost court unpopularity. It was this same belief in the necessity of love which made him impatient with English Christianity. Tractarians argued about the Patristic formulation of dogma. Broad Churchmen and High Churchmen were too stiff and formal. Evangelicals relied too much upon enthusiasm and the need for a 'felt' conversion. Colenso wanted a religion of love.

> But doubtless there were none of the grosser sins of Sodom and Gomorrah practised, openly at least, in Chorazin and Bethsaida in the time of our Saviour, and yet it will be more tolerable for the former in the day of God than for the latter; and Christian England may find herself amidst neglected privileges and abused power and wealth and influence, far more miserable and guilty in His sight than the heathen, who have had a very little light and have not quenched it.[2]

It is easy to forget, when one is dealing with the Colenso of the period from 1860 onwards that the man who was condemned as a rationalist and heretic was the man who was motivated in his study of theology by the desire to learn to love. It is easy, when a man is labelled by notoriety, to forget that religion honestly meant as much to him as to those who condemned him. Yet it is not difficult to trace in Colenso's thought, while he was still the handsome, charming, young Cambridge don, the elements that were to lead to his condemnation. It was not his incipient universalism alone. Colenso was already urging that the great men of antiquity ought to be read and understood as real people, human beings. Once this principle was applied to the Bible, as Milman's case showed, there was the beginnings of a critical approach.[3] Colenso was also haunted by the typical temptation of the theologian. He

[1] *Ibid.*, p. 27   [2] *Ibid.*, p. 24   [3] Cf. *supra*, p. 16

was afraid of pride in his intellectual accomplishments, first
fearing his own thoughts, because of the pride in calling them
'my own'; then seeing that to call them 'my own' was itself
pride. Then he came to see that they were to be treated as
belonging to God. It was not enough to fear the abuse of
intellect, and try to stifle thought itself lest it be abused. Intellect must be used since it was God's gift. 'It is a much more
difficult lesson perhaps to learn to use, than not to abuse'.[1]
Colenso's later opponents would have preferred him not to
have used his intellect at all.

A great deal of the emphasis on love and the growing sense
of intellectual liberty, Colenso owed to Maurice. Freedom was
one of the things, certainly, that meant most to Maurice—the
economic freedom of the poor, the freedom for men within the
Church to speak the truth, the freedom of the Church itself
from the pressure of outside authority and of vested interests.
Throughout his controversial ministry Colenso believed himself to be following Maurice's lead. But it was really only
Maurice's *conclusions* which Colenso accepted. All the context
in which they stood—the profundity of thought, the struggle
to arrive at the truth, the real agony of Maurice's mind—he
failed to borrow. Colenso took Maurice's conclusions and
superimposed them upon what were really liberal Protestant
presuppositions, which Maurice himself would have despised.

Maurice had no sympathy with the watery creed of the
'liberal', because he believed that man must be free from the
anxieties of loose speculation. The Church, the kingdom of the
free, must stand for the freedom of the community—must be,
in a sense, socialist. But the State must be the guarantor of the
freedom of the individual, to ensure that he was not coerced,
but free to think and to believe. Yet Maurice frowned on
democracy, preferring a modified form of the 'divine right of
kings' theory.

Colenso also came to be regarded as a champion of liberty,
the liberty of the liberal Protestant, the liberty for man to
exercise his divine reason freely, without restriction of any
kind. He came to advocate the control of the Church by the
State because such control could guarantee to the individual
the right to speculate to his heart's content. And precisely at

[1] Cox, *op. cit.*, I, p. 29

this point the tremendous difference between the two men is made clear. Maurice was the champion of the national Church against sectarianism; Colenso championed it against the Church Universal.

And yet the conclusions of the two men remained superficially similar. When, eventually, Colenso was excommunicated, he appealed to the Crown to defend his rights against the majority party in the Church. Maurice, who did not trust Church courts, would have approved of such an action at any time. But of the way in which Colenso made his appeal, Maurice said that it was the frenzy of an Erastian monomaniac. But all this lay twenty years in the future when Maurice married his friends and sent them off to Forncett. Colenso still was a 'Maurician', claiming to have accepted Maurice's hard-won position. He did not do so, of course, dishonestly. A great deal of Colenso's tragedy lies in the fact that he was a supremely honest man, with an inventive and independent mind, but lacking the profoundness of thought which might have kept his inventiveness within bounds. He pursued the rational (or what appeared to him to be rational) without regard for the reasonable. And yet, when all these reservations have been made, Colenso was still, at least at this period, closer to the position of Maurice and Coleridge and the Cambridge Platonists than to the conventional Erastian and Latitudinarian point of view.

The most valuable source for tracing the actual development of Colenso's theology during his time at Forncett is not his official biography, which contains very little that relates to this period of seven years, but the minute-book of the Depwade Clerical Society. Depwade was the rural-deanery within which Forncett fell, and the clerical society was formally constituted on 14 April 1846, though it had apparently already been meeting earlier than this.[1] The minutes are beautifully kept in a classical copper-plate hand, but apparently the members were less precise and formal for the rules agreed upon in April were rescinded in May 1846 and replaced by new ones. The society elected a 'director' to preside over its deliberations and the meetings took the form of discussion on passages of scripture,

[1] *Minutes of Papers Read and Proceedings at the Clerical Meeting, Depwade Deanery*, Book No. 1, p. 32

each member preparing a paper on the passage and reading it to the assembly. A mandatory clause in the constitution says 'That a cold Luncheon shall be taken at 2 o'cl: and the meeting resumed at 3'. Members were fined two shillings and sixpence for non-attendance.

Colenso was present at the inaugural meeting and first presented a paper, on 1 Timothy 2:3, 4, at the May meeting. His contribution was a flat assertion of universalism.

> We *all* have received life from Him, the 2nd Adam, as we received death from the first. We have all strength, if we will use it . . .
>
> This love of God towards His entire Intelligent Creation is confirmed by Analogy of Nature: the rain from Heaven, and fruitful Seasons given, not in mockery to doomed sinners, but in mercy to a ransomed race. . . .
>
> But it is not enough for us to live as pious Heathen or Jews: we must be conformed to the image of the Son of God, or else 'It shall be more tolerable for Sodom and Gomorrah etc'.[1]

To this the secretary appended the laconic note, 'N.B. This paper gave rise to considerable discussion'. We are not told what the discussion was, but it may not be entirely coincidental that the next speaker that morning stressed that 'Christ [is] the only way of approach to God'.[2]

Colenso's next paper dealt with 1 Timothy 4:5, and he spoke of the 'sanctifying' of God's creation, contrasting the Jewish approach to sanctification by a system of 'minute laws which extended to the ordinary matters of life and must have tended greatly to keep the faithful Jew alive to the reality of God's commands . . .', with the Christian method of sanctifying daily life. God, he says, 'gives us no longer dark commands to be obeyed at His word without a reason: but he calls us friends, unfolds to us His hidden meaning, and bids us obey, not in the oldness of the letter, but in the newness of the spirit'.[3] He picked up much the same theme in his third paper to the society, dealing with the duty of the clergyman to preach with life as well as lips:

> True piety, not the disturber but the soother and helper of common life; not an incongruous ingredient that must be mixed, with dislike and difficulty, in the cup of earthly joys and sorrows,

---

[1] *Ibid.*, pp. 40f   [2] *Ibid.*, p. 42   [3] *Ibid.*, pp. 57f

but that which will blend most naturally and entirely with every thought, feeling, and action.[1]

Thus his first three papers show quite clearly the theology developing in the mind of the new rector of Forncett St Mary: All men are redeemed by Christ, because God's love is for all; the chief difference between the Christian and the 'pious heathen' is the greater responsibility laid upon him; yet God's demands upon the Christian are not dark but reasonable; religion is a natural thing not obscure, nor irrational, nor extraordinary; and the mark of the Christian is joy.

In September 1846, Colenso talked to the society about 1 Timothy 5:21—'the elect angels'—taking the opportunity to explain how he understood the word 'elect'. This is a more obviously academic paper. He compares the passage from Timothy with a similar phrase in Josephus. There are several references to the original Greek. And Colenso does not question either the existence of angelic beings or the Pauline authorship of Hebrews. But the strongly anti-Calvinist temper of the man appears in his anxiety to define 'election' so that it will not exclude his own view of universal salvation. If angels can be elect, this can only mean that they are the angels who have not fallen. It is, as it were, the reverse of the Augustinian view. Augustine may argue that we are all fallen but God's grace destines some to salvation. Colenso argues that the angels are all elect but some damn themselves by falling away. And this is, he says, 'the universal meaning of the word 'Election'. It is still of grace because it still rests upon God's prevenient love. Man's reprobation now follows from his neglect of the grace given in Christ; his election rests upon him if he strives in the strength of that grace.

In an oddly prophetic passage he goes on to comment on 'St Paul's' injunction to Timothy to be impartial.

These words should remind us of the responsibilities of a Xtn bishop, and of our duty to receive with thoughtfulness and submission whatever may issue from our own chief pastor in the conscientious discharge of his office.[2]

Colenso's theological wrestling with the allotted texts must sometimes have puzzled his clerical brethren, who were far

---

[1] *Ibid.*, pp. 66f   [2] *Ibid.*, pp. 76f

more concerned with pious practicalities. The speaker who succeeded Colenso on this occasion, for instance, interpreted 'Drink no longer water, but use a little wine for thy stomach's sake and thine oft infirmities', to mean that 'Bishop Timothy' was 'an invalid' and that when the times of ordinations came round he needed all possible strength to face 'the additional weight of duty'—a truly eighteenth-century picture of a bishop's lot—a bottle of port at Embertide!

Yet there was a further shock in store for the members of the Depwade Clerical Society. At the meeting in November 1846 Colenso began to expound to them a kind of kenotic theory of the Incarnation, tinged with Nestorianism:

> 1 Timothy 6:15: 'In his own times': rather 'in its own times'. In such a mysterious way had the divine nature taken to itself the Human, in the person of Jesus Xt. that the latter knew not what the former did. The divine nature willed not to communicate to the human its own will and knowledge: to a fine human mind, such as Our Lord's was, all knowledge must be communicated from above: ideas must be acquired by gradual processes and communicated in time. This was the great Lesson which Our Lord's life was meant to teach, how a truly believing human being is supported from above. We may not confound Our Saviour's divine nature with His human, so as to view Him sustained in all His labours and temptations by His own divinity:— 'I will put my trust in Him' in dependence upon my Father, I will accomplish my mission. . . .[1]

It is a great pity that the secretary made no record of the details of the discussions following from the papers, for we have no precise means of knowing how the other clergy of the deanery reacted to Colenso's views. After his first year at Forncett, and in spite of the two-and-sixpenny fine, Colenso attended less and less frequently and his contributions to the deliberations became very rare indeed. He makes one more significant contribution, in June 1847, and this time his subject is Hebrews—the heavenly altar and the spiritual sacrifices. The points he stresses are that the heavenly altar is *one* and cannot therefore be represented by 'our multiplied communion tables'.[2] It has indeed no tangible analogue in the Christian

---

[1] *Ibid.*, p. 94   [2] *Ibid.*, loose sheets, p. 11

Church, it is probably to be understood as the Cross of Christ. The sin-offering, the atonement sacrifice, the Jew was not allowed to eat—'doubtless of this sacrifice we cannot eat; but there are other sacrifices, peace offerings . . . and sin offerings'. So we can offer to God our sacrifice of praise and thanksgiving and of confession and prayer, and Christ will offer these upon 'the same spiritual altar'. Plainly Colenso rejects any suggestion that there is a connection, in the Eucharist, between 'eating Christ's body and blood' and 'pleading his sacrifice'.[1]

Whether Colenso tended to stay away from meetings because he found his brethren too puerile, or because *they* found *him* too revolutionary, or whether he was simply too busy, we have no means of knowing. At least the civilities were preserved for when he became bishop of Natal the society gave him a silver salver. The new bishop's rather fullsome letter of thanks was read at the meeting of the society in January 1854.

> Though the seas roll between us we shall be all working, I trust, in the service of one Great Master, and if His love possess and rule our hearts that will keep us one in Him and keep alive in us a love to one another which many waters cannot quench.[2]

Though we know a good deal of what happened to Colenso's mind during this period, we know very little of what happened to his body. There is no account of day-to-day work done, just the merest scraps of information. The parish was very small. Even the undivided living of Forncett had not been a large one. The two churches, St Mary and St Peter, were less than a mile apart, and after the division Colenso's parish contained some 300 souls. It would seem that Colenso found himself somewhat frustrated by the backwardness of his people. Mrs Colenso later wrote of Forncett, 'The dense ignorance and stupidity of the English rustic . . . was enough to drive the teacher to the rising generation as the only hopeful soil'.[3] Certainly Colenso seems to have devoted a good deal of time and attention to his own parish school. The original village school had been at St Mary's since 1814. A division of endowments was made between this older school and a new one was to be

---

[1] Colenso later attacked all ideas of sacrifice as debased and undesirable; see Rees, *op. cit.*, p. 243.
[2] *Minutes of Papers Read* etc., single loose page   [3] Rees, *op. cit.*, p. 32

built at St Peter's. Colenso supplied the bricks for the new school at cost price—presumably he owned a brick-field as rector of St Mary's. He is also said to have made 'advanced' changes in the syllabus taught at St Mary's school, introducing chemistry and astronomy. In 1858, five years after Colenso left, a report on the school says 'the mistress teaches in a gentle winning manner. What is done is carefully done, though the attainments are not high'.[1] Presumably Colenso failed to make the parish school a great centre of new learning!

If Colenso's parish contained the original school, Forncett St Peter kept the old rectory, and the Colensos had to build a house for themselves. In the meantime they lived about two miles away in a rented house. All this meant that the already crushing debt which haunted Colenso, was further increased, and also that Colenso was continually distracted by having to move back and forth between his parish and the private pupils at his home.[2] He was presumably a conscientious parish priest, since he complains that he cannot do his work properly until he is able to live beside his church, but one suspects that the school and his own pupils were his chief interest.

Four of Colenso's children were born at Forncett. He was deeply concerned that they should be properly educated, not least in the Christian life. When Harriette, the eldest, was five her father wrote to ask a friend whether he thought it necessary to teach children about Hell.

> I *think* you will agree with me that to teach a child to love its heavenly Father and to dread His displeasure, the loss of His favour, and separation from His presence, as the most painful of all punishments, is the true Christian way of training it [*sic*] for His service here and His glory hereafter.[3]

We have a picture, then, of the brilliant Cambridge mathematician set down in a tiny country parish, amongst 'ignorant' rural people, and old-fashioned clerical colleagues. His 'Maurician' theology and his interest in new scientific knowledge drives him to interest himself chiefly in his private pupils, the

[1] I am indebted, for this quotation, to Miss M. B. Armstrong, headmistress of Forncett St Peter school. The whole of this paragraph is based on information supplied by either Miss Armstrong or Professor F. E. Vokes.

[2] Cox, *op. cit.*, I, pp. 41 & 44

[3] *Ibid.*, p. 46

village school and the instruction of his own children. He will see whether a conscientious application of his principles will develop a new generation to whom Christianity, rational, scientific knowledge and love will be a single whole—and a basis for a whole life. And he is appalled by the laxity of the Church life of many of his people.

It does appear to me that the Dissenters have just cause to complain of Church Baptism if it is so prostituted,—at any rate that we, ministers, are bound to set forward the Truth that, however charitable a work it is to bring the little ones to Holy Baptism (thank God, we do not believe them to be then only first taken under the love of God in Christ, though formally taken into the Christian Covenant and admitted to all its hopes and promises), still it is but a mockery of God for careless parents to bring their children to the font, or to get others to bring them, and that a true Christian cannot become a sponsor, except on these conditions, (1) that he shall have reasonable ground of charitable hope that the child will be Christianly brought up, (2) have the permission of free access to the family when opportunities permit, for observation and instruction of the child, and (3) have himself a fixed and hearty resolution by God's help to discharge his duty towards it.[1]

Such views as these, coming from Colenso, are something of a surprise. They appear at first sight to accord to Baptism an importance which he was not later willing to allow. But, in fact, it is not Baptism as a sacrament which Colenso is stressing; it is Baptism as a human action—'formal admission to the Christian covenant', 'not then first taken under the love of God in Christ'—and the importance of the sponsor's willingness to fulfil his promise.

The meaning of Baptism was at the time a point of theological controversy. In 1847 an Anglican clergyman of Calvinist opinion, G.C. Gorham, was presented to the benefice of Bampford Speke, which was in the gift of the Lord Chancellor. The bishop of Exeter, in whose diocese the parish lay, was Henry Philpotts, an old-fashioned High Churchman sympathetically disposed towards the early Tractarian movement. He examined Gorham, suspecting that he did not believe in Baptismal Regeneration, and finding his suspicions justified, refused to

[1] Cox, *op. cit.*, I, p. 41

institute him. The lawsuit which followed ended in the Judicial
Committee of the Privy Council finding that Gorham was
entitled to hold the views he did and remain a clergyman of the
Church of England. The judgment caused a tremendous stir.
Manning and R. I. Wilberforce (brother of the bishop of
Oxford) and many others seceded to Rome. It seemed clear to
Tractarians that the Privy Council, by interpreting Anglican
formularies as if they were clauses in an Act of Parliament, was
allowing too much doctrinal latitude to 'heretics' while giving
'catholics' no liberty at all in matters of ceremonial. Rubrics,
formularies and articles of religion when interpreted in this
way are bound to be treated as if their directions as to ceremonial were precise and exact, while theological statements
must seem vague and loose to the legal mind. It seemed, therefore, that the Privy Council was bound to favour doctrinal
divergence while prohibiting ceremonial innovation. Gorham
believed that the sacrament of Baptism only 'regenerated' if it
was worthily received, which meant that one could not really
think of infants being regenerated at all. Tractarians regarded
such theology with horror. The good Dr Pusey had, after all,
written at great length and with enormous learning in the
contrary sense in *Tracts for the Times*.

We have seen that Colenso was certainly no Calvinist. His
views on the Gorham case reveal very clearly what he
believed to be the true position of the Church of England. He
knew Gorham personally. He was interested because Bampford Speke was in his native Cornwall. And he believed that
Gorham was being persecuted. '. . . I have no sympathy with
his doctrinal views; but I love and esteem the man for his
meek and guileless simplicity, and I detest the malice and spite
and slander of his enemies'.[1] In other words Colenso believed
that the Church of England was committed to no one 'view of
Divine Truth' and that Gorham had a perfect right to hold his
Calvinist opinions. There is the authentic ring of Maurice in
this; though one may doubt whether Maurice would have been
so 'liberal' as Colenso.

It was not long, however, before Maurice himself was under
fire for his views on eternal punishment.[2] Colenso reacted precisely as he had done in the case of George Gorham. He himself

---

[1] Cox, *op. cit.*, I, p. 45   [2] See *supra*, p. 20.

still believed that eternal punishment must mean 'the undying hatred of God for all sin' and 'a perpetual retention in that state of all who should once be subjected to it'.[1] When Maurice was attacked, and particularly when he was viciously attacked by the Evangelical *Record*, Colenso dedicated a volume of *Village Sermons* to his friend as a token of his sympathy. He did not agree with Maurice's opinions, but he was ready to suffer in defence of Maurice's right to express them. Maurice warned him that he *was* likely to suffer and it was not long before the *Record* was condemning Colenso's sermons as 'singularly deficient in the clear exposition of definitive Christian doctrine'.[2] In a spirited defence of his views, Colenso publicly expressed two beliefs which were to become the basis of much of his later 'heresy'. He maintained that 'Modern Science' led one to a far deeper and better understanding of God and His works, and that it was wrong to 'uproot altogether the old religion of the heathen mind'. Reliance upon modern science and natural religion were to bring Colenso to the point at which his theology of the atonement and his biblical scholarship could be made the substance of the charges against him.

The *Village Sermons*, nine of them, are not particularly significant theological works. One wonders what the rustics of Forncett made of them, if indeed they really represent the kind of sermons Colenso used to preach in the village church. Family tradition said that the non-conformists, as well as Church people for miles around, used to come to hear him. It is always difficult, of course, to make a fair criticism of sermons of another age, and Colenso certainly seems to have maintained a good reputation as a preacher throughout his life, but *Village Sermons* do not strike one as having any particular impact. Nor are they an easy yardstick for measuring Colenso's theology at the time. There is an odd mixture of advanced and conventional ideas. Colenso had not yet entirely abandoned normal nineteenth-century opinions. But there is enough of his incipient universalism for one to be able to understand why the *Record* disliked them so much. For anyone looking to the sermons for an example of how Colenso interpreted his 'Maurician' theology to his villagers, the collection is disappointing. The Depwade

---

[1] Cox, *op. cit.*, I, pp. 48f
[2] *Ibid.*

Clerical Society minutes are a much more fruitful source of information.

Already, by the time Colenso sought to defend Maurice, he had accepted the bishopric of Natal. Throughout his ministry at Forncett he had been conscious of the call of the mission-field. His brother-in-law had headed a new mission to Borneo. Colenso felt that he ought to go himself—that he would have gone joyfully were it not for his debts. 'It is a sore punishment for past improvidence'.[1] Colenso's brother-in-law, T.F. McDougall, eventually became bishop of Labuan. He had been 'captivated' by the adventures of James Brooke who became governor of Labuan, commissioner in Borneo and rajah of Sarawak. The Church Missionary Society established the mission, and though Colenso could not leave Forncett he continued to interest himself in the work in Borneo, trying to find missionaries, and maintaining contact with his brother-in-law. The last of Colenso's entries in the baptismal register at Forncett records the christening of his sister-in-law's baby. The child's father is described as a 'clergyman' and the address given is 'Sarawak'.[2]

But since Colenso could not go off to be a missionary, he would help missions as much as possible from Forncett. Rather oddly the society which he chose to support was not the C.M.S., with which one would have thought him more likely to be in sympathy, but the S.P.G.[3] He became the local secretary of the Society. From 1844 to 1851 he edited the Society's series *The Church in the Colonies*—the very series in which Robert Gray of Cape Town published the journals of his visitations of his enormous diocese when trying to raise funds and obtain permission for dividing the area into three new bishoprics. And in his last year at Forncett Colenso became editor of *The Monthly Record*, published by the S.P.G. Ernest Hawkins, secretary of the Colonial Bishoprics Fund, was godfather to young Francis Colenso. Charles Bunyon, Mrs Colenso's brother, was closely connected with the inner councils of the S.P.G. When, therefore, Gray came to look for a priest in England to be the bishop of Natal, and tried to persuade another priest in the Norwich

---

[1] Cox, *op. cit.*, I, p. 42
[2] I am indebted to Professor F. E. Vokes for this information.
[3] Rees, *op. cit.*, p. 33

diocese to allow his name to go forward (Dr Hills of Great Yarmouth), it was natural that Hills, being himself unwilling, should suggest Mr Colenso. All Colenso's interest in missionary work and his connections with the S.P.G. and the Colonial Bishoprics Fund, the two bodies which had largely sponsored the work of the Church in South Africa, must have led Gray to suppose that he would be ideally suited to the work.

The editor of Mrs Colenso's letters has shown very clearly that Gray cannot have been entirely ignorant of Colenso's 'heretical' opinions.[1] If he was inclined to discount rumour, then Colenso's public defence of Maurice ought to have made the whole matter plain. Yet Gray was delighted with Colenso's enthusiasm, and almost fullsome in his praise of the bishop-designate.[2] James Green, the priest at Pietermaritzburg, was ever afterwards automatically prejudiced against anyone whom Gray praised, lest he should turn out to be another Colenso.

As regards hard practical questions of finance, Colenso was able to accept Natal, only because his debts had been almost miraculously cleared.

> Like Peter in the prison, my bonds have literally dropped off: I have completed the National School Arithmetic; and for this and my other remaining copyrights Longmans have paid me down £2,400, which has enabled me to arrange for the complete discharge of my obligations, principal and interest. . . .[3]

Yet it represented a considerable financial sacrifice to go to Natal. Apart from having to surrender the copyright to his popular arithmetic books, he was exchanging the secure income from his living, his pupils and his books, for the uncertainties of a poorly endowed colonial see where he would be responsible, personally, for the financial liabilities of the diocese. Years later Colenso wrote to Gray pointing out that it had been a real sacrifice to exchange Forncett for Natal, just when his affairs were relatively free from encumbrances,[4] and there is no reason to doubt his word in the matter. It is certainly true

[1] *Ibid.*
[2] See A. T. Wirgman, *Life of James Green*, 2 vols., 1909, I, p. 17.
[3] Cox, *op. cit.*, I, p. 47
[4] Natal Archives; Colenso Collection, 'Church Matters' 215; undated draft of letter from Colenso to Gray

that Gray was having the greatest difficulty in raising the money
to endow the see. He had come to England in 1853 and there
suffered a complete breakdown through overwork. The news of
his illness and the publication of his journals aroused a great
deal of sympathy. The Colonial Bishoprics Fund appealed for
£22,500, and Gray added an appeal of his own. The S.P.C.K.
gave him £7,000 and the S.P.G. a further £3,000. Smaller
sums came from private sources, but most of the money was
ear-marked for the new diocese of Grahamstown, in the
Eastern Cape. Only £3,000 was for Natal.

Colenso had asked for six months in which to make up his
mind, but before the period was over he had already decided
to go to 'the noblest field ever yet opened to the missionary
labours of the Church'.[1] The government was anxious to
Christianise and pacify the African tribes in Natal. The diocese was supported by powerful societies at home. It looked
as if Colenso was being offered an ideal opportunity to put into
practice those theological principles which had been taking
shape in his mind during his incumbency of Forncett St
Mary.

He seems to have taken some of the village people to Natal
with him. One of these settlers wrote home to Forncett later,
addressing his letter from 'New Forncett, Natal', and saying
that he had just received a visit from 'the Doctor' (i.e. Colenso)
and that he was 'too fond of the Kaffirs'.[2] Presumably, therefore, these emigrants were not part of Colenso's missionary
team. We do not know why they went to Natal with him; it
may have been no more than a chance to better themselves.
But it seems to suggest that the rector was popular with his
people.

Colenso was nearly forty when he was consecrated on St
Andrew's day 1853. He was now a married man with four
children, with something of a reputation as the author of well-
known arithmetic textbooks. He was, for the first time, free
from debt. He had had little pastoral experience, but had a
great pastoral heart. He believed passionately in the fatherhood
of God, the innate goodness of man and in the value of human
reason. He had an essentially mathematical mind and a fervent

---

[1] *Cox, op. cit.,* I. p. 47
[2] For the substance of this letter I am indebted to Professor F. E. Vokes.

belief in common sense. He was no immature youngster; nor was he too old to work energetically in a new field. He knew what he was undertaking; his brother-in-law would have told him just what a new mission was like. He arrived in Natal on 30 January 1854, just after his fortieth birthday.

CHAPTER 3

The Bishop of Natal

COLENSO left England at the end of 1853 and though he returned from time to time, sometimes for quite long periods,
his *home* was always thereafter in Natal. He was to reappear
on the English *scene* in 1862, not so much in person, but as
a name, a watch-word, a battle-cry, or a term of abuse. And
for the next twenty years, however much he was physically
located in an obscure settlement in Natal, he was part of
English Church history. He left England, a man with some
'odd' ideas; but he was obviously not regarded as dangerous,
or the careful Gray would not have selected him for Natal.
In spite of his *Arithmetic*, his friendship with Maurice, and
his work for the S.P.G., he was in no sense a well-known
personality. After ten years as a colonial bishop—and Natal
was not a 'plum' diocese, even amongst colonial sees—he
emerged again as perhaps the most notorious Anglican bishop
of his generation. The story of that ten years has little to do
with English Church affairs, but it explains how Colenso
gradually manoeuvred himself into a position of complete isolation. We have seen how Colenso's ideas, though they may
have been regarded as 'liberal' and disturbing, do not seem
to have prevented his living on cordial terms with his brother
clergy in the Depwade deanery. Those same ideas might in
any case have made much more of a stir when they were
propagated by a missionary and a bishop. But what made it
possible for Colenso to be formally delated for heresy and
for his excommunication to be regarded as a just and fitting
extirpation of vicious wickedness, was precisely the fact that
in Natal the bishop utterly failed to maintain constant cordial
relations with any considerable section of Church people. He
began by quarrelling with the missionaries, then with the laity,
then with the clergy of his diocese, and finally with his brother
bishops. And it seems clear that in the course of these contro-

versies he deliberately made alliances with old enemies, in order to attack new ones.[1] In part it was Colenso's opinions themselves which made him unpopular. In part it was the bitterness and narrowness of his opponents which was to blame. But it remains true that the bishop's own touchy, prickly nature, his belief (which we have seen developing[2]) that he was called to unpopularity, and his readiness to see himself as unjustly persecuted, were partly responsible. At all events Colenso's life from 1853 to 1863 consists of one bitter quarrel after another until his final excommunication seems no more than a concrete recognition of what had, in fact, already happened in practice.

Natal was not, at the time of Colenso's arrival, a large or well-established colony. The Voortrekkers (farmers of Dutch ancestry who emigrated from the Cape Colony to establish republics of their own in the interior) arrived in Natal in 1837. There was already a settlement of whites at Port Natal (later renamed Durban) and Captain Alan Gardiner, R.N., was established there in the curious position of a British magistrate with jurisdiction over British subjects, but outside British territory. It was entirely typical of colonial policy in South Africa at this period that the government should seek to retain control over its subjects while hesitating to annexe any further territory. Piet Retief, the Voortrekker leader, attempted to negotiate with Dingane, the Zulu chief, in order to acquire for his party an independent territory where the emigrant farmers would have sovereign rights. He was treacherously murdered in the process and an Anglican missionary called Owen, who witnessed the murder, barely managed to persuade the Zulu chief to permit him to depart unharmed.[3] Port Natal was destroyed by the Zulus two months later, and it seemed that white settlement in Natal was doomed.

Owen's missionary venture had been the brain-child of Alan Gardiner, a keen Churchman. He persuaded the Church Missionary Society to sponsor the mission, cajoled Dingane into permitting Owen to settle amongst his tribesmen, and

[1] See *infra*, pp. 77ff.   [2] See *supra*, pp. 38f.
[3] On Owen & Gardiner in Natal see C. Lewis & G. E. Edwards, *Historical Records of the Church of the Province of South Africa*, 1934, pp. 22ff & 303ff; J. du Plessis, *History of Christian Missions in South Africa*, 1911, p. 235ff. Owen's diary was edited for the van Riebeeck Society in 1924.

was then compelled to watch the mission disappear, after only
a few months of life, in the disaster of 1838. It was the only
Anglican missionary activity in Natal until Gray arrived at
Cape Town ten years later. When Colenso reached his diocese
in 1853, the murder of Retief, Owen's escape, and the destruction of Port Natal, were only fifteen years old. Natal was
still regarded as a somewhat tenuous foothold of the white
man in a barbarous Africa. It was cut off from the Cape Colony
by the still independent African territory on either bank of the
Kei river.

The Zulu armies of Dingane had been defeated in 1839 by
the Voortrekkers at the battle of 'Blood River' and a republic
had been set up. Intrigues within the Zulu royal family resulted in Dingane's murder and the accession of Mpande, a
protégé of the Trekkers. The boundaries of the little republic
were the Umzimvubu river in the south and the Umfolozi
in the north, beyond which was Zululand. Captain Jervis,
appointed by the Cape governor to take command of Port Natal,
had some hand in the initial negotiations over the establishment
of the republic, but British forces had been withdrawn at the
end of 1839. The republic regarded itself as an independent
state, with some pretensions to suzerainty over Zululand.

The capital was Pietermaritzburg, then only a small village,
in the centre of the new state and about fifty miles inland from
Port Natal. On the coast the climate is sub-tropical, with lush
vegetation, a steamy hot atmosphere, and all sorts of weird
and wonderful fruits. Farther inland, where the hills climb up
towards the great Drakensberg range of mountains, the climate
is less tropical and the capital city can be cold in winter, while
the port is still sweltering in the coastal heat. The mountains
are the inland frontier of Natal, in places an impassable bar-
rier, beyond which lies the Transvaal where the Trekkers were
eventually to create their South African Republic. From the
mountains to the sea run a succession of rivers, making valleys
between the hills inland, and lagoons behind the sandbanks of
the coast.

The republic lasted only for a short while. In 1841 the
British government formally notified the Trekkers that it would
not recognise the independent state of Natal. In 1842 British
troops arrived in Port Natal. Fighting broke out. Reinforce-
ments were sent into the territory. The republican government

showed itself incapable of maintaining authority and the country became a British colony in 1843.

The new colony was smaller in extent even than the republic had been. When the boundaries were defined in 1845 (and Natal was declared a dependency of the Cape) the northern frontier was set at the Tugela river, some distance to the south of the Umfolozi. The population of the colony was about 100,000, of which the whites comprised perhaps three per cent. A good many of the Trekkers crossed the Drakensberg again, into the interior and away from the searching fingers of the British authorities. The population of the colony became increasingly British, so that by the turn of the century Natal was preeminently the 'English' part of South Africa.

The colony was governed by a lieutenant-governor and an executive council of official members. Theophilus Shepstone, son of a Methodist missionary, was given charge of the affairs of the Africans in the colony. His policy was paternal and kindly, but in a sense reactionary since he hoped to settle the tribesmen largely in reserves, isolated from too much Western civilisation, and to maintain and use tribal authority and traditions. Shepstone was to figure prominently in Colenso's story. To the north of the colony was Zululand under Mpande; and to the south, the Pondos. Both were recognised as independent African states. In 1854, the very year in which Colenso first set foot in Natal, the British government abandoned the Orange River Sovereignty, between the Cape Colony and the Vaal river. This meant that Natal was completely cut off from British territory elsewhere, and two years later it was made a separate Crown Colony. There were obvious advantages in having a separate administration for so remote a territory. At the same time a legislative council, with a majority of unofficial members, was created—though responsible government was not granted to the colony until the end of the century. In the meantime the Cape had gained a measure of representative government in 1853 (responsible government followed twenty years later). These constitutional facts were to become important in the litigation which followed Colenso's excommunication.

The Church was not strong in the Colony. Owen's missionary experiences had not tempted other Anglicans to follow him into Natal. Bishop Gray, desperately trying to create some sort of order out of the ecclesiastical chaos of his vast diocese, had not much time to spare for Natal. In 1849 he sent a young man called James Green to be his commissary and rural dean in the colony. Green was then twenty-eight.[1] Gray had hoped that the colonial office would make Green colonial chaplain, but Lord Grey (the Secretary of State) actually appointed W.H.C. Lloyd. Green arrived first, by a short head, and settled in Pietermaritzburg. Lloyd took up his duties in Durban.

There was one mission station in the colony. Gray had visited Natal, still part of his diocese, in 1850.[2] He regarded the colony as the most important mission field in British South Africa. A government commission in 1846, the year after Natal was declared a dependency of the Cape, had proposed that African tribes should be settled in reserves or locations, equipped with hospitals and schools. Very little was done to implement the scheme, but it was suggested that the Church might take charge of the development of the 'locations' with financial assistance from the government. The active opposition of white settlers in Natal and the lieutenant-governor's lack of interest prevented the scheme from coming to fruition,[3] but Gray did establish a station at Umkomaas Drift in the south of the colony. A priest called Methuen was sent to open this station in August 1853. His staff consisted of two catechists and an 'agriculturist'. But Colenso had hardly arrived in his new diocese, in 1854, when Methuen was compelled to take his wife back to England for her health's sake. The mission was only a few months old.

Elsewhere in South Africa the Church was stronger in numbers, if still disorganised and uncertain.[4] Gray's chief pre-occupation was with order and discipline. He arrived in Cape Town to find that there were no established missions in the diocese. Clergymen were paid and appointed by the State, or by the State and the Society for the Propagation of the Gospel. Churches were built by a weird procedure which constituted joint-stock companies, paying dividends out of the pew-rents. The governor was *ex officio* the ordinary, exercising the judicial

---

[1] For a full but partisan biography of Green see A. T. Wirgman, *Life of James Green*, 2 vols., 1909.

[2] C. N. Gray, *Life of Robert Gray*, 2 vols., 1876, I, pp. 288ff.

[3] B. B. Burnett, *Anglicans in Natal*, 1953, p. 33

[4] See P. Hinchliff, *The Anglican Church in South Africa*, 1963, pp. 10ff for a fuller description of conditions before Gray's arrival.

and visitatorial powers of a bishop.[1] Each congregation was given legal existence by means of an ordinance of the colonial government. And each congregation was regarded as a local embodiment of 'The United Church of England & Ireland'. Gray was anxious to do three things: to divide the diocese so that each bishop might control a less unwieldy area; to create some kind of synodical government so that the Church in Africa could control its own affairs and, more important, accept responsibility for its own finances; and to establish missions, so that the great shame of the Anglican Church might be removed.[2] Once the diocese was divided in 1853 the chief mission fields lay outside Gray's reduced diocese of Cape Town. The metropolitan turned his attention to the matter of synodical government.

Gray had already got into the habit of calling so-called 'synods' of his clergy in the first years of his episcopate. He had begun to distrust the establishment even before he arrived in his diocese,[3] and as representative government in the Cape drew nearer he became more and more anxious lest a legislature, representing the majority, 'Dutch', section of the population should be in a position to dictate to the Church. The alternative was to make the Church a self-governing institution. His first 'synods' were informal gatherings of the clergy, not legislative assemblies. One of these meetings considered the possibility of asking the government to replace the various ordinances constituting the individual churches by a single general ordinance recognising the existence of the Church in the colony as a whole. This plan had to be abandoned when it was realised that, if the government were once invited to legislate for the Church, it might amend or repeal that legislation (without being invited) in a direction unacceptable to the Church itself.[4] This conclusion meant that, in fact, the churches recognised by colonial ordinances could not be touched by subsequent synods unless their trustees voluntarily accepted the decisions of the synods.

By 1851, just before he went to England to arrange for the

---

[1] *Classified Digest of Records of S.P.G., 1701–1892*, p. 269
[2] C. N. Gray, *op. cit.*, I, p. 192
[3] *Ibid.*, p. 125
[4] *Ibid.*, p. 212 and see P. Hinchliff, *op. cit.*, p. 40f.

division of the diocese, Gray had decided that it was no good
waiting for either the colonial or the imperial government to
pass an Enabling Act to allow synods to meet. He was not
willing to follow the example of Bishop Selwyn in New Zealand in 1844, whose synod consisted of clergy only. Gray was
determined that the laity should assume responsibility for their
own Church.[1] He warned his diocese[2] that he intended to
summon a synod, that the synod would consist of the clergy
and of laymen representing the communicants of the various
parishes, and that it would be a legislative body whose resolutions would be mandatory. In their turn, several of the clergy
and laity warned their bishop that they would not be willing
to be drawn into any such synod at all. At the time when
Colenso was consecrated the position had not altered. It was
three years more before Gray actually issued the summons for
the synod.[3]

Colenso, meanwhile, had to take over his diocese. Since
Methuen left the single mission station within a matter of
weeks after Colenso's arrival, the clergy of the diocese consisted, for all practical purposes, of Green and Lloyd. It would
be difficult to conceive of a more oddly assorted pair.

Green had been at Durham University in its early days and
had then moved to Cambridge. Like Colenso he was a mathematician of ability, but he lacked Colenso's brilliance—or perhaps it was Colenso's application and earnestness that he
lacked.[4] His theological training Green acquired by reading
under a clergyman in Berkshire and he was ordained by Bishop
Blomfield in 1844. After four years in the diocese of London
he went out to South Africa to serve under Robert Gray. He
was a Tractarian of the most advanced kind. (In 1850 this did
not mean that he used eucharistic vestments.) Whereas Gray
was far more the old-fashioned High Churchman, Green was

---

[1] See correspondence between Gray and Archbishop Sumner in C. N. Gray,
op. cit., I, pp. 311ff. But Gray also said (at a later date), 'If they are very anxious
to come I must invite them. If they are indifferent, they will forfeit their
privilege . . .', Keble College, Oxford; Keble Papers (91), Gray to Keble,
17/12/1863.

[2] In a Pastoral Letter dated 15 November 1851 (C. N. Gray, *op. cit.*, I,
pp. 344ff)

[3] Pastoral Letter dated 15 November 1856, and printed with *An Address
delivered by the Right Rev. the Lord Bishop of Cape Town at the opening of the
First Synod*, 1857.

[4] A. T. Wirgman, *op. cit.*, p. 2, 'he went mad upon the boats. . . .'

definitely a product of the Oxford Movement. He made himself something of an expert in the canon law, and advised Gray on a good many aspects of the constitutional system the bishop was creating.[1] His theology was medievalist. Towards the end of his life he was to advance a quite fantastic theological explanation of university degrees and graduation as a basis for the creation of an examining body in the Province.[2] He saw everything in dramatic, romantic, blacks and whites. He was a Bernard struggling with an Abelard—an Athanasius at grips with a new Arius. He looked back on the great Church of the middle ages and he tried to behave as he thought men behaved when the Church dominated society, when ecclesiastical courts were materially powerful, when excommunication was a fearful threat with material consequences.

Green and Colenso disliked each other from the start. Colenso made a rather clumsy attempt to get rid of Green; the hints he dropped were elephantine. Gray was caught in an awkward position. He had to tell Green that Colenso would prefer to have another priest in Pietermaritzburg, but he tried to do it in a way which would not hurt Green.

> My own opinion is that neither of you fully appreciate each other. I think you have quite failed to see the beauty of his character, and the real nobleness of his disposition. He is a most devoted servant of God, and full of love for all that is good, and all good men.[3]

This panegyric was an honest account of Gray's real love for Colenso. But he went on to say, what a metropolitan ought never really to say to a thirty-three year-old priest about his bishop: 'He acts, when a cooler and more cautious man would be thinking whether he ought to act'. Green was Gray's choice for Natal. Even after the new bishop arrived, Green was still in a favoured position as 'Gray's man'. Colenso had made it clear that he would prefer Green's absence. And Green was from the very start ready to complain of Colenso's every action. It was not a promising beginning.[4]

[1] *Ibid.*, p. 14
[2] See P. Hinchliff, 'The Theology of Graduation' in *Studies in Church History*, I   [3] Wirgman, *op. cit.*, I, p. 17
[4] The principal sources for the first few years of Colenso's episcopate are A. T. Wirgman, *Life of James Green* and G. W. Cox, *Life of Bishop Colenso*, but since both are primarily controversial works the greatest care must be taken

Lloyd, in Durban, was a very different class of man. He was a Church of England parson to the backbone. He was old-fashioned. He was a Church and State man. When Colenso committed 'Biblical criticism', Lloyd was genuinely shocked. He attempted to prevent the bishop from entering his church. But when the courts proclaimed Colenso to be the lawful bishop of Natal, Lloyd felt he had no choice but to accept the court's decision and renew his loyalty to Colenso.

> Most talkative of them all and certainly most amusing was Mr. L., the English clergyman here. This charming ecclesiastic has been exceedingly attentive and kind. He is a thorough specimen of the good old type of country clergyman, of good birth, social instincts and genial sympathies.[1]

It would seem, from later events, that Lloyd did not even use the surplice in conducting services, and that he was somewhat rash in practical affairs.[2] He was, in fact, a colonial chaplain of the old type—very much a part of the English government, used to the quiet, comfortable, endowed existence of English country parishes, opposed to the innovations of the Tractarians, a firm believer in the Establishment, conscientious, kindly and hearty. He was plainly a good man, but not Colenso's sort nor the perfect team-mate for Green.

Colenso's visit to Natal in 1854 was a preliminary tour to investigate conditions and to see exactly what was necessary for the proper running of his new diocese. He decided that the mission station at Umkomaas Drift was not central enough to serve as his headquarters. In any case, the work there was hardly yet begun. The sensible thing seemed to him to be to move the station to a point nearer Pietermaritzburg. He was granted 8,500 acres of Crown land just outside the capital.[3] On this site were established both Bishopstowe, Colenso's residence, and Ekukanyeni, the chief mission station for the diocese. From one single centre Colenso planned to oversee both the missionary and the normal parochial work of the diocese.[4] He

in using anything other than the original documents which both authors fortunately quote extensively. Most of the letters printed in Cox, *op. cit.*, are also in the Campbell Library, Durban; Colenso Folios.

[1] Quoted in B. B. Burnett, *op. cit.*, p. 28.
[2] *Infra*, pp. 69f.   [3] Burnett, *op. cit.*, p. 39
[4] For Colenso's missionary plans and principles I am indebted to a thesis by B. B. Burnett, *The Missionary Work of the First Anglican Bishop of Natal*

ordained R. Robertson, one of the catechists from Umkomaas Drift, and left him in charge of the wild, unbroken site of the future Ekukanyeni. Robertson was to become the great missionary to the Zulus. Like most of the outstanding men in the diocese, he was to quarrel with Colenso, and eventually asserted his independence of the bishop. Already by 1854 he had acquired a valuable knowledge of the Zulu language and was the one real missionary at Colenso's disposal.[1] Robertson's was an intensely personal ministry. He loved people. He could mould and shape and convert them by love. His whole life was given to Zululand where, quietly and without figuring much in ecclesiastical politics, he built up a strong Christian community which was eventually to serve as the foundation of a new missionary diocese.[2]

Colenso made a very thorough tour of his see. Wherever he went he questioned Africans about their history and their religion. The history seems to have been somewhat garbled, either by Colenso or his informants. The bishop was impressed by the people as a whole, a little shocked at the 'be firm with the Kaffirs' attitude of most of the white settlers, but ready to be taught by Shepstone 'that too much familiarity . . . did much mischief in making them pert and presuming'.[3] He was excited by the possibility of using African religious customs as a foothold for Christianity, planning to officiate himself, if possible, at the Zulu feast of the first fruits so as to convert it into a kind of harvest festival.[4]

After three months Colenso returned to England. He had made his debut as 'an ambassador of Christ'.[5] He had made a thorough examination of the diocese and seen its weaknesses and deficiencies. He had made the acquaintance of Theophilus Shepstone and begun the alliance which was to take the two men a long way together until at last the inevitable quarrel separated them. It was now time for him to go back to England,

(Rhodes University, Grahamstown: M.A. thesis) parts of which were subsequently published in the same writer's *Anglicans in Natal*. See also J. W. Colenso, *First Steps of the Zulu Mission*, 1860.

[1] Burnett, *Anglicans in Natal*, pp. 39, 41, & 50f

[2] See P. Hinchliff, *The Anglican Church in South Africa*, pp. 63, 70, 96, 133, 165.

[3] Cox, *op. cit.*, I, p. 55

[4] *Ibid.*, pp. 58f

[5] See *Election of a Bishop*, reprinted from the *Natal Mercury*, 1866, p. 66.

to raise money for the diocese, and to recruit his team for the work. In England he published the journal of his visitation, *Ten Weeks in Natal*.[1] The book provoked the first attack on Colenso's theology.

Colenso refused to regard the heathen African as a wicked savage. His attitude to the feast of the first fruits was typical of his missionary approach. The African already knew a good deal about God; the missionary ought to use that knowledge. In his journal, which was intended to serve as a piece of propaganda for the diocese, he advocated using the Zulu word for the 'high god', in translating the Bible, instead of a word which seems to have been coined by missionaries on the eastern Cape frontier.[2] He also maintained that the Church ought to allow polygamists to be baptised. It seemed to him to be a sin against Christian charity to present the convert with a choice between foregoing baptism or putting away his extra wives. He hated hell-fire evangelism, for the same reason. It was a sin against the God of love. The storm aroused by his *Ten Weeks in Natal* did not subside quickly. Polygamy, in particular, was a controversial issue.[3] Pamphlets on the subject continued to appear for years.

The bishop returned to Natal in 1855 with his missionary team, including the new archdeacon of Natal, Charles Frederick Mackenzie.[4] Mackenzie has lately been the subject of a brilliant study, in which he is described as:

> . . . the simplest of men, if the epithet *simple* is used in its complimentary sense. Though an able mathematician, he was in a manner an unlearned man. He was content with a simple, practical faith. He barely felt the need of philosophising about faith, of studying Christian history or Christian thought, he was uninterested in theological argument and believed himself incompetent, he took no pleasure in metaphysics. His was the logic of the heart not of the head. . . . He had no guile and no capacity for compromise. He said what he thought when he thought it.[5]

[1] *Journal of a Ten Week Visitation of the Colony of Natal*, 1855
[2] See E. W. Smith (Ed.), *African Ideas of God*, 1950, pp. 98ff and cf. pp. 102ff.
[3] See Campbell Library, Durban; Colenso Folios, E.E.; papers relating to polygamy.
[4] There had been a not very serious suggestion that Maurice might become archdeacon of Natal, see Rees, *op. cit.*, p. 36.
[5] O. Chadwick, *Mackenzie's Grave*, 1959, pp. 37f.

Like Green, Mackenzie was a Tractarian; but of an older, gentler type than Green. He was inclined to dither in a crisis, but he was completely selfless, self-effacing and humble.

Another new recruit already established in the colony by the time Colenso returned was Henry Callaway.[1] Callaway was again a very different type from Mackenzie. He was by nature brisk, efficient, clear-thinking, and capable of expressing his opinion caustically on occasion. Callaway had been a Quaker. He was a doctor of medicine. When he heard that Colenso had gone to Natal he offered his services to the new bishop, returned to the Anglican Church and was ordained. He went to Natal and took charge of Ekukanyeni until Colenso's return, but found it difficult to work in close proximity to the bishop and soon set up a mission station of his own. He admired Colenso; perhaps he owed his missionary vocation to Colenso's influence. But he differed from the bishop in important theological matters, and particularly over polygamy.[2] He remained loyal to Colenso as long as possible, refusing to be drawn by the bishop's opponents into the hysterical controversy which developed so soon.

The principal *dramatis personae* for this part of Colenso's life were now all upon the scene. There was the bishop himself; liberal in theology, passionately concerned for the gospel of love, with a chip on his shoulder and an active inquiring mind. There was Gray, the metropolitan, born and brought up in the High Church tradition, mistrustful of his own academic abilities,[3] conservative, yet sympathetic towards the Tractarians, a great administrator and pastor, always anxious to see the best in men. There was Green at Maritzburg—a narrow 'catholic', inclined to dramatise himself and his situation, honestly horrified by Colenso's liberalism, and one of the hardest working priests in South Africa. There was Mackenzie as archdeacon, something of a dreamer, and the gentlest of all Colenso's clergy. Lloyd at Durban typified the old Church of England parson at his best. Robertson, the missionary who came up from the bottom of the ladder, was earnest, hardworking, devoted. Callaway, the other missionary, was clear-cut,

[1] For a life of Callaway see M. S. Benham, *Henry Callaway*, 1877
[2] See H. Callaway, *Polygamy: a bar to admission to the Christian Church*.
[3] On this point see P. Hinchliff, *The Anglican Church in South Africa*, 1963, pp. 27f.

decisive, more of a genuine scientist than Colenso, but intensely loyal to the man whose theological judgment he could not entirely trust. It was an explosive mixture, and Colenso was to be the spark.

The bishop had already indicated that *Ten Weeks in Natal* was not the last of his attempts to set out his missionary theology. When he brought his new team to Natal in 1854 he had occupied their time on board by various courses of study, including a series of lectures on the Epistle to the Romans.[1] These were a deliberate attempt to expound, on the basis of scripture, the gospel which the bishop proposed to preach to his heathen flock. At the time they seem to have caused no stir at all. Perhaps Mackenzie, the one really well-educated person in the audience, felt himself inadequate to the task of arguing with Colenso. Certainly he was the last person in the world to begin his ministry under a new bishop by charging that bishop with heresy.

Later, when Colenso was involved in a controversy over eucharistic theology, Mackenzie wrote, 'The Bishop has lately preached and published two sermons, which I do not at all like. . . . I am not learned nor well read, and so am diffident of my own opinion. . . .'[2] In any case Colenso and Mackenzie shared a common zeal for a religion of the heart. The bishop would seem to his archdeacon to be a good man and, if his theology was unusual, the 'unlearned' and diffident Mackenzie was not likely to question its orthodoxy. But these lectures later formed the basis of Colenso's commentary on Romans and when the book was published it precipitated the famous heresy trial.

The new bishop's first task on dry land was to establish the settlement at Bishopstowe and Ekukanyeni. The site was a magnificent one.

> . . . upon a long sweep of hill, surmounted by other lower rises on each side, but over-topped to the north at right angles by a higher range into which one end of its own ascends. Upwards to the north, downwards to the east and west, swept wide the plantations of trees, grown by ourselves, those to the west bounded by a sluggish stream, white with lilies every autumn, across which a long low bridge with heavy weeping willows led to the steep

---

[1] G. W. Cox, *op. cit.*, I, p. 135
[2] U.M.C.A. Archives, London; letter from Mackenzie dated 17/3/1858

and winding drive, bordered on either side by choice and foreign shrubs.[1]

Colenso's original home no longer exists, except for part of the old chapel which is now an outbuilding of a farm-house, but the site is still magnificent. There is a dusty, winding road out of Pietermaritzburg and then, from the top of the hill, the view towards the city on the one side and the hills and mountains stretching away on the other. Here Colenso brought his family. Frances Colenso, with intellectual tastes, fond of the society of intelligent people, brought up amongst nice things and a comfortable if not luxurious way of life, was five months gone with their fifth child. She had no home, as yet, only the barest of shelters. The elder of her two little girls was six; the two boys were still hardly more than babies. It must have seemed to the gentle Mrs Colenso that she had condemned her small family to a Robinson Crusoe kind of life. The family stayed in Pietermaritzburg for a while, while some sort of shelter was being built at Bishopstowe. Even when they moved out there, their home was the very simplest and roughest little cottage. The bishop had a summer-house for a study, where he worked at his sermons, his translations, and his elementary Zulu textbooks. The timber was cut and the bricks were made on the site itself; and the bishop did his share of the labour. Trees were planted, a chapel constructed, the beginnings of a farm laid out. It was a hard, exacting life for the whole family.

The bishop deliberately chose to live outside his see city, so as to be his own chief missionary. Like most early South African bishops he was obliged to shoulder a two-fold task. On the one hand he had to care for the white settlers, to whom the Church was one of the precious sentimental links with England, 'home', the 'old country'. Inevitably, for such people, the Church had to be run on lines as much like 'home' as possible. There must be parishes, vicars, churchwardens, and *no interference from the bishop*. Colenso was never entirely able to satisfy the demands of this prickly, expatriate churchmanship, but he tried from the first to model his oversight of white congregations, as far as possible, upon the pattern of the English system. He was at hand; but he was outside even his see city.

[1] Cox, *op. cit.*, I, pp. 76f

But the missions were different. Colenso had not come to
Natal to be an English bishop (and it was the irony of history
that he was driven, in the end, into precisely this position) but
to be a missionary. In white parishes clergymen would be
licensed and then allowed to behave like English incumbents,
but Ekukanyeni was to be the real centre of all missions. The
bishop himself would be the director, immediate as well as
ultimate, of all mission work. And from Ekukanyeni the ten-
tacles would spread out till they covered every 'native reserve'
in Natal. For various reasons the plan failed to work. Callaway
and Robertson, the first two men to start new subsidiary
mission stations, both eventually broke free from Colenso's
direct control. Yet Ekukanyeni was the model mission station.
It contained a printing-press, a school, a theological college, a
farm, a smithy, a carpenter's shop, a brick-field, and a church.
By 1861 the bishop had spent over £11,000 on the establishment and equipping of the station. It was the show piece of
Anglican missions in Southern Africa.[1]

The bishop's labours were prodigious. He threw himself
with enthusiasm into the work of creating the tools necessary
for missionary preaching.

Less than three months after his party's arrival in the Colony
Colenso advertised in the colonial press a Zulu-English Dictionary, a Zulu Grammar and a revised version [in Zulu] of St
Matthew's Gospel. This very zealous and bustling man achieved
an astonishing amount in the linguistic field in the first seven
years of his episcopate, and this in addition to establishing a new
mission and administering a Diocese. There is no suggestion that
his work was shoddy or carelessly done. His production of works
in Zulu had equalled those of the most influential missionary
body in the Colony at that time, and one which had been active
in Natal long before his advent. He had translated the entire New
Testament, and the books of Genesis, Exodus and Samuel in the
Old. He had published, with financial aid from the Government,
a dictionary of 522 pages, various Zulu reading books, a Zulu
Liturgy, a tract on the Decalogue, and readers in Geography,
Geology, History and Astronomy, apart from sundry Grammars
—a truly herculean labour.[2]

[1] See *Classified Digest of Records of S.P.G.*, 1701–1892, p. 330
[2] B. B. Burnett, *op. cit.*, pp. 45f

Within a year of the bishop's arrival with his family and team of workers there was the first really serious quarrel in the diocese. Colenso constituted a cathedral chapter in 1856. Green became dean of Pietermaritzburg, Mackenzie was archdeacon, and Callaway and J. D. Jenkins were installed as canons. Jenkins was a fellow of Jesus College, Oxford, and something of a liturgist and theologian. He became chancellor of the new cathedral.

In the same year there was trouble in Durban. The bishop moved Lloyd away from St Paul's, the church in Durban, and sent Mackenzie to take charge. His ground for this interference was that St Paul's congregation had got into serious financial difficulties. The bishop helped to make up the deficit, but, in return, demanded the right to control the church according to his own wishes. In view of later events, the bishop's wishes seem rather odd. He sent Mackenzie to Durban with specific instructions to introduce the Prayer for the Church, a collection, and the use of the surplice.[1] At the time these were contentious matters. All three South African bishops were anxious to do away with pew-rents and the control over churches and services which these rents gave to the laity. The laity, who had had to manage their own affairs for nearly half a century, resented what they regarded as the high-handed behaviour of the bishops. There was trouble in all three dioceses.[2] In Cape Town it took the form of an active opposition to Gray's plans for a synod. In Port Elizabeth it resulted in the establishment of a dissident congregation. And in Durban there were open riots. Colenso's effigy was burnt in the market square. Newspapers ranted at the bishop's 'popery'.

Civil despotism is bad. Military despotism is worse, but spiritual despotism is worst of all and this, it would seem, is the despotism under which we live. The Bishop is practically our ruler. His word is law. People of Natal, who love your Queen and the glorious constitution which elsewhere, wherever the sun shines, guarantees liberty of conscience and the right of self-government, will you in this little corner of Her Majesty's Dominions, few and

---

[1] 'The Bishop . . . asked me if, now that I saw conciliation was of no use, I would introduce the offertory and the surplice': U.M.C.A. Archives; letter of Archdeacon Mackenzie, partly quoted in H. Goodwin, *Memoir of Bishop Mackenzie*, 1870, p. 112.
[2] Hinchliff, *op. cit.*, p. 49

feeble as you are, will you suffer your Sovereign's honour to
be tarnished and your dearest rights to be crushed under the
iron hoof of a petty, despicable despotism, skulking under a
Bishop's Lawn while it wields the tyrant's sword? No, never,
never, never. Rouse ye. Quit ye like men—like free born Englishmen.[1]

A 'Church of England Defence Association' was formed to
resist the bishop and to preserve the principles of the Reformation. (It subsequently claimed to have converted the bishop to
its own point of view.)[2] Questions were asked in the Natal
legislature, and Colenso had to insist that the Church in the
colony was not established and that the legislature had no
rights over it.[3] Mackenzie was in an intolerable position. He
was not the right man to fight such a battle anyway. He was
not entirely convinced that the bishop had kept his word to the
vestry of St Paul's.[4] He was the object of a vicious and slan-
derous attack. An eccentric and fanatic, Patrick Carnegy, laid
a charge of murder and conspiracy against the archdeacon. The
charge, of course, failed. Carnegy was tried for perjury and
found 'not guilty on grounds of insanity'.

In the meantime Green had been writing to Gray. The
correspondence gave a most confused and confusing picture of
what was happening. Green accused Colenso of introducing
innovations into the Church services. These innovations seem
to have been the use of the Ante-Communion service (with the
Offertory and Prayer for the Church) after Evensong as well
as after Matins, and the introduction of a petition for missions
and the heathen into the Prayer for the Church itself. At the
same time the people of St Paul's were complaining of
Colenso's innovations—by which they meant the surplice, the
Offertory (i.e. a collection), and the Prayer for the Church.
Green used all these at Pietermaritzburg. He seems to have
given Gray the impression that, while the Durban congregation was 'protestant' and rebellious, the bishop was much to

---

[1] Burnett, *op. cit.*, p. 57. Letters dealing with St Paul's, Durban are to
be found in the Campbell Library; Colenso Folios, N. The date on the file
(1885–6) is misleading. Some of the letters date from 1856.

[2] *Correspondence between Bishop Macrorie and the Rev. A. K. D. Edwards*, 1896,
Introduction

[3] C. Lewis & G.E. Edwards, *Historical Records*, p. 314

[4] See Mackenzie's letter, already cited, in U.M.C.A. Archives. I am greatly
indebted to Canon Broomfield for having copies made of such parts of Mackenzie's letters as are not printed in H. Goodwin's *Memoir*.

blame for what had happened. Gray advised Colenso to adhere
strictly to the Prayer Book; but it is not clear that Gray had
distinguished between the two different, but similar, charges
of innovation. He blamed Colenso for bringing out the wrong
kind of people to work in his diocese and for giving way at the
wrong moment. He was probably right in his last complaint.[1]
But the other was almost certainly groundless. Lloyd had not
been brought out by Colenso. In any case, Mackenzie persuaded Colenso to withdraw his afternoon Offertory and Ante-
Communion and, apart from these curiosities, Colenso and his
archdeacon were only doing what Green and Gray already did.
The bishop's nerve, however, seems to have been shaken. He
began to defer, for a time, to Green's judgment,[2] and, though
Carnegy had proved an unreliable witness, he gave way also to
the Durban laity. He restored Lloyd to St Paul's, sent
Mackenzie out into the country districts, and allowed the vestry
of St Paul's to have its way. He even began to draft a bill for
the Natal legislature, which would have had the effect of giving
that assembly control over Church affairs.[3] But he had made
his first enemies.

His next clash was with Green and the Chapter. It began
with two quite separate issues. A priest called Crompton, an
advanced Tractarian, asked for leave to celebrate in his own
house since he found that the Eucharist was very infrequently
celebrated in Durban. He was also anxious to restore the use
of vestments. Colenso was unwilling to allow this request.
Thereupon Crompton wrote to 'petition your Lordship to
cause the Holy Sacrifice of the Eucharist to be more frequently
offered in the Church in this place'.[4] Colenso again refused;
and Crompton's language must have seemed to him in the
highest degree 'un-English'. Crompton then announced that he
regarded Colenso as no longer a bishop of the Catholic Church
and himself as free to disregard his injunctions. Gray, Green
and Mackenzie all, at this stage, backed the bishop and condemned Crompton's contumacy.[5] Gray never withdrew his
condemnation,[6] but the others subsequently changed their

---

[1] See C. N. Gray, *op. cit.*, p. 395 for Gray's complaints.
[2] U.M.C.A. Archives; Mackenzie's letters, 7/4/1856
[3] A. T. Wirgman, *op. cit.*, I, p. 33
[4] *Ibid.*, p. 34
[5] *Ibid.*, p. 35
[6] Letter dated 16 April 1867, in C. N. Gray, *op. cit.*, II, p. 302

6

minds. Green's biographer devotes a considerable space to an attempt to justify Crompton's actions.

The matter which caused Green to change his opinion was a controversy about eucharistic theology.[1] In 1857 the bishop came to suspect that the dean, as his examining chaplain, was failing candidates for orders on the grounds that they did not hold the Tractarian teaching on the Real Presence. The bishop maintained that, since the examining chaplain was his deputy, he ought to be requiring candidates to hold a doctrine of the Eucharist such as the bishop himself would approve. Green, on the other hand, seems to have believed that the dean of a cathedral chapter ought *ex officio* to be the diocesan expert in theology—the person to whom application might be made when a definition in some doctrinal matter was required. The nub of their actual theological difference was that whereas Colenso believed that our Lord's manhood is communicated to believers *in exactly the same way* at the Eucharist and at other times, Green believed that there was no such communication 'in ordinary assemblies' of the faithful. Green had again been in touch with the metropolitan, informally, and Gray once more committed himself somewhat unwisely to certain criticisms of the bishop of Natal. The dean, Gray said, was 'too ready to take offence': but Colenso was 'hasty, irritable, and perhaps imperious'—'the sins and infirmities which beset those who have power and authority'.[2]

The argument between Colenso and his dean dragged on into 1858.[3] The climax came when Colenso, having warned Green of his intention, preached on the subject of the Eucharist at an ordination in his cathedral. Green did not communicate because he believed that Colenso's views were formal heresy. The bishop wrote to ask whether Green intended to make a regular practice of this withdrawal from communion with his own bishop, and Green summoned the Chapter (a somewhat unconstitutional and presumptuous act) to advise him on his reply. When Colenso saw the minutes of this meeting he was so angry that he forbade the Chapter to have any further communication in the matter with him at all. Green referred the

---

[1] W. Rees, *Colenso Letters from Natal*, has a chapter on the early controversies, but it is a series of inaccuracies. The eucharistic controversy is said to have been 'on the sacrament of baptism', p. 60   [2] Wirgman, *op. cit.*, I, p. 36
[3] *Ibid.*, pp. 52ff & Cox, *op. cit.*, I, pp. 97ff

whole thing to the metropolitan, warning Colenso that he proposed to do so, but not telling him what form the missive actually took. The formal presentation is a long document containing extracts from Colenso's sermons and was signed by Green and Canon Jenkins. Green's biographer presents the whole story in a confusing and partisan manner, but it is plain, when the letters are arranged in their proper chronological order, that Green's presentation of his bishop was sent to Gray at a time when Colenso believed that Green was merely referring the matter to the metropolitan (and to the archbishop of Canterbury) as a difficult theological question on which an authoritative opinion was required. Colenso's chief concern was for Gray. The metropolitan was in England. He was tired and he was very busy. Colenso was desperately sorry that he should be burdened with such an unpleasant matter at this time. Green was anxious lest he should be too weary to make a forthright stand for the truth.

Gray sent two replies to Green. The first, in May 1858, was an informal one. He told Green he had consulted Bishop Wilberforce of Oxford, who was convinced that the dean's view was heretical on the point of the communication of our Lord's manhood to the faithful outside the Eucharist.[1] Colenso's teaching was characterised as 'vague and unsatisfactory', but the real blow was the use of the word heresy to describe Green's own teaching. The formal reply followed a month later. Gray refused to allow proceedings against Colenso for heresy. He said, and Wilberforce's tactful diplomacy probably lies behind his statement, that Green's language went beyond that of the Church, while it was probably orthodox in itself, and that Colenso's teaching was dangerously vague but not actually heretical. Unkindest cut of all, from Green's point of view, was a quotation from the decrees of the Council of Trent cited in Colenso's favour.[2]

There the matter had perforce to rest. It had had two important consequences. It had made Colenso suspicious of the Tractarian clergy in his diocese, and of Gray in so far as he sympathised with them. It also drove Colenso to question Gray's authority as metropolitan. There was no formally constituted province of South Africa at this time, no clear-cut rules,

---

[1] Wirgman, *op. cit.*, I, p. 61
[2] *Ibid.*, p. 65

no constitution providing for such things as the trial of bishops or the authority of the metropolitan. Colenso maintained that although Gray was metropolitan by letters patent (and the patent gave him specific visitorial jurisdiction in Natal)[1] he was not an 'independent metropolitan' 'by Church authority'. Colenso believed that he and Gray were both 'in a certain sense within the *Province* of Canterbury' in terms of Gray's patent, and in spite of the oath of canonical obedience to Gray which he had taken at his consecration.[2]

The eucharistic controversy in Natal was responsible, also, for the first breach in the friendship between Colenso and Maurice. In 1856 Colenso still considered himself a 'Maurician'.[3] In the same year Maurice wrote to Mrs Colenso, 'Tell the Bishop, with my kindest love, that the battle [over missionary methods] he is fighting is ours also; nothing less than the battle whether the devil or the Father of our Lord Jesus Christ is God'.[4] But when Colenso's sermons on the Eucharist were published in 1858, Maurice dissociated himself from the bishop's teaching. Colenso was shocked. He accused Maurice of not having read the sermon in question. And the reason he gave illustrates perfectly how Colenso misunderstood Maurice's teaching, even when he was most strongly influenced by it. Colenso says that Maurice cannot have read his (Colenso's) sermon because he has read a sermon of Maurice's and agrees with every point save two—that Christ's presence in the sacrament is of a different kind than at other times; and that the sacrament transcends all other modes of intercourse with God! Colenso simply could not believe that Maurice really agreed with Green.[5] Between 1858 and 1860 the salutation in Colenso's letters to Maurice changes from 'My dear friend' to 'Dear Mr Maurice'.[6]

It is worth noting that at this stage Colenso had committed himself to several opinions which he was later to find most inconvenient. In the troubles at Durban he had asserted the

---

[1] An abstract of the patents is given in E. Hawkins, *Documents Relative to the Erection and Endowment of Additional Bishoprics in the Colonies, 1841–1855*, pp. 65ff. Gray's letters patent are in the Diocesan Library, Cape Town.

[2] Cox, *op. cit.*, I, pp. 100f

[3] Letter quoted in W. Rees, *Colenso Letters from Natal*, p. 58

[4] Cox, *op. cit.*, I, p. 91

[5] *Ibid.*, pp. 113ff

[6] Campbell Library, Durban; Colenso Folios; I 5-14

desirability of certain 'High Church practices' and had maintained vigorously that the Church in the colonies was not established. In the eucharistic controversy he had argued that the archbishop of Canterbury had an appellate jurisdiction in South Africa and that Gray's authority was defective because he was metropolitan by royal letters patent only and not by Church authority. From all these opinions he was, in the press of later events, to depart either openly or by implication.

In the period following the controversy over eucharistic theology two other matters developed which had the effect of widening still further the breach between Colenso, on the one hand, and Gray and the Tractarian clergy in Natal, on the other. At the same time Colenso came closer to the laity. It would seem, though his biographer deliberately minimises this as much as possible, that the bishop now deliberately sought the backing of the very laymen in Durban with whom he had so violently quarrelled in the first years of his episcopate.[1] The two fresh controversies developed concurrently, but it is more convenient to consider each in turn.

Bishop Gray's visit to England at the time when Green presented Colenso for heresy had as its primary purpose the establishment of a missionary diocese. Gray believed that the Province[2] ought to be sponsoring missions outside its borders, and that such missions ought to be headed by a bishop.[3] He was anxious to have Zululand, to the north of Natal, proclaimed as a missionary diocese and to send a bishop into the territory with a team of missionaries. He persuaded the Secretary of State for the Colonies to allow the consecration of a bishop to take place in South Africa[4] and he asked Colenso whether he would commend Archdeacon Mackenzie as the new bishop. This Colenso did, warmly and willingly. Unfortunately at this point Mackenzie and Green began to side openly with Crompton in his rebellious attitude to the bishop and Colenso withdrew his commendation. For a time it was proposed that Mackenzie should still head the mission, but as archdeacon not as bishop. This compromise broke down

[1] Cox, *op. cit.*, I, pp. 103f
[2] Using the term 'Province' in a loose sense
[3] Hinchliff, *op. cit.*, p. 69f.
[4] Bishopscourt Archives, Cape Town; Memoranda EHD III; Summary of the facts relating to the Organisation of the Church of the Province.

because Gray believed that new missions outside the boundaries of British South Africa should be a provincial responsibility and headed by a provincial official under the authority of the metropolitan. To Colenso this seemed as though Gray were about to appoint a deputy to work on the boundaries of the diocese of Natal—an outpost of Tractarian Cape Town on his own frontier. Zululand was, if it was to be an archdeaconry at all, an obvious dependency of Natal, not of Cape Town over a thousand miles away. The bishop of Grahamstown, a staunch Evangelical called Cotterill, sided with Colenso in pouring scorn on Gray's pretensions to exercise metropolitical jurisdiction beyond the limits of British territory (i.e. where his letters patent could not possibly confer any authority whatsoever).[1]

It would seem that Colenso also feared that, once it was agreed that Mackenzie should lead a mission and should be answerable only to the metropolitan, Gray would consecrate him sooner or later whether Colenso agreed or not. The bishop of Natal tried every expedient to prevent this situation from arising. He seems to have thought of proposing Callaway as bishop of Zululand. He suggested that he should himself resign Natal and head the new mission. He obtained the support of the S.P.G. for the scheme[2] and set off on a tour of the African territory. He came to the conclusion that the time was not ripe for a Zulu mission at all. There was too much unrest and suspicion in the country. He sent Robertson to start a centre at Kwamagwaza, but that was all.[3] In the meantime the delay had effectively prevented Gray's scheme from maturing. Under Livingstone's influence the metropolitan agreed to place the new mission in central Africa. The English universities provided the money necessary and Mackenzie went to be the first bishop on the Zambezi.

The other matter in dispute at this time concerned synodical government. Like both his brother bishops in South Africa, Colenso 'longed for the time when the whole body of the clergy and the laity who should come to my help, should together

---

[1] Cox, op. cit., I, pp. 338ff. The validity of the letters patent and not the question of whether Mackenzie should be consecrated in England or South Africa (cf Rees, op. cit., p. 61) was the point at issue. Convocation officially requested Gray to consecrate in South Africa, by a resolution of 8 June 1860.

[2] Classified Digest of the Records of S.P.G., p. 337

[3] Ibid., and also Cox, op. cit., I, p. 120

make their own laws, and change the government of the Church
in this diocese from an apparent despotism under a single head,
or from a state of anarchy and confusion, to one of orderly and
constitutional rule'.[1] Gray had already summoned his first
synod in Cape Town, and had provoked a violent protest
against synodical government on the grounds that it was an
innovation, illegal, and likely to cause a separation from the
Church in England. Colenso sought to make his assembly rather
different from Gray's, which had consisted of three 'houses'—
the bishop, the clergy and representatives of the laity. The
bishop of Natal called a conference to discuss the actual form
the assembly should take. The conference itself consisted of
both clergy and laity. The bishop asked them to decide whether
it was 'desirable that at regular intervals a body *similar to this*
should be convened, for deliberating and deciding upon matters
properly falling *within its cognisance*'.[2] The words italicised[3]
were the real cause of the trouble, for Colenso had specifically
stated that the conference was an advisory not a legislative
body, that the clergy and laity together made up the assembly,
and that the matters 'falling within its cognisance' were those
defined in a bill brought before the Imperial Parliament by the
archbishop of Canterbury, passed by the Lords, rejected by the
Commons, and finally withdrawn altogether in 1856. This bill
had specified that colonial Church synods might not legislate
on matters relating to doctrine, the Bible, the Prayer Book, or
the Articles, but on order and discipline—disputes, finances,
education and missions, patronage and property. In itself this
was not a contentious provision, but it meant that questions of
'heresy' were not to come within the purview of the assembly,
but that the discipline of the clergy was to be handled by a
body in which clergy and laity sat together and where the clergy
could be swamped by the laity. This did not appear to Green
and his friends to be a synod in the sense in which synods
existed in either the primitive or the medieval Church. One
could not be an Athanasius or a Bernard if one were forbidden
to discuss doctrine. One could not imagine Athanasius or
Bernard allowing the laity to dictate to the clergy. And in any
case the bishop would not be bound to accept the decisions
of the assembly, if its function was purely advisory. In Cape

---

[1] Cox, *op. cit.*, I, p. 103   [2] *Ibid.*   [3] The italics are mine.

Town a measure might be blocked by any of the three houses. In Natal the laity could overwhelm the clergy, and the bishop possessed an absolute veto.

There can really be little doubt that Colenso deliberately devised this form of synodical assembly in order to gain the support of the Protestant and Erastian laity against the Tractarian clergy. It was a consequence of his capitulation after the Durban troubles. In his preliminary remarks to the members of the conference the bishop hinted that he was prepared to go over completely to the point of view of the dissidents.

> I would here place myself wholly in the hands of the conference, assured that you will consider both what is due to my office among you, and what is due to the peace and welfare of the parish of Durban, and, with it, of the whole Church in this diocese.[1]

As the conference contained a majority of laymen this was really a plain hint that the bishop was ready to give way to lay opinion on the points at issue. It was a triumph for the 'Church of England Defence Association'.

The conference,[2] largely under the influence of Durban laymen, voted against the creation of a synod on the Cape Town pattern and for a Church Council on the lines Colenso had proposed—'a body similar to this'. Green, Mackenzie, Jenkins and Robertson withdrew from the conference—more than half the clergy of the diocese.

This preliminary conference met on 20 April 1858. The first meeting of the Church Council was set for 13 March 1859. The four dissident priests issued a formal protest against the proceedings.[3] Gray encouraged them in their action and they themselves began to side with Crompton against Colenso, thus helping to bring the Zululand bishopric scheme to nothing. The Church Council drew up a long resolution condemning the action of Green and his supporters. This document, also, was sent to Gray. The metropolitan would take no action to interfere in the internal arrangements of the diocese, but he clearly believed that Colenso had behaved in an improper manner.[4]

The squabble dragged on into the 1860s. Mackenzie went

---

[1] Cox, op. cit., I, pp. 103f

[2] Campbell Library, Durban; Minutes of a Conference of Clergy and Laity in the Diocese of Natal, convened on 20 April 1858

[3] Wirgman, op. cit., I, pp. 76f   [4] Ibid., p. 80

to his missionary diocese and his death. Colenso appointed another priest to take Jenkins's place on the Chapter and tried, yet again, to get rid of Green. Gray proposed a compromise, which Colenso was willing to adopt, but which Green rejected.[1] The Council continued to exist, but it could never be an entirely effective instrument for Church government so long as a large proportion of the small body of clergy refused to recognise its authority. Colenso even had some difficulty in persuading Lloyd and the parish at Durban to support the Council.[2]

But in 1861 these lesser controversies were all swamped by the furore consequent upon Colenso's publication of his commentary on Romans—*St Paul's Epistle to the Romans: newly translated, and explained from a missionary point of view*. It was no chance that this work became the storm-centre of the whole controversy. It was a fuller and more elaborate version of the lectures delivered by Colenso to his party of mission-workers in 1854. It was a deliberate attempt, as the lectures had been, to expound a missionary gospel, the essential faith to be preached to the heathen. It was a deliberate statement of doctrinal policy made by the most important missionary in South Africa.

One might have thought that Romans was the least likely, of all the books of the New Testament, to serve as a basis for the liberal and universalist teaching of the bishop of Natal. St Paul's opening chapters show how man ought, by nature, to have a knowledge of God, but the Apostle goes on to argue that by perverting his ideas of God man has perverted his own nature, and is now unable to know God by the light of nature alone. The epistle is the favourite source-book for those who advance the doctrines of justification by faith alone and of predestination. It would seem an unpromising field for someone who wanted to emphasise the importance and value of natural religion, and presumably it was the very unpromising nature of the material which led Colenso to make the epistle the crux of his argument. If he could interpret Romans in a manner favourable to his view, he had captured the enemy's citadel. We have already seen how, in his days at Forncett, he dealt with the doctrine of election. He now proceeded to deal in a similar

[1] *Ibid.*, p. 94
[2] Natal Archives, Pietermaritzburg; Colenso Collection, 136, Correspondence; Colenso to Lloyd, 21/6/1858

manner with the whole of St Paul's teaching. It was a deliberate attempt to demonstrate how the bishop of Natal interpreted St Paul's gospel to the heathen who had never heard the gospel before.

The commentary is a small book, closely printed. The work was done by the Ekukanyeni press, and clearly the workmen there had not yet achieved a very high standard of artistry in lay-out or in binding. But the book is, nevertheless, surprisingly attractive. It is written in an easy, readable style, less dated than a good many Victorian works of theology. The bishop's debt to Maurice is marked, but, again, Maurice's thought seems to have lost some of its foundations in the borrowing. Maurice had revolted against the penal substitution theory of the Atonement. He denied that Christ died in order to take upon himself the *punishment* due to human sin. He denied that Christ died to placate an angry Father, blindly demanding his pound of flesh from humanity.[1] Colenso followed Maurice, but went further to deny that God really has any righteous anger against sin at all. He spoke of Christ's paying 'the debt of nature which sin had the right to demand of Him'.[2] He puts 'nature' in the place of 'the devil', but it is not clear what he means by 'nature'. It would seem that he means 'human nature' as a sort of universal or generalisation, for he asserts that Christ's death pays the debt to nature once and for all and redeems all men everywhere, from their birth hour, whether they have heard of Christ or not. All men, without exception, are united in Christ's death from their birth, just as all men were once united in Adam's death from their birth. Baptism is no more than a proclamation of the accomplished fact that all men share already in Christ's death and resurrection. The Christian knows this: he has no other advantage.

Reacting against the excessive subjectivism of much missionary preaching, the bishop asserted that the Atonement was an entirely objective event. He hardly allows any place for a personal application of salvation at all. The heathen Zulu is redeemed before he has ever heard of Christ; to preach is to place before him the pattern of Christ's love.[3]

[1] F. D. Maurice, *Theological Essays*, E. F. Carpenter, 1957, p. 112f
[2] J. W. Colenso, *Romans*, pp. 96ff & 102ff
[3] Colenso, *op. cit.*, pp. 113f, 117ff, & cf pp. 75 & 156

It must be said, in fairness to Colenso, that his theology was, in part, developed as a necessary corrective to the teaching of a great many other missionaries.[1] He rightly maintained that to offer the heathen a choice between conversion and a dramatic picture of eternal damnation was to attempt to frighten them into the faith. But this is only part of the story. The commentary on Romans is the logical development of the ideas Colenso borrowed from Maurice and tried to make his own while he was at Forncett. It also draws together and makes a coherent whole of those other views he had expressed from time to time while he had been in Natal.

Colenso's teaching is defective because it makes no real distinction between the holiness of God and man's sin. It makes Christ's atonement belong only to history, not to the here and now. It minimises the necessity for conversion and makes Baptism irrelevant, for he sees no difference between being in the Church and in the world. It makes 'nature' the source of sin, but because he did not believe in the doctrine of original sin, Colenso virtually teaches a dualism of God and nature. Because he did not attach much importance to Baptism, he could logically maintain that the break with polygamy ought to come with the second generation of Christians. His belief that all men were redeemed from their birth, ties in with his belief that all men have some true knowledge of God. It explains, too, why he found it difficult to distinguish between Christ's sacramental presence in the Eucharist and his presence 'wherever two or three are gathered together'. Having denied that salvation is a *personal* necessity for every man, he denied the existence of the Church apart from the human race as a whole, and also denied the reality of the sacraments. Anything less like Maurice's teaching in its whole aspect would be difficult to imagine and Colenso himself admitted that he did not expect Maurice to agree with the whole of the commentary.[2]

It is terribly difficult to give a fair picture of Colenso's theology in such a very compressed review of a crucial piece of writing. Contrary to the common opinion, it was *Romans* and not his Old Testament criticism which really brought the attack on Colenso to a head. It was for his doctrine of the Atonement that he was again formally delated, this time successfully,

[1] Cox, *op. cit.*, I, p. 119
[2] *Ibid.*, p. 126

and it is important that Colenso's *Romans* should not be distorted by personal prejudice or by too much compression. Perhaps the only fair way to treat the book is to give a substantial extract from it and show how his accusers used it against him, so that the opinions of both sides may be fairly assessed.

The first schedule of the articles of accusation brought against Colenso included part of the following passage from the bishop's commentary.

This was the Sacrifice of faith and obedience, offered by One in our nature, and perfect unto the end, which our Father's Loving Wisdom had prepared. In this way Our Lord took part with that death, which sin had brought upon all, and He came to take our nature and to become one of us, whom He was pleased to call His brethren; it was needful also that He should pay the debt of nature, the debt which Sin (according to the Apostle's bold personification in the next chapter) had the right to demand of Him, if He was really willing to be a true Son of Man. And now that He, our Head, has paid that debt, we are free. We are made partakers of His death, are reckoned to have died, to have paid this debt to Sin, because He died. This is the doctrine of St Paul. We shall die, indeed, still, but no longer as paying a debt which we owe to sin, no longer as incurring a part of the curse of our fallen nature. The sting of death is taken away for us. We shall die now because our Father wills it. He wills that all His children shall pass, as their elder brother has passed before them, through death into life.

But we are anticipating here the matter, which the Apostle will bring before us more fully in the next chapter. Let the expression, however, once more be noted. The Apostle does not say that *God is reconciled to us* by the death of His Son, but that *we are reconciled to God*. The difference in the meaning of these two expressions is infinite. It is our unwillingness, fear, distrust, that is taken away by the revelation of God's love to us in His Son. There is nothing now to prevent our going with the prodigal of old, and throwing ourselves at His Feet, and saying, 'Father, I have sinned; but Thou art Love'.[1]

The words from 'Let the expression . . .' down to the end of the passage quoted were cited by the accusers as evidence for the bishop's 'maintaining that our Lord did not die in man's

[1] Colenso, *Romans*, pp. 96ff; commenting on Romans 5:10

stead, or to bear the punishment or penalty of our sins, and that God is not reconciled to us by the death of His Son' and that he 'impugns and contradicts the Catholic faith as expressed in the articles, etc., as above set forth and referred to'. The 'articles, etc., referred to' were Article II *Of the Word or Son of God, which was made very Man*, (in which there appear the words, 'to reconcile His Father to us'), Article XXXI—*Of the one Oblation of Christ finished upon the Cross*, and the opening sentence of the prayer of consecration from the eucharistic liturgy of the 1662 Prayer Book.[1]

Quite apart from the comic sound (to modern ears) of Anglo-Catholics quoting the Articles against Colenso, it will be noted that the accusers seem to misunderstand, perhaps wilfully, the point which Colenso was trying to make. They miss the aspects of the bishop's teaching which is most obvious to the modern reader. And they put the stress, not on the point with which the bishop was really concerned, but alter the emphasis slightly, and give the impression that Colenso was denying the Atonement altogether, rather than one particular way of teaching the meaning of the Atonement.

One other point about Colenso's *Romans* is worth making. We have already seen how Colenso in attempting to explain 'election' to the Depwade Clerical Society, did not question the existence of angels nor the Pauline authorship of the Pastoral Epistles.[2] In the same way he now makes none of the attacks on the conventional approach to the New Testament which we might expect from the notorious liberal biblical critic. There is nothing of the Strauss approach. The Pauline authorship of the Pastoral Epistles is taken for granted.[3] It is assumed that Acts is an historical account, accurate in detail.[4] To most modern scholars his approach would seem naïve and childlike. Colenso was not yet prepared to use critical methods in Biblical exposition—or at least not in expounding the New Testament.

When the commentary appeared Colenso gave copies of it to the two senior clergymen in the diocese, Dean Green and Archdeacon Fearne. These two men were old enemies. Fearne had succeeded Mackenzie as archdeacon. He had sided with

---

[1] In the printed report of the *Trial of Bishop Colenso*, published in Cape Town in 1863, p. 5. See also C.N. Gray, *op. cit.*, II, pp. 594f.
[2] Cf *supra* pp. 43f.   [3] Colenso, *Romans*, p. 3
[4] *Ibid.*, p. xii

Colenso on the Church Council issue and, on at least one occasion, he and Green had indulged in public controversy.[1] Now, however, these two took concerted action against the bishop. They wrote to Colenso on 25 October 1861 protesting that the book struck at the roots of the doctrine of the Atonement and asking the bishop to submit it to the metropolitan's judgment.[2] Colenso replied two days later, rebutting their objections, and saying that he could not regard the objections of an advanced Anglo-Catholic and an extreme Evangelical as sufficient reason for submitting the book to Gray.[3] Green then sent copies of the correspondence to the metropolitan.

Gray was undoubtedly in a most awkward position. He had tried not to take any formal or official part in the Natal troubles, but he had not been able to avoid sympathising with Green and had written to him unofficially on several occasions, making his views quite plain. He knew that Colenso did not regard him as the real metropolitan of an independent province. He referred the whole matter to the archbishop of Canterbury, sending him a copy of Colenso's book. He had already tried to persuade Colenso to withdraw the work, but Colenso, of course, had refused to allow himself to be muzzled by private request. This device having failed, Gray hoped that the English bishops would condemn the book in convocation or that the archbishop would try Colenso in some quasi-patriarchal court. The English bishops met in May 1862. Gray was then already on his way to England. During the voyage he heard the first rumour that Colenso had yet another revolutionary book ready for publication.[4] The bishop of Natal followed the metropolitan very shortly and, once they were both in England, the affair rapidly ceased to be a private South African controversy.

---

[1] 'Revd. Mr. Fearne preached—sensation—Mr. Green preached a counter sermon in the evening'. Shepstone quoted in B.B. Burnett, *Anglicans in Natal*, p. 65.
[2] A.T. Wirgman, *Life of James Green*, I, pp. 107ff
[3] *Ibid.*, pp. 112ff. The Evangelical Bishop Cotterill of Grahamstown also abandoned Colenso's cause once his views on such matters as penal substitution and fundamentalism became known.
[4] C.N. Gray, *Life of Robert Gray*, II, p. 27

CHAPTER 4

The Old Testament Critic

THE first part of Colenso's *Pentateuch and the Book of Joshua, critically examined*, had been set up and roughly printed before he left Natal in 1862. It was intended that this first edition should serve both as practice for an African apprentice printer whom Colenso was training[1] and also as an advance notice of his researches which could be placed in the hands of his friends and others before he finally committed himself to publication in England.[2] It was considerably revised before the definitive edition was issued.

Colenso's work on the Old Testament is almost invariably described as negative, hurried and not particularly valuable. This is a misleading judgment. The truth of the matter is that his books reflect precisely the pilgrimage of the bishop himself. He began as a fundamentalist with doubts—that is to say he subscribed to the conventional view of the day, but he was not entirely happy about it. When challenged he was forced to consider the matter thoroughly. He became convinced that the Bible could not be verbally inerrant. For reasons which seemed good to him, he believed that he ought not to hide his opinions. The first part of his work was, therefore, published immediately. The later, more constructive and positive contribution which he had to make was something of an anti-climax and was more or less disregarded. This was not his fault. A purely academic personage might have kept the whole thing till it could be published together. Colenso felt that a missionary bishop could not do this. Once he had ceased to be a fundamentalist he published his reasons, however negative, at once.

His opinions came as a shock even to his closest friends and colleagues. In January 1861 the bishop of Natal was in Cape Town for the consecration of Mackenzie as bishop on the Zambezi. The bishops also met in synod and discussed a draft constitution for the South African province. Colenso was present

---

[1] G.W. Cox, *Life of Bishop Colenso*, I, p. 193   [2] *Ibid.*, & cf. p. 188

and subscribed the resolutions passed by the synod. His biographer maintains that he had not at that time begun his work on the Old Testament, nor even to read seriously the critical works of English and German scholars.[1] At the same time Bishop Gray said of Colenso:

> I am very anxious about Natal. His views are dangerous. I fear that we may have taught in Africa 'another Gospel which is not another'. It is curious and painful to see how the reaction of his mind from the utter Calvinism in which he was brought up, is driving him to the contemplation of God solely as Love, the Loving Father of all creation. . . .[2]

It is clear that Gray is here talking of Colenso's 'speculation' which led eventually to his commentary on Romans. About a year later he wrote to Bishop Wilberforce saying that about 300 copies of the commentary had been sold in Cape Town, where 'chiefly among the Dutch, rationalist views are spreading'.[3] Theological 'liberalism' was indeed a problem in the Dutch Reformed Church in the Colony at this time. Between 1862 and 1864 there were several lawsuits in which ministers of the Dutch Church were accused of heresy and the local authorities became very wary of importing clergy from Holland where rationalism was believed to be undermining the whole life and faith of the Church. In the very same month in which he first alluded to his fears 'about Natal', Bishop Gray delivered a charge[4] to his clergy in which he dealt with the subject of 'Rationalism'. He says that 'it has crept into and is being disseminated within' another communion. He fears that it may penetrate even the Anglican Church, but he in no way hints or suggests that it is being held or taught by one of the South African bishops. This may not be conclusive proof that Colenso had not yet begun his critical study of the Old Testament, but for what it is worth it suggests that Colenso's biographer is probably right when he says that the first part of *Pentateuch and Joshua*[5] was produced between January 1861 and April 1862. If Colenso had begun to question the historical accuracy

[1] Cox, *op. cit.*, I, p. 487
[2] C. N. Gray, *Life of Robert Gray*, II, p. 21
[3] *Ibid.*, p. 26
[4] *Visitation Charge of the Lord Bishop of Cape Town*, Cape Town, 1861, p. 13f
[5] 160 pages in the Longmans' edition of 1862

of the Old Testament before 1861, he does not seem to have told anyone of his doubts. A little more than a year later his reading and thinking was done, the book was written, and a first draft had been printed. It was a formidable undertaking, and it involved a revolution in the bishop's own mental and religious attitudes.

It has been suggested that Colenso began his work on the Old Testament or had at least begun to think along critical lines, before he left England.[1] The memoirs of Lord Courtney of Penwith contain a reference to a sermon preached by Colenso which revealed an unconventional attitude to the Old Testament. But if the passage is read properly it will be seen that the unconventional thing about Colenso's approach is not that he used any of the methods or results of criticism, but that he was willing to attack as immoral the actions of Old Testament characters, of whom the Old Testament itself approved.

Colenso's own account of the revolution in his thinking is contained in a letter addressed, but not sent, to Dr Harold Browne, the Norrissian Professor of Divinity at Cambridge, who later became bishop of Ely. Browne was a friend of Colenso's, but he became in the end one of the most prominent critics of the bishop's work. Colenso wrote his letter (in 1861) but did not post it because he feared that Browne might be compromised or embarrassed by being asked to comment on the problems which were worrying Colenso. The bishop of Natal categorically says that in January 1861 he had not begun to enter upon his inquiries. He had already planned to tackle the problem, but had at that time no idea of the conclusions at which he was likely to arrive.[2] The doubts were there, but had been shelved until there was time to investigate them thoroughly. And this is an explanation which will fit well enough with the other evidence.

The point is of some importance since the trustworthiness of the account given by Colenso and by his biographer are necessarily called in question by accusations and counter-accusations bandied about during the controversy. It is desirable to be able to show just how Colenso arrived at his opinions. It is also important to realise how short was the period Colenso gave to his first steps in biblical scholarship. It illustrates his

[1] S.C. Carpenter, *Church & People*, pp. 504f
[2] *The Pentateuch and Book of Joshua*, Part I, 1862, p. xiii.

impetuosity, and his prodigious capacity for hard work, and it explains some of the naïveties of the published book as well as the shattering effect it had upon Colenso's friends and colleagues.

Colenso's own account is as follows.[1] A long time before, probably in his days as a tutor at Cambridge when he first began to take theological studies seriously, he had been 'uneasy' about certain parts of the Old Testament. He does not say which parts. It is likely, though, that what he learnt from Maurice of God as 'Loving Father' made him feel uncomfortable about some of the more bloodthirsty passages in the Pentateuch. In his English parish he was so busy that he was able to 'settle down into a willing acquiescence in the general truth of the narrative, whatever difficulties might hang about particular parts of it'. Pastoral duties required him to expound the Scriptures devotionally, morally and doctrinally, but not necessarily to comment on the historicity of the narrative.

But once he came to Natal the problems became more acute. He used his African converts to help him with the work of translating the Bible, and they asked him questions as they went along. We know that he had already translated Genesis and Exodus by 1861, and it seems that it was these two books in particular which raised doubts in the minds of both the bishop and his converts. One of these converts, William Ngidi, became famous as the 'intelligent Zulu' who 'converted' Colenso, by pointing out that the Old Testament seemed to be in no way superior to the folk tales of his own people. Colenso was asked whether he really believed that Noah could have gathered all the animals into an ark of the size described in Genesis. And he realised that in any case what he had learnt of geology—particularly from Sir Charles Lyell's work—meant that it was extremely unlikely that there had ever been a *universal* deluge at all. He was also asked whether the Mosaic laws on the subject of slavery,[2] could really emanate from 'the merciful Father of all mankind'. And he realised that to explain these passages as written by Moses under the misapprehension that they had been put in his mind by divine inspiration was to place 'a very great strain on the cord which

[1] *Pentateuch and Joshua*, Part I, pp. vff
[2] Cf Ex. 21:20f

bound me to the ordinary belief in the historical veracity of the Pentateuch'.[1]

Such problems having arisen, Colenso could not teach his flock what he himself doubted. Maurice had taught him to hold to the truth fearlessly. Maurice had taught him to love the heathen because they were the children of the Loving Father. The bishop felt himself bound to probe into the problem until he found some answer to these doubts. His attempts to describe the torment to which he was subjected gives one some idea of the dreadful sense of insecurity which his doubts created. 'Should all else give way beneath me I feel that His Everlasting Arms are still under me.'[2] If God was Truth, then to search for truth could not destroy faith.

This was the point Colenso had reached when the bishops met for the consecration of Mackenzie in January 1861. In the meantime the famous volume *Essays and Reviews* had appeared. The contributors to the volume included Frederick Temple, the future archbishop, who wrote a mild article arguing that biblical scholarship must be adult and mature, using fully the gifts of the Spirit and human intelligence. Rowland Williams described some of the German critics' findings, including the hypothesis that the Pentateuch was not a single literary whole written by Moses, but was a collection from various sources. Baden Powell made an attempt to reconcile Darwin's evolutionary theory with Christianity, but at the cost of dispensing with the miraculous. H.B. Wilson pleaded for the widest doctrinal latitude in the National Church. C. W. Goodwin attempted to show that the picture of the universe as presented in the Bible ought not to be regarded as scientifically inerrant. And Mark Pattison wrote an historical survey of the development of religious thought in England in the seventeenth and eighteenth centuries.

There was a public outcry against the book, which was treated as an invitation to apostasy. Some 8,500 clergymen appealed to the archbishop of Canterbury to institute proceedings against the authors. Two of the essayists, Wilson and Williams, were tried in the Court of Arches and were both suspended for a year. They appealed to the Judicial Committee of the Privy Council and this court reversed the judgment of Dr Lushington, the Dean of Arches. In the meanwhile the

---

[1] Cox, *op. cit.*, I, p. 495   [2] *Pentateuch and Joshua*, Part I, p. ix

bishops had met in February 1861 and condemned the book, and their condemnation was embodied in a pastoral letter issued by the archbishop.

Colenso's preface to his *Pentateuch and Joshua* was written between Lushington's judgment and the appeal to the Judicial Committee. It appears that Colenso had read *Essays and Reviews*. He seems to have been still clinging desperately to the conventional view of inspiration, because he seems to have read all the answers to the essayists, hoping to have his doubts allayed. But he felt that no-one tackled the real difficulties and he was sickened by the evasions and personal remarks of the orthodox.[1] He ordered a large quantity of books, mostly by German critics (and including the works of Hengstenberg, the conservative scholar) in order to be in a position to investigate the whole matter for himself. And he began to wonder whether he could continue to hold his bishopric.

Colenso's heroic course of reading seems to have begun with the *History of the Old Covenant* by Kurtz who, like Hengstenberg, opposed the findings of the critics. Colenso was impressed with his earnestness and zeal, but not with his attempts to answer the problems.[2] So he turned next to Ewald's *Geschichte des Volkes Israel*, in the German. Here he was more impressed by the author's erudition, though he did not agree with all his conclusions. While Colenso freely cites other authors on both sides, Ewald's name hardly appears at all in *Pentateuch and Joshua*. Dissatisfied with Ewald, Colenso turned to Hengstenberg's defence of the traditional position, only to be even more dissatisfied, not to say disgusted, with what he found there. He later told F.D. Maurice how much he despised Hengstenberg's approach.

> For Hengstenberg's works, certainly, I do feel something like contempt, for his arguments are often dishonest—I can use no milder term—and that with a prodigious affectation of honesty and censure of others as suppressing the truth from interested motives.[3]

Pentateuch and Joshua is full of comment on and criticism of Hengstenberg's point of view. As Hengstenberg was a convert from 'rationalism' to 'orthodoxy' and displayed some of the

---

[1] *Pentateuch and Joshua*, Part I, pp. ixff
[2] *Pentateuch and Joshua*, Part I, pp. 62f   [3] Cox, *op. cit.*, I, p. 196

extremist fury of the convert, Colenso's distaste is perhaps excusable. He comments harshly on Hengstenberg's attempts 'to force the text of Scripture to say what it plainly does not say' and compares Hengstenberg unfavourably with Kurtz because, being dishonest himself, he continually accused his opponents of dishonesty.[1]

At this point Colenso wrote the first draft of Part I of his book. It is obviously a work written in some heat. It shows the revulsion which Colenso felt for any attempt to conceal or twist what he believed to be the truth. The 'dishonesty' of the traditionalists seems to have affected him very deeply. He uses the word 'fiction' to describe those parts of the Old Testament which were not historical.[2] To sort truth from fiction seemed to him to be his principal vocation at this stage. He 'had no longer any doubts'.[3] It was his duty to lay before the Church at large an account of the course his own inquiry had taken, showing plainly what conclusion he had arrived at and by what steps he had done so.[4] And his conclusion was that the Old Testament, and particularly 'the account of the Exodus', 'whatever value it may have, is not historically true'.[5] He began to revise his draft work for publication in England and in order to do this he embarked upon a further course of reading in the German critics.

We are able to date this stage in Colenso's studies almost exactly. The bishop had a great friend, Dr W. Bleek, who was the curator of the museum and library in Cape Town. He had been introduced to Colenso by F.D. Maurice and had gone out to South Africa with him.[6] He shared the bishop's interests in African languages and customs, and he was the son of Friedrich Bleek, the German Biblical scholar. In the preface to *Pentateuch and Joshua* Colenso says, 'While rewriting it with a view to publication, De Wette's *Einleitung* and Bleek's excellent posthumous work, *Einleitung in das A.T.*, have come into my hands'.[7] On 29 July 1861 the bishop wrote to the younger Bleek:

I shall be very thankful if you will send me the books you speak of. I have never seen De Wette though, of course, I have heard

---

[1] *Pentateuch and Joshua*, Part I, pp. 24f
[2] He later substituted the word 'unhistorical' in the published version, see his letter to Maurice in Cox, *op. cit.* I, p. 196.
[3] *Pentateuch and Joseph*, Part I, p. xvii   [4] *Ibid.*, pp. xviiff
[5] *Ibid.*, p. xix   [6] Rees, *op. cit.*, p. 151   [7] p. xvi

of him. I have just finished three thick tomes of Ewald and have four more to read. I disagree with him in every page and am extremely disappointed with (in my opinion) the utter want of judgment which he shows in his criticisms. I have scarcely got a single new idea from him and certainly think him one of the wildest and rashest yet one of the most positive[1] critics I have ever met with. I shall be much interested with [sic.] your father's book and De Wette's. . . .[2]

A fragment of Bleek's reply survives as a quotation in a letter from Colenso to Maurice:

You will see that your estimate of Ewald pretty nearly agrees with my father's, as you would also find if you read Bleek's last work.[3]

And Colenso goes on to comment:

Ewald, in fact, is far wilder in his hypotheses and far more rash in his conclusions than I should wish to be. It is not because he is *too* conservative that I cannot agree with him, but just for the very contrary. Nevertheless, I had long ago struck out from my book every word that might give pain to a great and good man, though I do not at all doubt that what I have said of him, supported as it is by Bleek's calm judgment, is perfectly true. . . .[4]

It will be recalled[5] that in Germany at this time Ewald, De Wette and Bleek were not regarded as extreme or radical critics. Even Ewald held that there was a unity of authorship, whether Mosaic or not, in the Pentateuchal books. Colenso, then, was clearly not adopting a particularly radical position. He was associating himself with the centre party in Germany and with the more conservative De Wette and Bleek rather even than with Ewald.

During the whole of the time that *Pentateuch and Joshua* was being printed in rough form in Natal, Colenso continued with his reading of German and English works, revising and adapting his own work as he went along. Even after he arrived in England in the middle of 1862 he was continually consulting works, both critical and conservative, which had not been available to him in the colony. References which he gives in the body of his book indicate the thoroughness with which he

---

[1] From the context it seems probable that 'positive' is here used in the sense of 'cock-sure'.

[2] Campbell Library, Durban; Colenso Folios; A. 152

[3] Cox, *op. cit.*, I, p. 191   [4] *Ibid.*   [5] See *supra*, p. 15

digested the writings of other scholars. One of them in particular, who is quoted again and again by Colenso, deserves special notice. This was Abraham Kuenen, a Dutch authority on the Old Testament, whose *Historisch-Kritisch Onderzoek* Colenso describes as 'a work of rare merit'.[1] Kuenen was at this time a disciple of Ewald and his work was translated into English in 1865 by Colenso 'by whom Kuenen was much influenced'.[2] The association between Kuenen and Colenso was more direct and personal than in the case of the other continental scholars whom the bishop read. Kuenen stayed with Colenso in England in 1864[3] and he was clearly a great admirer of the bishop's. He defended Colenso against the charge that his work was 'obsolete and antiquarian' by pointing out that Ewald and others had been compelled to revise their conclusions by the force of the bishop of Natal's criticisms.[4] Indeed Kuenen suggests that it was Colenso's work which led him to the conclusion that certain narratives of the Pentateuch (from the Priestly documents) which had been believed to be the oldest part was in fact the latest and so, perhaps, prepared the way for Kuenen's assertion that the 'P' source of the Pentateuch was the last addition to the whole.[5] And Kuenen's eulogy of Colenso after the latter's death leaves no doubt about the wholeheartedness of his admiration for the bishop as scholar and as missionary.[6] Kuenen's comments, even if some of their enthusiasm is discounted, suggests that the relationship between Colenso and continental scholars was not all one-sided.

Colenso seems, himself, to have felt that a charge of impertinence might be brought against a missionary bishop from an obscure diocese who presumed to enter the field of Old Testament scholarship. The comparatively short time within which his work was produced and the limited facilities available to him could and did lead to the accusation that it was a hasty and ill-considered work. He was out of touch with biblical scholarship in England and on the continent. He had very few books at his disposal.

[1] *Pentateuch and Joshua*, Part I, p. xvi

[2] F. L. Cross (Ed.), *Oxford Dictionary of the Christian Church*, reprinted 1958, art. *Kuenen*

[3] Cox, *op. cit.*, I, p. 250 & cf p. 79, which suggests that Kuenen visited Colenso in Natal also.

[4] Cox, *op. cit.*, I, p. 626   [5] *Ibid.*, p. 627

[6] *Ibid.*, pp. 81f

The bishop of Natal sought to defend himself in advance against this charge by giving six reasons why *he* should be the person to attempt this work.[1] His missionary work had made him more aware of the problem than most of his contemporaries. Old Testament studies, and Hebrew in particular, had been much neglected in England. Critical discussion had been chiefly concerned with the Creation, Fall and Flood narratives which could be interpreted as allegorical, and the accuracy of the 'historical' parts of the Old Testament had not been challenged. English scholarship had been either irreverent or evasive. German scholarship, where it had been or was being translated, was mostly of the conservative type. If it was of the other school it took too much for granted and there was no work which would present the essentials of the problem to the intelligent layman. And Colenso adds[2] that he was compelled to do his work so quickly in order that his views might be made plain, in an open and honest fashion, as soon as possible. He was able to complete it in so short a time because all he had really had to do was to state the facts and draw the obvious conclusions. No great erudition was required in order to discover the plain inconsistencies and impossibilities of the biblical narrative.

He attempted also to defend himself in advance against two other charges, both of which became real issues later in the controversy. One of these charges was that it was illegal for a clergyman of the Church of England to hold the views set out in *Pentateuch and Joshua*. But, as Colenso points out, Dr Lushington in the *Essays and Reviews* case had held that 'unfeignedly believe in all the Canonical Scriptures' (in the ordination promise made by deacons) simply meant 'believe that the Holy Scriptures contain everything necessary to salvation and that to that extent they have the direct sanction of the Almighty'. Colenso believed himself to be, on the whole, justified by the judgment so that there was no absolute necessity for him to resign. He told Maurice,' Certainly, till Lushington's judgment was delivered, I did feel a great difficulty about the words in the Ordination Service of Deacons. The judgment, and Stephen's reasoning, have removed that difficulty. I see that we cannot mean to express 'unfeigned belief' in the historical

[1] *Pentateuch and Joshua*, Part I, pp. xxiff
[2] *Ibid.*, p. xxxii

veracity of the story of the Exodus any more than in the historical veracity of Job or the Song of Solomon'.[1]

The other matter was more serious. If our Lord, in his incarnation, believed that Moses had written the Pentateuch (John 6:46, Luke 20:36 etc.) then either this guarantees the Mosaic authorship or our Lord was mistaken. And if our Lord really was God would he have been able to make such a mistake? Did not Colenso's work 'impugn His veracity'.[2] The bishop began his answer by making two smaller points, which in fact weaken his real case by evading the central issue. Perhaps our Lord only meant that certain parts of the Pentateuch were Mosaic, 'reverent criticism to determine what passages give signs of *not* having been written by Moses' is permissible. Or perhaps our Lord was merely accommodating his words to the popular language of the day. But Colenso's real defence rests upon the same 'kenotic' view of the Incarnation which we have already seen him expounding to the Depwade Clerical Society. 'He took our nature fully, and voluntarily entered into all the conditions of humanity, and among others, into that which makes our growth in all ordinary knowledge *gradual* and *limited*'.[3] If Christ's childhood was a real childhood he cannot have possessed more information about the Pentateuch than is proper to a child. To suppose that He later acquired 'full and accurate information on these points' is itself difficult. 'Why should it be thought that He would speak with certain *Divine* knowledge on this matter more than upon other matters of ordinary science or history?'

Colenso's actual work on the Pentateuch is chiefly concerned, as he said, with setting out the facts and letting them speak for themselves. By far the greater part of the passages with which he deals are concerned with matters of historical *fact*—with contradictions and impossibilities rather than with moral difficulties like the question of slavery. The point which became notorious was the matter of the tabernacle in the wilderness. Leviticus 8:14 says that the whole assembly of Israel was gathered at the door of the tabernacle. Colenso argues that this must mean, on a literal interpretation, that they came within the court of the tabernacle because they had to witness a particular ceremony taking place inside the tabernacle. The

[1] Cox, *op. cit.*, I, p. 195, but cf p. 181
[2] *Pentateuch and Joshua*, Part I, p. xxx   [3] *Ibid.*, p. xxxi

author of 'Colenso's Arithmetic' has a wonderful time calcu-
lating the mathematical implications of this.

> But how many would the *whole Court* have contained? Its area
> (60 yards by 30 yards) was 1800 square yards, and the area of the
> Tabernacle itself (18 yards by 6 yards) was 108 square yards.
> Hence the area of the Court outside the Tabernacle was 1692
> square yards. But the 'whole Congregation' would have made a
> body of people nearly 20 miles—or more accurately, 33,530 yards
> —long and 18 feet or 6 yards wide; that is to say, packed closely
> together, they would have covered an area of 201,180 square
> yards. [He has already calculated this on the basis of allowing an
> area 24 by 18 inches for each person.] In fact, the Court, when
> thronged, could only have held 5000 people; whereas the able-
> bodied men alone exceeded 600,000.[1]

The figure of '600,000 able-bodied men' also gave rise to
vigorous argument. Numbers 1:3 was the source for the figure
and Colenso calculated that, on this basis, the *total* number of
Israelites, including women and children, must have been
something like the population of London which at that time
was about 2,000,000.[2] Therefore, says Colenso, it would have
been quite impossible for Moses and Joshua to address 'all
Israel' (see Deuteronomy 1:1 and Joshua 8:35). Again and again
in his correspondence with Maurice and others the figure
600,000 recurs, as though this was the point which aroused
most bitterness.

Colenso also worked out that the number of sheep the
Israelites possessed in Egypt must have required some twenty-
five square miles of grazing land and that, if the Israelites were
scattered over so wide an area, it would be quite impossible
for the instructions about the Passover to be circulated amongst
them in the time allowed in the book Exodus.[3]

When he has considered eighteen such points the bishop
comes to a chapter called 'The War on Midian', and here,
perhaps, the purpose of his work becomes plain. He has so far
been concerned merely with proving as a matter of sheer fact
that the Exodus narrative is not historically accurate and was
not therefore written by Moses. Having done this he is now
able to say:

---

[1] *Pentateuch and Joshua*, Part I, p. 34
[2] *Ibid.*, p. 36   [3] *Ibid.*, p. 60

But how thankful we must be, that we are no longer obliged to believe, as a matter of fact, of vital consequence to our eternal hope, the story related in N[umbers] xxxi, where we are told that a force of 12,000 Israelites slew all the males of the Midianites . . . and then, by command of Moses, butchered in cold blood all the women and children. . . . The tragedy of Cawnpore, where 300 were butchered, would sink into nothing, compared with such a massacre, if, indeed, we were required to believe it.[1]

The purpose of Colenso's researches becomes plain. He was not merely concerned to show that a man of common sense could not accept the narrative as reliable, he went on to draw the conclusion that if it was inaccurate then we were not required to believe that God behaved in a bloodthirsty and cruel manner. This is entirely consistent with the ideas which underlay his commentary on Romans.

This point is made explicit in his 'Concluding Remarks' to Part I.[2] Colenso promises to undertake more positive critical study in Part II, attempting to suggest the manner and date of the authorship of the Pentateuch. More important, he attempts also to provide an alternative to the 'aching void' left by his demolition of the traditional view of inspiration. He refers the reader to his commentary on Romans and says that he believes the essential core of the Christian religion (which he had tried to expound there) remains unshaken by his new views on biblical criticism.

The main essence of that teaching is that our righteousness is wholly of 'faith', a living trust in God's Love,—that we *must* all, and we *may* all, depend entirely on our Father's Mercy, and come as children to His Footstool, continually, for light and life, for help and blessing, for counsel and guidance, and, if need be, for 'loving correction' which 'shall make us great'.[3]

Colenso believed that his work might be of positive value for the missions of the Church. The Bible need no longer be treated as a revelation of scientific and historical facts but as 'containing a message from God to our souls'. There was no need to teach children or heathen to do more than to search in the Bible for what God already says to them in their hearts. It became possible to look for the Spirit of God elsewhere than in the Bible—in Cicero or in Sikh or Hindu writings—where

[1] *Ibid.*, pp. 143f   [2] *Ibid.*, p. 147   [3] *Ibid.*, p. 148

also men have learned 'living truths' by 'the direct teaching of the Spirit of God'. And on that revolutionary note Colenso's first part ended.

The second part[1] fulfils part of the author's promise. A more positive note is struck. He shows how one can separate the writings in the Pentateuch in which God is called Elohim from those in which he is called Jehovah. He affirms 'with some degree of confidence' that Samuel was the author of the document which uses the name Elohim. The other source was probably written in the reign of Solomon. Deuteronomy was written in the reign of Josiah, perhaps by Jeremiah. Colenso is firmly among the critics. He has theories of his own to expound. He is no longer merely the iconoclast. As his work continued he became more scholarly, more technical, and more elaborate. By the time Part V[2] appeared Colenso had distinguished a 'second Jehovist' and a 'second Elohist' among the authors of the Pentateuch. One quotation from this part will suffice to show that the bishop had become a far more technically competent scholar during the four years between 1861 and 1865.[3]

The portions which still remain of Genesis, when the parts due to J_2 and D shall have been removed, amounting to 1134 verses . . . are so homogeneous in character that we are unable to distinguish any marked difference in style and tone between different sections of them, except in one respect. A glance at xx 1-17 will show that in this section the name 'Elohim' is used *exclusively (six* times), *viz.* in v. 3, 6, 11, 13, 17, 17; and the same phenomenon occurs again in xxi 6-22, where we have 'Elohim' *nine* times, v. 6, 12, 17, 17, 17, 19, 20, 22, and no 'Jehovah'.

It is impossible, however, to assign those passages to the original Elohist, because they exhibit no trace of his style (except for the use of the Divine Name), and contain also a number of decidedly Jehovistic formulae.'[4]

Passages in which there is some attempt at interpreting the results of critical scholarship begin to appear. Colenso maintains, for instance, that the early Hebrews offered worship to

[1] Published by Longmans, Green in 1863. It is somewhat longer than Part I, consisting of some 380 pages.

[2] Published in 1865

[3] Part V also shows an apparent acquaintance with Hebrew not evident in the first part. It is a book of 320 pages, containing a detailed critical and literary analysis of Genesis, and concluding with two very learned appendixes.

[4] *Pentateuch and Joshua*, Part V, p. 58

God 'in the same low form in which it already existed among the Canaanite tribes' and that it was only the 'long-continued efforts of those great prophets, whom God raised up', the calamity of the Exile, and contact with 'those Divine Truths which were taught in the Zoroastrian religion' which finally created the Judaism of the post-Exilic period.[1] And, having argued at great length about the reason for the introduction of the name 'Jehovah' to take the place of 'Elohim' in the religion of Israel, Colenso draws from his reconstruction of events the lesson that one is not to despair if the heathen, or new converts, or even some Christians, seem to have a lower view of the nature of God than one has oneself—one is to accept this rather as a stage towards a fuller and deeper understanding and to use it accordingly.[2] In other words the bishop has reached the stage where his studies have, for him at least, a positive religious value.

There is one last issue raised in the fifth part of the work which deserves special attention because it was to be one of the charges brought against him at his trial. Colenso elaborated the point, already mentioned, that the Bible is God's Word, not because it is infallible in matters of science and history, but because it speaks God's Word to men's hearts. Then he says:

> But, when we say 'the Bible contains God's Word', we do not mean, as some have supposed, that we may 'pick and choose' among the contents of the Bible,—that we can separate the books or portions of the Bible, which *are* God's Word, from the books and portions which are not. We mean that throughout the Bible the Word of God will be heard by the listening ear and the obedient heart. . . .[3]

And yet it must be admitted that the bishop was not really above criticism on this point and that he does not seem to have settled the problem for himself, for on the very same page he uses language which suggests that he *did* think that critical scholarship could sift and remove the 'false' bits of the Bible. 'Thus', he says, 'we need not be disquieted, though the progress of criticism should take from us much in the Scriptures, which perhaps, without sufficient reason, we had hitherto

---

[1] *Ibid.*, p. 300   [2] *Ibid.*, pp. 300ff   [3] *Ibid.*, p. 311

regarded as infallibly certain and true. . . .'[1] So long as this blatant contradiction remained unresolved in Colenso's thinking, his opponents might be forgiven for accusing him of 'picking and choosing'.

Having obtained some idea of just what Colenso's Pentateuchal criticism was like, it is possible for us now to pick up the story of his life at the point where he and Gray both went to England to settle the matter of the commentary on Romans. The Colensos sailed first:

> They packed all their most valued possessions and set out with the feeling that quite possibly they were bidding a last farewell to a much-loved home and people. . . . After a farewell service in the little wooden chapel, the journey down to Durban was accomplished by ox-waggon, in the same patriarchal fashion as the journey up seven years ago, and lasting for three days. Part of the 'trek' was by night, when the Bishop beguiled the weariness of the little party with talk about the stars and with stories of the wanderings of Ulysses. Passage by sailing-vessel rather than by the then monthly steamer was chosen for economy's sake. It was an interesting voyage. The Medusa, though small, was a capital sailer, outstripping every vessel we fell in with.[2]

But Gray sailed on the steamer, deciding on this course at short notice, and arrived in England some weeks ahead of his colleague.[3]

The English bishops had already decided on a course of action.[4] Bishop Wilberforce, Bishop Hamilton of Salisbury and Bishop Sumner of Winchester seem to have led the attack on Colenso. Tait, the bishop of London, a great stickler for legality and the sacrosanct character of English Common Law, tried to postpone action. An interesting, and momentary, alliance between Wilberforce and Thirlwall of St David's pressed for matters to be settled. Thirlwall was reputedly a great 'liberal' who had been dismissed from his Cambridge fellowship for advocating that dissenters should be admitted to degrees.[5] Tait was also generally regarded as a 'liberal', but in the

---

[1] *Ibid.* [2] Mrs Colenso's account; from Cox, *op. cit.*, I, p. 171
[3] C. N. Gray, *op. cit.*, II, p. 28
[4] What follows is based on Wilberforce's account, quoted in C. N. Gay, *op. cit.*, I, p. 175.
[5] But Thirlwall had on other occasions turned against those who looked to him to support liberal opinions. See A. R. Vidler, 'Rowland Williams' in *Theology*, LXIII, 479, pp. 177ff.

Colenso case his concern was far more for what he thought of as legality and justice, than for liberal theology as such. In later years he seems to have believed that if Gray had acted in accordance with the processes of the English courts, Colenso would have been convicted of heresy.[1] Certainly he feared that the chief effect of *Essays and Reviews* and *Pentateuch and Joshua* would be to frighten the really religious liberals into reaction. He thought Thirlwall likely to be the only bishop able to stand firm and prevent the 'widespread alienation of intelligent men'. 'The great evil', he said, 'is that the liberals are deficient in religion, and the religious are deficient in liberality'.[2]

On this occasion, as once before in the matter of *Essays and Reviews*, Wilberforce succeeded in persuading the bishops to take a firm line. When Colenso arrived the English bishops were to 'open personal communication with him'. They were to try and show him the error of his ways and to ask him to withdraw his book. If he would not, then they would 'request him not to officiate in our dioceses'. Tait and Thirlwall now fought a delaying action—not about the heterodoxy or orthodoxy of *Romans*,[3] but as to the advisability of concerted action against Colenso on any grounds. But Wilberforce's plan was adopted. Gray was informed of what was afoot as soon as he arrived and Archbishop Sumner complimented him on the 'mildness and conciliatory spirit which you have united with the firmness and decision exhibited in the whole of your distressing correspondence with the Bishop of Natal'.[4]

This was not Colenso's reaction when he reached England and (what seemed to him to be) a very clever trap was sprung. He received two letters, one from Gray and the other from Wilberforce. Both invited him to discuss his book with the English bishops. But while Wilberforce spoke of 'loving and unprejudiced discussion of differences', Gray gave Colenso the impression that he was being 'convened' before a bench of bishops.[5] Colenso was only willing, under these circumstances, to meet the bishops one at a time—to make it clear that they

---

[1] R. T. Davidson and W. Benham, *Archibald Campbell Tait*, 2nd ed., 1891, I, pp. 362f   [2] *Ibid.*, I, p. 337
[3] *Pentateuch and Joshua* was not yet in question.
[4] C. N. Gray, *op. cit.*, II, p. 28
[5] Cox, *op. cit.*, I, pp. 174ff

met as equals, not as accused before a court. Gray replied again, 'I do not see how they can consent to meet you one by one, merely in a private way, or treat the grave statements you have made as open questions'. By this Gray meant that the bishops had taken an official decision to meet Colenso and to invite him to suppress his 'heretical' work. They could not treat 'heresy' and 'orthodoxy' as equally valid. But Colenso saw Gray's letter, perhaps justifiably, as meaning that the case was pre-judged. It was first suggested that he should meet the archbishop of York (Longley), Wilberforce, and Jackson of Lincoln. Subsequently St Asaph was mentioned, but Colenso's comment was, 'I hardly felt that with a Prelate of his advanced years a discussion upon my commentary would be likely to lead to any practical result. . . .'.[1] Apart from proposing that he meet Longley, Wilberforce and Jackson singly, Colenso had one other suggestion to make. 'To the Bishop of St David's [Thirlwall], whom I myself mentioned to Bishop Gray, and whose learning might, indeed, have been profitably consulted by us, my proposal, as his lordship has informed me, was never in any way communicated'.[2]

This last comment is typical of the whole long controversy. Colenso regarded every event in such an absolutely different light from his opponents that it was quite impossible to hope for reconciliation. The bishops believed themselves to be defending the truth. They had agreed that Colenso's *Romans* was heterodox. They had deputed some of their number, headed by the archbishop of York (Archbishop Sumner of Canterbury was dying), to persuade Colenso to withdraw the commentary. They were anxious not to make any official pronouncement in case the matter should go to trial. They were hardly likely to agree to send Thirlwall, one of the two bishops who had opposed this plan for dealing with Colenso, to act as their representative in carrying it out. But it is easy to see that Colenso might be convinced that the bishops had condemned him in his absence, were keeping sympathisers on the bench away from him, and were trying to silence him without using the due and open processes of the law. The whole negotiations broke down completely.

Archbishop Sumner died towards the end of 1862. Longley

---

[1] Cox, *op. cit.*, I, p. 183   [2] *Ibid.*

succeeded him at Canterbury and Colenso's first part of *Pentateuch and Joshua* appeared in the public bookshops on 29 October of the same year. It was a great success. Nearly 8,000 copies sold in three weeks.[1] A recent writer has described this as 'success as a publication, and yet the Bishop had committed what proved to be an irretrievable blunder'.[2] The first part of Colenso's book set out merely to destroy the literalist position. Any positive criticism was to come in the later volumes.[3] But in the meantime this created the impression that Colenso's work was merely negative and destructive, and that it was, moreover, of a purely petty and niggling kind. Maurice sneered at Colenso for treating history as a branch of arithmetic. Even Dean Stanley, who was a great liberal and supported Colenso's right to his opinions, criticised Colenso as entirely negative in his approach. Stanley was also appalled by Colenso's apparent willingness 'to write himself down as a heretic'.[4] It was too easy to answer the bishop without taking his problems seriously. He could be brushed aside as a mathematician masquerading as a theologian.

Longley, Colenso's old headmaster at Harrow, took action in 1863. He had been formally approached by the S.P.G. for advice on whether the Society ought to continue to support Colenso. In February he called a meeting of English, Irish and Colonial bishops to discuss the whole matter. In the same month the case of the Reverend W. Long was heard in the Judicial Committee of the Privy Council, though judgment was not delivered till later in the year. This judgment was to prove enormously important for Colenso's future.[5]

At Longley's meeting most of the bishops were only too ready to condemn Colenso's Pentateuchal criticism. It seems to have been almost forgotten that it was the commentary on

---

[1] This is Colenso's own estimate—see Cox, *op. cit.*, I, p. 236. Rees, *op. cit.*, p. 73, says, 'Within six days of its appearance, ten thousand copies, running to four editions, were sold or ordered'. This seems to be based on a misreading of another of Colenso's letters—Cox, I, p. 233.

[2] Rees, *op. cit.*, p. 73

[3] Rees, *loc. cit.*, speaks of Colenso's later volumes as 'textual criticism', but this is wrong. Colenso was never a great Hebrew scholar and his interest in variant readings is very slight. He is far more concerned with source criticism, authorship, style and date.

[4] R. E. Prothero and G. C. Bradley, *Life and Correspondence of A. P. Stanley*, 1893, II, p. 100 (Stanley to Jowett)

[5] For an account of the Long case see *infra*, pp. 118ff.

Romans which had originally led Gray to consult Sumner. Phillpotts of Exeter and Wilberforce of Oxford pressed for a joint, corporate, action by all the bishops, inhibiting Colenso from officiating in their dioceses. Thirlwall of St David's objected, and Tait of London and one or two others (while agreeing that Colenso's teaching was undesirable) hesitated to approve the motion. Thomson the archbishop of York, opposed it on the grounds that it was not the proper legal method. The resolution was finally carried by twenty-five votes to four.[1]

The bishops met again on 7 February. As before almost the whole of the discussion turned on *Pentateuch and Joshua*. Gray had to remind the meeting that *Romans* must be considered too. Tait replied that it was not his business to condemn a book he had not read (Tait had proposed a resolution disapproving of *Pentateuch and Joshua*, Part I) and said 'when I do read, I wish to read good books'.[2] Feelings seem to have been roused. Tait accused Longley of being actuated by personal motives, and Gray of being unfair to Colenso. Eventually a committee was appointed to draw up a statement on behalf of all the bishops. The statement was presented at a further meeting a few days later and was signed by forty-one bishops, the only dissentient being Thirlwall of St David's—who at the second meeting had declared that he regarded Colenso's position as untenable. The signatories included, significantly, Thomson, Tait and Prince Lee. The nub of the statement, which took the form of an open letter to Colenso, was the argument that since *Pentateuch and Joshua* could not be reconciled with the promises of the ordinal, Colenso ought to resign.

Colenso treated the 'round robin' from the bishops with contempt. If he had ever seriously considered resignation, this attempt to prejudge the issue (as it seemed to him) only made him obstinate in his determination to fight on. The real scandal, he said, was caused by those 'who maintain a state of things in the Church opposed to the plainest results of modern science'.[3] He was removed from the list of vice-presidents of the S.P.G. and elected to the Athenaeum at about the same

---

[1] The dissidents were Thomson, Tait, Thirlwall and Prince Lee of Manchester.
[2] C. N. Gray, *op. cit.*, II, pp. 31ff, contains an abstract of the proceedings of the two meetings, based on his father's notes.
[3] Cox, *op. cit.*, I, p. 236

time. And, all still in February 1863, Part II of his work appeared in the public bookshops at about the same time as Lyell's *Antiquity of Man*. Lyell and Colenso became close friends at about this time.

About the middle of the month action was taken in Convocation. Archdeacon Denison of Taunton, a High Churchman, who had himself been prosecuted for his eucharistic theology, moved the appointment of a committee to investigate Colenso's teaching. He was seconded by Dr McCaul, of King's College, London, whose son had publicly announced that he had 'picked a hole' in Colenso's scholarship.[1] Professor Harold Browne of Cambridge, moved an amendment which affected tactics rather than principle, but the original motion was carried. Tait and Thirlwall opposed the motion in the upper house, but were overwhelmingly defeated.

The committee sat until May 1863, drawing up its report. Letters which passed between Archdeacon Denison and Archdeacon Bickersteth of Buckingham indicate that the committee planned its tactics very carefully so as to gain the sympathy and support of as wide a cross-section of Convocation as possible.[2] Edward Bickersteth was prolocutor of the lower house, brother of the Robert Bickersteth who became bishop of Ripon, and a distant connection of Colenso's. The relationship in no way modified his zeal. Bickersteth, like Denison, belonged to the 'High' party, but they arranged that the report should also be sponsored by prominent Evangelicals.

The report was forwarded from the lower house to the upper and certain resolutions were adopted. The resolutions really said three things. Colenso's *Pentateuch and Joshua*[3] was described as subversive of faith in the Bible as the Word of God. No direct action would be taken by Convocation because the work was to be considered by an ecclesiastical court elsewhere. The general public was warned that the book was dangerous.

Colenso might dismiss the resolutions of Convocation as 'the very best thing they could [do] for me'.[4] He might shrug his shoulders at the attempts of the Church Union to whip up feeling against him. Yet, again and again, in his more private

[1] Cox, *op. cit.*, I, p. 234
[2] Three letters bound up in a volume called *Colenso I*, in the Cape Town Diocesan Library, Bib. e. 398
[3] 'The said book'. *Romans* was not included in the condemnation.
[4] Cox, *op. cit.*, I, p. 238

letters he shows that he is not really the brash heretic ready to withstand the armies of Christ with a cold, unfeeling front. He felt that a fearful storm was about to break over him. His friends and relations were hesitant. His brother-in-law, the bishop of Labuan, had written to Tait:

> Poor J.W.N.[atal], he is much in my thoughts. I hope his coming to England will dispel the fogs Natal seems to have generated in his mind. If he had been here in my place, he would not have had time for encouraging these doubts and mists, and perhaps inter-course with Eastern people would have been a good corrective.[1]

While his relations could think that Colenso's Old Testament work was really the kind of thing which the devil provides for idle hands, and his friends were saying 'Caution! Caution!', Colenso was not entirely unaware that he might be purchasing for himself a splendid but lonely isolation. He established himself and his family in rooms in Blackfriars and later in Kensington. Part of the time he spent travelling about the country, staying with friends who would have him. The elder girls were sent to school at Winnington Hall in Cheshire and Mrs Colenso seems to have taken the other children to stay there from time to time.[2] Winnington was a progressive school, at times a thought too progressive for the advanced Mrs Colenso who did not think Carlyle's *Frederick* suitable reading for an 'unmarried English woman'. But at least the school provided a haven where the echoes of the controversy were softened by distance. Family life could go on more or less as normal. Mrs Colenso could write her husband letters which, even though they might have to refer to controversy, could still deal with the happy, ordinary things.

> My own dear Love,
> . . . . This fair weather is capital for the boys, they are out after a rabbit, the skeleton of which is wanted for anatomical study by the young ladies![3]

But it could not have been pleasant to be living in hired rooms for an indefinite period, nor to be on uneasy terms with their own relatives who either ignored the subject or tried earnestly to bring the erring sheep back to the fold. Nor can it have been

[1] R. T. Davidson and W. Benham, *op. cit.*, I, pp. 362f
[2] Rees, *op. cit.*, p. 70   [3] *Ibid.*, p. 78

pleasant to be told by Mrs Colenso's mother that they had better not hire rooms in a particular street because that was where Maurice lived.

Perhaps Maurice's reaction was the thing that hurt Colenso most.[1] He had sent his old friend one of the preliminary copies of his book. The very same *Record*, which had once attacked Maurice, also somehow acquired a copy and denounced it with virulence. But Maurice was on the side of the *Record* this time. He was horrified by some of Colenso's less wise expressions (e.g. the use of the word 'fiction' in describing parts of the Pentateuch). He claimed that no clergyman of the Church of England had any right to expound such views as Colenso's. He accused Colenso of misappropriating funds provided for missions to produce a work which would undermine the faith of millions. While Stanley encouraged Colenso so to modify his more extreme language that 'no indiscretion of expression or exaggeration of argument should lead off the public scent' from the bishop's real intention,[2] Maurice roundly condemned Colenso as dishonest and arrogant.

Eventually Maurice seems to have met Colenso face to face and to have told him that 'the consciences of Englishmen will be very strongly impressed with the feeling that you ought to resign your bishopric'.[3] This was just the sort of argument— the appeal to the public conscience of *Englishmen*—likely to influence Colenso. There seems indeed to have been a time when the bishop seriously considered resignation. He modified parts of his book so as to remove the expressions to which Maurice and Stanley both took exception. But his reply to Maurice's strictures was to say that there might be many who would feeel that Maurice was just as dishonest in retaining his own living. Maurice immediately took this retort very deeply to heart. He wrote to Charles Kingsley that he felt he must resign. He still believed that 'some of our scientific men and secularists' might be saved. 'Arguments about a Creator will fall dead upon them. A message from a Father may rouse them to life.'[4] But at the same time he wrote to Stanley that he felt obliged to dissociate himself from Colenso lest he be regarded

---

[1] The correspondence is printed in Cox, *op. cit.*, I, pp. 188ff; see also Campbell Library, Durban; Colenso folios, I, 5-14.
[2] Cox, *op. cit.*, I, p. 192 and cf Rees, *op. cit.*, p. 72
[3] F. Maurice, *Life of F.D Maurice*, II, p. 422
[4] *Ibid.*, p. 428

by the public as a hypocrite of the same kind—preaching the morality of the Old Testament but inwardly treating it as a mass of fictions and forgeries. In the end Maurice was persuaded not to resign by Colenso's brother-in-law, Charles Bunyon, who argued that resignation would look like an unanswerable attack upon a man who was already overwhelmed by vicious criticism on all sides. But it was a very long time before any sort of relationship was re-established between the two men, and then it was on a cold and formal level.

It is interesting that Pusey later attacked Colenso in almost exactly the same way as Maurice did and was met with almost exactly the same kind of answer. To Maurice's complaint that mission funds were being used to print apostate books, Colenso replied, 'According to *your* reasoning, I myself have committed a crime in spending my time in writing such a book, since, according to your view, I was not "sent out" . . . for such purposes'.[1] Pusey argued along very similar lines. 'Had he been *Mr* Colenso still the book would have been still-born. Now it is read by tens of thousands because he is a Bishop. It is his office of Bishop which propagates infidelity'.[2] Colenso and Pusey exchanged salvos over a period of some years. When Colenso's 'case' had been concluded Pusey called on him to resign, even though the secular courts had upheld his cause. Pusey argued that Colenso's teaching could not be reconciled with that of the Church of England, and Colenso turned on Pusey precisely the same *et tu quoque* argument he had used on Maurice. He had less love for Pusey than for Maurice and was correspondingly more brutal. Pusey cared less what Colenso thought of him than Maurice did, and the bishop's riposte was in this case less wounding. Colenso wrote to Pusey, reminding him of what the great Tractarian had written in the *Guardian* in the 1840s when his sermons on the doctrine of the Real Presence had led to his being inhibited by the University of Oxford. Pusey had then said that he would 'defend [his] opinions though he suffered the loss of all things; and that [his] opinions could *not be* proved contrary to the doctrines of the Church of England'.[3]

Attacks on Colenso came from all sides. Most people held

---

[1] Cox, *op. cit.*, p. 194
[2] R. T. Davidson and W. Benham, *Archibald Campbell Tait*, 1891, I, p. 337
[3] Campbell Library, Durban; Colenso Folios; K.30.—Colenso to E. B. Pusey, 6/6/1867

an extremely conservative and traditional view of the inerrancy of Scripture. Bishop Gray of Cape Town believed that 'there *are* difficulties in Holy Scripture—difficulties which have probably been permitted to be there to try the humility and faith of God's people, to invite them reverently to examine and inquire—which are chiefly difficulties to the half-informed and irreverent'.[1] William Magee (later to be archbishop of York) held similar views. Inconsistencies were in the Bible 'by God's special providence' so that man would not try to find mathematical certainty in his faith.[2] Bishop Wilberforce's attitude has become notorious through his debate with Huxley. People like Milman and Stanley were more encouraging, particularly when they were satisfied that Colenso's work was not to be purely destructive.[3] But Harold Browne, the very Cambridge professor to whom Colenso addressed the letter subsequently printed as the preface to *Pentateuch and Joshua*, published in 1863 a work entitled *The Pentateuch and the Elohistic Psalms in reply to Bishop Colenso*. It was one of many such books.[4] But it has a particular importance because it comes from a distinguished scholar, with no personal axe of controversy to grind, and one who was less biased and bigoted than most of the bishop's opponents.

In July 1863, for instance, Browne was writing to a friend:

> I know not what you think, but I certify that I fear more the less open assault upon the faith than such plain-spoken words as those of Colenso. He tells us plainly what he thinks and means. Others, with much to admire and even to love, write piously and pleasantly, and yet at last it is doubtful whether they mean Christianity or Pantheism.[5]

[1] C. N. Gray, *op. cit.*, I, p. 423
[2] D. Nicholls in *Church Quarterly Review*, CLXIII, No. 348, p. 340
[3] Cox, *op. cit.*, I, pp. 240ff
[4] See e.g. J. C. Knight, *The Pentateuchal Narrative Vindicated from the Absurdities charged against it by the Bishop of Natal*, 1862; J. C. Knight, *The Incredibilities of Part II of the Bishop of Natal's Work upon the Pentateuch; a lay protest*, 1863; C. Pritchard, *Vindiciae Mosaicae, A Letter to the Right Rev. Bishop Colenso*, 1863; F. Ashpitel, *The Increase of the Israelites in Egypt shewn to be probable from the Statistics of Modern Populations, with an examination of Bishop Colenso's Calculations on this subject*, 1863; J.B. Turner, *An Answer to the Difficulties in Bishop Colenso's Book on the Pentateuch*, 1863. The first author listed was an assistant at the British Museum; the second was secretary to the Royal Astronomical Society.
[5] E. Harold Browne to Archdeacon Bickersteth, bound up with Browne's *Pentateuch and Elohistic Psalms* in the Diocesan Library, Cape Town, Bib. e. 398

The letter contains also a reference to the committee appointed by convocation to investigate Colenso's writings, and to Bishop Phillpotts of Exeter's charge attacking Colenso. Browne approved of neither of these things.

In private, then, Browne was neither bitter nor inclined to fulminate against Colenso. Colenso's biographer accuses him of being dishonest in his public controversy with the bishop of Natal,[1] but at least it does not seem that Browne was motivated by any personal animus.

Browne's book in reply to Colenso's Part I begins with the argument that if Christ believed Moses to have written the Pentateuch, then he must have done so. This was the conventional reply—to throw the blanket of Christ's divinity over as much of the Old Testament as possible. As Browne said, 'Our religion is the religion of Christ, not the religion of Moses',[2] but 'The sapping of the foundation seems to threaten that the superstructure will follow. Moses first, and a greater than Moses afterwards'.[3] His argument is that, setting aside instances of 'accommodation' (where our Lord adapted His language so as to make it understandable to the people of his time) there are certain clear cases where one has simply to choose between saying 'Christ was right' or 'Christ was wrong'. His humanity, even a perfect humanity, might be *limited* in its knowledge, but the fact that He was God as well would preserve that limited knowledge from positive error. (This is the answer to Colenso's contention that it was Christ's human, limited mind that was capable of error).

'If therefore our Divine Lord . . . was not in error about a most important *religious* truth, there was such a man as Moses, there were such laws as the laws of Moses, there was such a prophet as Moses, and there remained writings of Moses.[4]

Plainly this argument does not protect the whole of the Pentateuch, for our Lord cannot be proved to have cited the whole of those books as of Mosaic origin. Browne rather brushes aside the question of 'how much of the Pentateuch is covered by our Lord's appeal to it', and so he devotes the rest of his work to considering particular points raised by Colenso.

---

[1] Cox, *op. cit.*, I, pp. 409ff
[2] Browne, *Pentateuch and Elohistic Psalms*, p. 2
[3] *Ibid.*, p. 1   [4] *Ibid.*, p. 15

There is a good deal of discussion of the arithmetical sections of the bishop's work—whether it was possible 'where marriages were early and fecundity great' for the people of Israel to grow as rapidly in Egypt as Genesis and Exodus imply.[1] There is much argument about the name Jahweh—whether Samuel 'forged' it or not. (This section includes a delightful consideration of whether Eve spoke Hebrew.[2]) Yet, on the whole, Browne's reply is impressive even to the modern reader. He is not simply taking refuge in the taboos of Christ's divinity. Nor is he a mere literalist, defending the Scripture as the *words* of God. He is aware that 'it was no part of the Divine purpose in the mission of Moses that he should teach the Israelites geology or astronomy'.[3] He is not perturbed by the modern discovery that man has been on the earth for longer than 6000 years—'far more formidable problems occur both in life and religion' than these. So much for Colenso's claim that the whole book of Exodus is incredible because it conflicts with modern science.

The other principal difficulty was the moral issue—did God command, or did he not, the barbarities and atrocities for which the Old Testament claims his sanction? Browne does not directly answer this question. Instead he compares the laws of the Old Testament with other codes of conduct—ancient and modern, Christian and heathen—'they may put to shame the humanity of Christian Europe to this very day'.[4] 'Apparent anomalies in a code of such amazing antiquity as the Law of Moses, are not reasonable grounds for denying its excellence'.

This is, indeed, typical of Browne's approach. He will not, where he can avoid it, chop arithmetic with Colenso. Just as he refused to argue that our Lord's reference to the Law of Moses guarantees every verse, so he will not attempt to prove the historical accuracy of every incident in Exodus. It is the broad outline, the existence of Moses as lawgiver, the journeying of Israelites from Egypt to Palestine, the general excellence of the Mosaic law, which he upholds. His second lecture contains a dissertation on inspiration which is well worth reading, even now.[5] Exaggeration in numbers may not disprove the general veracity of a history; but it might suggest that the writer of it is not divinely inspired. But this is only the case if we believe

[1] *Ibid.*, p. 21   [2] *Ibid.*, pp. 42ff   [3] *Ibid.*, p. 80
[4] *Ibid.*, p. 83   [5] *Ibid.*, pp. 30ff

that 'every letter was the direct utterance of the Most High', and this Browne will not allow. The results of modern criticism forbid the belief that God dictated every letter and *then preserved it miraculously in transmission.* We know there are variant readings. We know that some parts of the New Testament are of doubtful authenticity. Yet we believe that 'the writers of our sacred books received a Divine teaching, a supernatural illumination, a direct and miraculous inspiration, and that their writings have been preserved to us, and for our instruction by a special Providence' but not so as to 'warrant us in denying every human element in the mind and writings of those taught by it'.

All this is worth remembering because of the fundamentally false picture one is often given of the controversy over Colenso's Pentateuchal criticism. The bishop is represented simply as one who checked the sums of the Bible and found them wanting.[1] His opponents are depicted as obscurantists anxious to prove that the hare chews the cud.[2] There was a great deal in Colenso's writing which was arithmetical quibbling and which could be answered, as Browne pointed out, by saying that errors had crept in in the transmission of the text. Many of the bishop of Natal's opponents *were* obscurantists, defending the last ditch with a blind, almost hysterical determination to preserve the verbal inerrancy of Holy Writ. Both the arithmetic and the literalism can be made to appear comic now, and very little of what was worth while in the views of either party has been preserved. Colenso's admirers are anxious to exculpate him at all costs; the heirs of the 'orthodox' tend to slip smoothly through this part of the story without stopping to assess what was valuable on either side. But Colenso has something positive to say. He argued that the Priestly Code was the latest of the Pentateuchal sources and that the book of Daniel was written in Maccabean times. He pointed out the close connection between Jeremiah and Deuteronomy; and all these and other matters like them are valuable for a real understanding of what the Old Testament is saying. The best of his opponents, like Browne, were willing to accept what seemed to them to be

[1] 'If Colenso's voluminous books of biblical criticism do not perhaps give a satisfying account of the Bible as a source of religious authority, they do answer the question, what is the value of the Bible as a mathematical treatise?', A. O. J. Cockshutt—*Anglican Attitudes*, 1959, p. 94.

[2] Rees, *op. cit.*, p. 77

the positive and reasonable conclusions of criticism and to realise that one of the most important of all the fruits of the discussion was that what mattered was not the minutiae of mathematics but 'the great outline of God's early dealings with man and with his own peculiar people'.[1] The tragedy is that while men remember the quarrel about the number of Israelites who could be squashed into the temple, no-one remembers that Colenso began to wrestle with a kenotic Christology long before the time of Gore and Weston, and that Browne attempted a formulation of the ideas of inspiration and revelation which would allow for a proper balance of both human and divine elements. We have become accustomed, in this century, to maintaining the view that orthodoxy (i.e. truth) lies in maintaining the human part as well as the divine in the Incarnation, the Church, the sacraments and the Bible. It seems to us a new and important discovery, but it is worth remembering that both Colenso and the best of his opponents perceived that this was a necessary corollary of the critics' work and were fumbling with just this problem.

Maurice described his feelings, on first reading Colenso's book, as shock and horror.

> To have a quantity of criticism about the dung in the Jewish camp, and the division of a hare's foot, thrown in my face, when I was satisfied that the Jewish history had been the mightiest witness to the people for a living God against the dead dogmas of priests, was more shocking to me than I can describe.[2]

No doubt the vast majority of Christians felt a similar shock of horror. This would account for the hysterical abuse to which Colenso was subjected—and no-one would now seek to excuse or exculpate those who hurled insults at the bishop. At the same time it was a tragedy that Colenso published his Pentateuchal criticism at the precise moment when his *Romans* was being examined for heresy. The real issue at stake was whether a missionary bishop should be allowed to preach a universalist gospel as official Anglican doctrine. As soon as *Pentateuch and Joshua* appeared, all this was forgotten. 'Biblical criticism' was an easier heresy to pin on Colenso. People felt more strongly about it. Conservative bishops could be whipped up in a

---

[1] Browne, *op. cit.*, p. 33
[2] F. Maurice, *Life of F. D. Maurice*, I, p. 174

frenzy of moral indignation about it. It was easy to explain to the general public, and to win popular sympathy, if one said that one could not allow a Christian bishop to attack the Bible. Maurice might forgive incipient universalism; he could not forgive 'biblical criticism'.

And so Maurice's assessment of the situation passed into history. Colenso was labelled as quibbler and iconoclast. The controversy about biblical criticism completely overlaid the much more important and earlier issue concerning the theology of the Atonement. In the indictment against Colenso the question of the inspiration and authority of the Bible tended to overshadow every other issue. People condemned Colenso for the wrong reasons. And he was praised and defended for the wrong reasons, too. Men hailed him as the champion of common sense and anticlericalism.[1] But always it was his work on the Pentateuch which was remembered; it was 'the quantity of dung' which stuck. One recent writer does not mention the original 'heresy' for which Colenso was indicted, and treats the whole thing as though Old Testament criticism was the only issue raised.[2] What nearly everyone forgets is that Colenso was not a mere iconoclast. 'The mighty witness for a living God' was as much Colenso's concern as it was Maurice's. From Colenso, seeking to free the God of truth from a web of false witness; to Maurice, fighting for Christian liberty and love; from Gray's passionate concern for the Church and its faith, to Browne's honest search for the hand of God in history; a great many men were trying to bring truth to light. The episode was not really a tragi-comic quarrel about the hare's foot and the Jewish birthrate.

[1] Rees, *op. cit.*, p. 75   [2] A. O. J. Cockshutt, *op. cit.*

CHAPTER 5

The Heretic

To the Right Reverend John William Colenso, Doctor in Divinity, Lord Bishop of Natal, and a Suffragan Bishop of the Province of Cape Town.
My Lord,—By direction of the Lord Bishop of Cape Town, I hereby cite you to appear before the Most Reverend Robert, Lord Bishop of Cape Town and Metropolitan, on Tuesday, the seventeenth day of November, one thousand eight hundred and sixty-three, at eleven o'clock in the forenoon, in the vestry of the cathedral church of Saint George in Cape Town, then and there to answer certain charges of false, strange and erroneous doctrine and teaching, preferred against you. . . .

ON 18 May 1863 this citation was issued in Cape Town. The substance of the charges against Colenso (set out in detail in a schedule attached to the citation) were summarised in general terms claiming that by the 'writing, printing and publishing, and the sale within this Province' of *Romans* and the first two parts of *Pentateuch and Joshua*, Colenso had attempted to 'maintain, set forth, teach, inculcate and express beliefs, doctrines, views and opinions in opposition to and at variance with the doctrine and teaching of the United Church of England and Ireland, as set forth, expressed and maintained in the Book of Common Prayer, the Sacraments and other rites of the said Church, the 39 Articles of Religion and the Canons Ecclesiastical . . .'.[1]

Robert Gray returned to Cape Town after the bishops' meetings arranged by Longley, arriving in South Africa in the middle of April 1863. He had already been investigating the possibility of citing Colenso for heresy. At the meeting on 4 February Longley had asked him whether he intended to institute proceedings against Colenso. Gray's reply was that he had consulted various prominent legal authorities including Sir Roundell Palmer and Sir Robert Phillimore, and they had

---

[1] Printed report of the *Trial of Bishop Colenso*, p. 2

advised him that he could take action if it could be proved that Colenso's books had been sold in the South African province and provided that the Long case did not result in a weakening of the authority of his letters patent.[1]

It has already been pointed out that the Privy Council judgment in the Long case was not delivered until 24 June 1863. Gray could not remain in England indefinitely. The case had been heard before the Judicial Committee from 9 to 13 February, when Roundell Palmer and Phillimore appeared for Gray. Once the case was concluded and the English bishops had drawn up their 'round robin', Gray had to return to the Province. Nor was he willing to wait indefinitely before issuing the citation. The Privy Council judgment was expected almost daily. Gray waited three months, and then took action. But the delay was not really as long as it looks. The fast steamship to England from Cape Town took about a month to do the journey. News inevitably travelled very slowly. Moreover, it would have taken Gray some time to have the necessary documents drawn up and to arrange for the prosecution. The truth is that he did not really wait for the judgment in the Long case at all, but proceeded to arrange for Colenso's trial almost as soon as he returned to Cape Town. At the time when the citation was formally issued he could not even have heard that the Convocation of Canterbury had condemned Colenso's writings.

Gray was, of course, under pressure. The South African clergy, in particular, were clearly in favour of a formal trial—though oddly enough the man who might have been expected to take the lead in this matter, proved to be curiously reluctant. Henry Callaway sent Dean Green a copy of *Pentateuch and Joshua* early in 1863. Green, in reply, urged on him that it was no longer the duty of the Natal clergy to present their bishop for heresy. He was out of the way. He was no longer feeding his flock with 'poison' from the pulpit. It was the metropolitan's job to cite Colenso of his own volition ('*sua sponte*' is Green's phrase) '*He* must drink of this cup; for this cause came he to this hour'.[2] Green even argued that the clergy of Natal should not send any kind of protest or statement to the metropolitan. In March he wrote to Gray himself, 'If, as you say, you need

---

[1] C. N. Gray, *op. cit.*, II, pp. 34f
[2] A. T. Wirgman, *Life of James Green*, I, pp. 130ff

a *promoter*, you need but *one*, and he had better be taken from your own, or from the Diocese of Grahamstown, where the clergy are not related to the Bishop as we are. If your Dean were the promoter, the Bishop would feel that pure motives only influenced him'.[1]

One can imagine Gray's exasperation on receiving this reply. It is clear that he has been *asking* Green to act as promoter, but, since *Romans* was the real source of all the trouble and since Green had written to him to complain of *Romans*, Gray was perhaps justified in assuming that Green would intend to delate Colenso formally if given the opportunity. It looks very much as though Gray acted on Green's advice about finding another promoter, for the charges against the bishop of Natal were finally made in the name of the dean of Cape Town, the archdeacon of Grahamstown and the archdeacon of George.[2]

The whole thing has an unpleasant sound. Gray had asked the archbishop of Canterbury to sit in judgment on Colenso's teaching. Having obtained a condemnation of that teaching from the English bishops, the accuser then turned judge and, not content with this, sought for someone whom he could persuade to act as accuser, in turn. Colenso might be forgiven for feeling that this was a travesty of justice and that he could not submit himself to any court which was so clearly prejudging the issue.

In justice to Gray, however, it must be said that these same events were patient of quite another interpretation. Green had complained of Colenso's *Romans*. Gray had then asked for a ruling from the archbishop of Canterbury because on the first occasion when Green delated his bishop for heresy[3] Colenso had argued that Gray was not a real metropolitan, but that they were both suffragans of Canterbury. The new archbishop and other English bishops (including even the redoubtable Tait) had asked why Gray was not undertaking to hear the case himself. The matter had been referred back to Gray's jurisdiction and the decision of Convocation would eventually make his responsibilities even more clear. He felt himself obliged to take action and he felt that in order to hear the case there must be someone to present it to the court. He therefore turned back

---

[1] *Ibid.*, p. 137
[2] The archdeaconry of George was then part of Gray's diocese; it is now a separate see.   [3] *Supra*, p. 73

to Green as the person from whom, in a sense, the first accusation had come. Green was now unwilling to act and Gray felt
obliged to find someone else. The clergy of the diocese of Cape
Town had sent him an address on his return to South Africa
in which they said that they were 'prepared to take [their] share
—in giving efficacy to the Church's power of discipline, and
putting her laws in force'.[1] It did not seem wrong to Gray to
ask them to take that share: 'I need scarcely say that if, after full
consideration of the subject, you still feel that you ought to
frame articles against the Bishop, and present him for his
writings, I shall feel it my painful duty to cite him. . . .'[2]

It is interesting to note that the clergy of Natal, in spite of
Green's hesitations, sent a similar petition to the metropolitan
at about the same time.[3] The divisions in the diocese of Natal
were becoming more and more obvious. Dean Green was
inclined to think that the chapter ought to act as the supreme
authority in the diocese in the absence of the bishop.[4] Colenso
in fact appointed Theophilus Shepstone to act on his behalf,
with power of attorney, and with strict instructions to prevent
Green from getting possession of any of the property of which
Colenso was trustee.[5] Petition and counter-petition, clergy
against laity; the tiny white Anglican community in Natal was
being broken up.

The really puzzling thing about Gray's action is not whether,
as Colenso thought, he was being dishonest and hypocritical,
but that he was not prepared to wait until his legal authority
was no longer in question and the Privy Council had pronounced judgment in Long's case. The answer lies partly in
Gray's own character; partly in the facts of Long's case itself.

The Reverend W. Long was ordained deacon by the bishop
of London and sent to the Cape Colony by the S.P.G. in 1846,
when he was made colonial chaplain at Graaff-Reinet in the
eastern division of the Cape Colony.[6] He was ordained priest
by Bishop Gray and later sent to be rector of St Peter's Mowbray, in the environs of Cape Town itself. This living had been
endowed by the first incumbent, the Reverend John Hoets, who
asked in return that he and his heirs should possess the right

[1] C. N. Gray, op. cit., II, p. 56   [2] Ibid., pp. 56f
[3] Ibid.   [4] Wirgman, op. cit., I, p. 132
[5] Cox, op. cit., I, p. 241
[6] Bishopscourt Archives, Cape Town: Index of letters to S.P.G.; B. Hawes
14/12/1846

to nominate his successors according to the English pattern of patronage.[1] Gray was most unwilling to accede to this request. His whole plan for the development of a South African Church depended on cutting away as much as possible of the English Establishment. He agreed that Hoets might choose the next two incumbents. After that the gift would revert to the bishop. Hoets nominated Long as his immediate successor.

It has already been pointed out that Gray had trouble in the diocese of Cape Town over the constitution of a diocesan synod. Some of the laity suspected the bishop of having leanings towards Rome. They also resented any attempt to have a local legislative body foisted on them, which might compel them to accept an ecclesiastical order which would be illegal in England. Hitherto Anglicans in South Africa had regarded themselves as belonging to individual congregations of the Church of England, not to any South African branch, province or diocese of an Anglican Communion. They were Englishmen. They were living abroad, it is true, but they were still Englishmen. In no sense were they 'South Africans'—'South Africa' did not then exist, of course. The sort of religion they wanted was English Christianity, the Church of England as it was established 'at home'. The intensity of the opposition roused by Colenso's early actions indicates very plainly just how sharp their fear was that a bishop might arbitrarily change the whole appearance of that Protestant, Established religion to which they were accustomed.

When Gray first spoke of summoning a synod, some of the clergy and laity warned him that they would not be willing to accept any such body unless the law compelled them to do so. In 1856 the bishop issued the summons to the clergy of the diocese and mandates to the various parishes instructing them to elect lay representatives. A petition was drawn up which protested that the bishop was attempting to do something which would be manifestly illegal in England, for the English Convocations could not meet, do business, nor pass mandatory legislation without the authority of the Crown.[2]

The position in England at this time was that Convocation, after the long period of forced inaction, was just beginning to

---

[1] C. Lewis and G. E. Edwards, *Historical Records of the Church of the Province of South Africa*, 1934, p. 150
[2] *Correspondence between the Lord Bishop of Cape Town and F. R. Surtees*, 1857; the petition is printed as an appendix.

revive. In neither Canterbury nor York had the Convocation had any power at all. Proctors were elected every time Parliament was summoned. In Canterbury the Convocation assembled for certain formal ceremonies and was then prorogued. In York the prorogation came even more rapidly.

In the 1830s agitation began for the revival of the powers of the Convocations. Some attempts were made to insist that the proceedings should not be mere formalities. In the '50s there appeared a flood of pamphlets arguing that a vital, active Convocation would stimulate Church life, protect the Church against Papal aggression, and free it from the tyrannical control of the State. By 1851 the possibility of the revival of Convocation had become a sufficiently live matter for Robert Gray to think it worth his while to attempt to claim a seat in the upper house of Canterbury.[1] Bishop Samuel Wilberforce, Gray's friend, agent and mentor, was one of the leading figures in the movement for revival, with Blomfield and Philpotts. The Society for the Revival of Convocation was founded by a layman called Henry Hoare. Archbishop Sumner firmly opposed the move until 1854, and the government also seems to have done its best to prevent any revival. Convocation itself compelled both the archbishop and the law officers of the Crown to allow it as much activity as was not actually forbidden by law —and this was found to give a good deal of latitude. The making of new canons was specifically prohibited: apart from this Convocation could do a great many things. From 1855 Convocation asserted its right, within this limitation, to conduct its business. The fact that no royal licence would be granted to it to allow it to legislate meant that its own constitution could not be amended to make it a more representative body. Although this particular matter was not to be dealt with until the present century, 'letters of business' enabling Convocation to amend a canon were issued in 1861. The battle was not yet over because it soon became apparent that the royal assent to canonical legislation would not be automatic. Archbishop Tait seems always to have preferred that matters should be dealt with by Parliament, rather than by Convocation. There were always those

[1] Bishopscourt Archives, Cape Town: Memoranda E.H.D. III; Summary of facts relating to the Organisation of the Church of the Province. Gray's patent indicated that he was in some sense a subordinate of Canterbury. His failure to gain admission to Convocation showed he was not a 'suffragan' in the normal sense.

who were ready to condemn Convocation as a clericalist and obscurantist body. But by the late 1850s it was clear that the English Convocations were to be active bodies again, and it is significant that the battle was fought, not by the Tractarians,[1] but by the advocates of efficiency like Blomfield and the old-fashioned High Churchmen like Wilberforce. Gray's sympathies were, as has already been pointed out, much more like those of Wilberforce than of the Tractarians proper.[2]

In the colonies the Convocation fever affected a good many bishops. In New Zealand Bishop Selwyn was experimenting with some sort of synodical government. Inquiries came from Canada about the legal position of synods in the colonies. In Australia an enabling act was passed which allowed the Church to hold synods. Several attempts were made to pass a bill through the Imperial Parliament which would regularise the whole position. But in the end nothing was done and the government itself seems to have been uncertain about whether anything ought to be done. The Church in Canada was informed that no enabling act was needed.[3]

It was extremely difficult for the imperial authorities to duplicate the English situation in the colonies. Even when the authorities were sympathetic (as Gladstone was in 1852) they had to solve a genuine dilemma. The government might grant a measure of independence and establish a civil legislature in one of the colonies. If it also established an ecclesiastical legislature in the same colony it would have called into being two legislative bodies deriving their authority from the same source and, although that authority might normally be exercised in different spheres, it was conceivable that they might conflict. The only alternative was to make the one body directly subordinate to the other, and this was not likely to be welcomed by the very people who were agitating for the creation of synods. The authorities hesitated to create in the colonies the parallel system which had obtained in theory in England, but which had gradually been done away in practice. Parliament had come to exercise, through the cabinet, more and more of the ecclesiastical prerogatives of the Crown. The only alterna-

[1] See E. W. Kemp, *Counsel and Consent*, 1961, p. 172.
[2] *Supra*, p. 10 and cf A. T. Wirgman, *James Green*, I, p. ix
[3] 'Statutable aid is not necessary and, if not necessary, it is highly inexpedient'—quoted in C. N. Gray, *op. cit.*, I, p. 411.

tive was to ask the colonial legislature to pass an enabling act —and this Gray would not countenance.

Under these circumstances Gray's attempt to create a diocesan synod in the Cape Colony was bound to cause unrest. The local distrust of bishops, and the English dissension about Convocation, made a good many people feel that he was doing something revolutionary and probably wrong. The dissidents did everything in their power to prevent the assembling of the synod. Since the attorney-general of the colony gave it as his opinion that there was nothing illegal in a bishop's summoning of the clergy for consultation, the opposition concentrated on the question of lay representatives. They attempted to persuade the parishes to refuse to elect and in a number of cases they were successful. Tempers ran high. Very rude things were said in public about the bishop. Synodical government was an issue about which quite ordinary men and women developed violent and unrestrained opinions.[1]

Three clergymen in the diocese joined in the protests. They appeared at the synod, but only to object to the summons, and then withdrew again. One of the three was William Long. His objections were that synods were an innovation since the time when he had been ordained and licensed; that they were illegal unless authorised by the Crown; that they could not be forced upon those who were not willing to accept them: and that they imposed an unjust limitation on the rights of members of the Church.[2]

One of the odd things about the whole of the Long case was that there was no obvious schism. Even after the case was over, Long continued to attend informal meetings of the clergy and the services which preceded the official synods. What he would never do was to admit that Gray had the right to compel him to attend a session of a legislative body whose acts would be binding upon him or upon his parish. At this stage Gray ignored the protest and his relations with Long continued as before. The bishop seems to have felt that Long was not entirely honest in his assertion that he was maintaining the 'laws and constitutions of the Church',[3] but there was no open breach.

[1] An account of some of the meetings to elect lay representatives is printed in *Correspondence between the Lord Bishop of Cape Town and F. R. Surtees, Esq.*
[2] Lewis and Edwards, *op. cit.*, p. 150
[3] C. N. Gray, *op. cit.*, I, p. 419

The year after Gray held his first synod the so-called 'Eton College Case' was heard in the English courts. The normal convention of the time was that the Crown exercised the right to nominate to any ecclesiastical benefice vacated because the previous incumbent had been given preferment by the Crown, irrespective of the rights of the patron of the living. In time the Crown came to exercise this right even in cases where the preferment was to a bishopric in the colonies. Thus if an English incumbent was nominated to a colonial see the living vacated by him would be filled by the Crown, and the patron of the living would have no say in the matter at all. This actually happened in Gray's case—in spite of the fact that the endowment of the see had come from private donations and the bishop-elect had been chosen by the Colonial Bishopric's Fund committee. The Crown had played no part at all, except to issue letters patent, but it had gained the right to nominate the next incumbent of the parish of Stockton-on-Tees.

In the Eton College case the college attempted by legal action to prevent the Crown from superseding the normal right of a patron in such a case. Lord Campbell, when the case was heard in the Queen's Bench, held that the *Established* Church of England could have no legal existence in the colonies, particularly where there was a separate legislature. This threw a completely new light on the whole situation at the Cape. Dr Phillimore, the great expert in canon law, advised Gray that one of the implications of this judgment was that the courts of the Church in South Africa were not a part of the system of Church courts in England and no automatic appeal could lie from Gray's court to the Court of Arches in the province of Canterbury.[1]

There were other important implications too. When Gray summoned his synod for the second time in 1860 he felt obliged to alter the declaration that he had required from laymen who proposed to vote in the election of representatives. Previously he had required them to state that they were 'members of the United Church of England and Ireland'. This requirement had in itself been a cause of great resentment. Englishmen felt that their religion ought to be 'taken as read'. They had never been asked to *declare* that they belonged to the

---

[1] Bishopscourt Archives, Cape Town; Memoranda E.H.D. III, *loc. cit.*

English Church before. But now Gray asked them to state that they were 'members of the Church of the Diocese of Cape Town in union and full communion with the United Church of England and Ireland'. If his previous actions had given rise to a fear that membership in the English Church would depend upon the whim of the bishop, the wording of the new declaration only made those fears more acute. Yet Gray was simply trying to comply with what he believed to be the legal implications of Lord Campbell's judgment.

Long again refused to attend the synod, repeating the substance of his earlier protest and adding expressions reflecting the fear that the 'Church of the Diocese of Cape Town' might be drifting away from the old English Church at home. This time Gray took action, determined to test his authority. Long was summoned to appear before the bishop's court on 4 February 1861.

Gray's action was somewhat daring. He had been warned that his court stood apart from the system of Church courts in England. It owed its existence to, and its procedure was regulated by, the enactments of that very diocesan synod of 1856 which Long had refused to attend. Long was to be tried by a court whose very genesis he had protested against. But from Gray's point of view there was really no alternative except to tolerate a complete lack of discipline. Sitting with five of his clergy as assessors, he found Long guilty of disobedience and sentenced him to three months suspension, without loss of salary. Long only appeared before the court to protest against its jurisdiction. He refused to obey the sentence of the court and was finally deprived of his benefice altogether for his persistent contumacy.[1]

Long then applied to the Supreme Court of the colony for an interdict, to restrain the bishop from evicting him from the church at Mowbray. Gray appeared before the civil court in person, rather than run the risk of having a lawyer who might not understand all the implications of canon law.[2] The chief justice held[3] that Long had bound himself to obey the bishop by accepting a licence from him. Once that was allowed then

---

[1] Lewis and Edwards, *op. cit.*, p. 150
[2] *Speech by the Bishop of Capetown in the Supreme Court of the Colony,* 1861
[3] See *Report of the Case of the Reverend Mr. Long,* 1861, and Bishopscourt Archives, Cape Town; Folio 1—Complete record of Long *v.* Gray.

all the rest followed and Gray was within his rights in depriving Long for disobedience. But the court also held that the legal position of bishops holding letters patent in the colonies was so complex that Long was hardly to be blamed for not understanding what his obligations were.

Long appealed to the Privy Council and the judgment was delivered two years later, when the Colenso case had come to the fore. On 24 June 1863 the Judicial Committee, presided over by Lord Kingsdown, reversed the judgment of the colonial court.[1] A sharp distinction was made between a bishop's authority as bishop, and his jurisdiction as bishop of a particular area. The Crown might make lawful bishops at will. It could only give them coercive jurisdiction in a specific area under certain conditions. In some cases colonial bishops had been given jurisdiction by Act of Parliament, but this had not happened in Gray's case. His first letters patent had been superseded by the second letters patent, issued when Colenso was consecrated, and the second letters patent were *ultra vires* because by the time they were drawn up the Crown had already granted representative government to the Cape Colony. It had already surrendered the right to certain prerogative powers. The only way that Gray could exercise jurisdiction over the clergy in the colony was by some sort of contract between them. The first synod had, in effect, created a contract of a kind, but Long had never consented to it. He could not, therefore, be compelled to recognise the synod nor its decisions and Gray could not punish him for refusing to do so. But the Judicial Committee refused to deal with any matter of 'spiritual authority' and recognised Gray's right *as bishop* to inhibit Long. Long was, in fact, assured of his temporal rights. He could not be given cure of souls unless Gray was willing to license him again.

A more complicated situation would be difficult to imagine. Wilberforce advised Gray to settle the matter in a charitable fashion by restoring Long to his cure and continuing in the same relationship with him as between the two sessions of the Cape Town synod. This Gray did. Wilberforce also believed —quite mistakenly—that 'To apply this [judgment] to the Colenso case seems to me easy and direct. He has taken the oath

---

[1] A copy of the judgment is in the Bishopscourt Archives and it is also printed in an appendix to C. N. Gray, *op. cit.*, II.

of canonical obedience to you;—this being a voluntary act he cannot question your jurisdiction'.[1]

Colenso was, as it proved, rather shrewder in his assessment of the implications of the Privy Council judgment. He did not reply to Gray's citation (which had been served on him by a proctor of the Doctors' Commons on 1 July 1863) until 5 October. He was still in England and was not proposing to return to South Africa in time to appear at his trial in Cape Town. He sent the metropolitan a letter rejecting his claim to jurisdiction and asserted that Gray had 'no legal right to take cognisance of the charge in question'.[2]

Gray nevertheless persisted in his determination to proceed with the trial. That he should have had the courage, or the foolhardiness, to stick to his guns in spite of the uncertainties arising from the Long case may seem surprising in retrospect, but Gray believed that he had no alternative. Like Colenso, Gray is a controversial figure. He is conventionally represented as saint and hero or narrow bigot; just as Colenso is represented as courageous liberal or wicked heretic. In neither case is the picture a just one.

In the South African prayer book Robert Gray is the only 'local worthy' who is commemorated in the kalendar.[3] There is a fashion in the Province for calling things after him, and undoubtedly he is an heroic figure for the South African Church. In his own day he was regarded by both sides in the Colenso dispute as 'prejudiced', which probably means that he did his best to steer a middle course, in spite of the fact that Colenso's theology distressed him terribly. Colenso's opinion, that Gray was biased and had prejudged the issue, has already been referred to. Dean Green regarded Gray as too conventional and lacking in courage.

Bishop Gray had been educated in the traditions which had come down from Constantine. Through all those ages the Church had been in intimate connection with the State: the conception of the Church moving freely in the kingdoms of the world, disconnected from the civil power, now so familiar to us, may be said to have been at that time in an embryo state, undeveloped

---

[1] C. N. Gray, op. cit., I, p. 534   [2] Cox, op. cit., I, p. 279
[3] 1 September. The only other person approaching 'local' interest is Bernard Mizeki, an African from Portuguese East Africa, who was converted in Cape Town, and worked as a missionary in Rhodesia where he was martyred.

into shape. In addition the Bishop's mind was strongly conservative in character. . . .[1]

Modern attempts to assess Gray's character are just as varied, and just as unsatisfactory. He has been described, with turgid sentimentality, as the helmsman of the ship of the Province. 'With Robert Gray at the helm, and sometimes in grave peril, she continued her course'. 'He had been led to a far country which had demanded from him great physical endurance, great moral courage and an unconquerable spirit. He had been given a heart both stern and gentle, humble, courteous and kind'.[2] He has also been represented as aggressive and domineering. 'It was impossible for a man of Gray's convictions, and headstrong temperament, to seek any accommodation with Evangelicals, and he made no attempt to seek unity within his diocese except by imposing his will upon all'.[3] With less partisan feeling he has been described as a traditionalist with a tendency to exaggerate the importance of events and situations in which he found himself. 'Himself an Etonian, the son of a bishop, Gray's mind had been formed in a purely Anglican atmosphere. A nervous, bookish, ungregarious boy, loneliness had tended to make him ignorant of the views of others, while his natural tendency to self-dramatisation made him overlook their importance when they were known'.[4]

None of these descriptions, the sentimental, the bitter or the literary, really does justice to Gray. He was not an unconscious Erastian, for one of his earliest decisions as a bishop was to do everything in his power to free the Church from the disabilities imposed upon it by the State connection. His attitude was, rather, that he ought to work within the limits of the traditional position for as long as it was humanly possible. He was neither physically nor intellectually a giant, though he was capable of a considerable obstinate courage. He mistrusted his own judgment,[5] particularly in intellectual or academic matters,

---

[1] Quoted from a sermon by Dean Green in Wirgman, *op. cit.*, I, p. ix. But Gray and Green had disagreed violently over the consecration of Colenso's successor and never quite recovered their original friendly relations; see P. Hinchliff, *op. cit.*, p. 102.

[2] A. Brooke, *Robert Gray*, 1947, pp. 113 & 151

[3] Rees, *op. cit.*, p. 56

[4] A. O. J. Cockshutt, *Anglican Attitudes*, p. 95

[5] And even his most fervent admirers concede that he hated to admit that his decisions had been wrong; see A. Brooke, *op. cit.*, p. 123.

and he suffered from more or less continual illness. He was not a bigot and he was capable of treating 'Evangelical' clergy with great consideration and kindness. He was not, strictly speaking, a Tractarian at all, but a High Churchman of a somewhat older school.[1]

The assessment of Gray as a self-dramatiser has, perhaps, some truth in it—but only in the sense in which the same description might be applied to almost every man of his generation. It is easy to generalise about the 'Victorians', and most generalisations are wrong. But romanticism was in the air. Most men thought of themselves in dramatic terms. Perhaps the *earnestness* of the Victorians[2] deprived them of a sense of humour, and a sense of humour means a sense of proportion. Even the much more eighteenth-century Colenso was inclined to exaggerate the dramatic importance of events. His correspondence with Maurice[3] contains phrases, in the letters of both men, which to modern ears have a ring of unreality and artificially created drama. So Colenso says:

Can you suppose that I have not daily and hourly beloved forms such as these before my eyes—that I should pursue the path I am taking, if I did not think and most entirely believe that they from their higher places look down and breathe their blessing upon my work, while struggling here on earth—(amidst much infirmity, and every kind of temptation to give up the struggle and be content to lie)—to be true to the Living God and His truth.[4]

If Colenso saw himself 'hourly' as a sort of latter-day author to the Hebrews, surrounded by a great cloud of departed relatives and friends cheering him on, Pusey, as we have seen, saw himself as a latter-day St Paul ready to 'suffer the loss of all things'.[5] Tractarians tended to die of broken hearts. Newman's secession was the climax of a genuine drama and a great deal of dramatising. Shaftesbury described the Parisian Sunday as a 'wholesale, resolute, national desecration of the Lord's Day. Whether it be disbelief or disobedience, the result is distressing, and weighs one down with the reflection that millions are set in

---

[1] I have attempted elsewhere a more detailed assessment of Gray's character; see P. Hinchliff, *op. cit.*, pp. 27ff. Gray's comments quoted in C. N. Gray, *op. cit.*, II, p. 170, indicate that he did not identify himself with the Tractarian party.
[2] Cf *supra*, p. 27
[3] *Supra*, p. 107
[4] Cox, *op. cit.*, I, p. 189
[5] *Supra*, p. 108

open resistance to the Most High, and are bent on giving the victory to the flesh over the spirit, to time over eternity, to the god of this world over the God of the other'.[1] Gray did dramatise himself and his situation, but so did most men of the time, and none more than James Green in Pietermaritzburg.[2] And what of the judge of the Natal court who formally pronounced Green an 'outlaw'! Indeed it is probably true to say that it was the combination of moral earnestness and the strong sense of the dramatic which made all the religious controversies of the mid-nineteenth century, and not Colenso's alone, such bitter and violent struggles.

On the other hand, Gray was certainly a romantic, in a way that Colenso was not. Church history was his 'favourite study'.[3] He developed a romantic veneration for the Church of the patristic age. When he was given the opportunity to create an Anglican Church in a new continent, the patristic Church was the model on which he planned to shape it—or, at least, the patristic Church as Gray imagined it to have been. He was also heartily sick—not of the Establishment itself, but of the one-sidedness of Establishment and the difficulties it created for the Church of England.[4] And his views were perfectly plain. He had made no attempt to hide them. If it can be argued that Gray ought to have known of Colenso's 'unsatisfactory' theology,[5] then it is equally true that Colenso ought to have been fully aware of Gray's idea of the proper organisation and government of the Church. Colenso had, after all, helped to frame the constitution of the embryo province.[6]

Gray and Colenso had been very close friends up to the time of Colenso's departure for England after the publication of *Romans*. Each admired the other, sincerely and openly. Each made just sufficient reservations, at the same time, to make it clear that the admiration was a genuine thing—not mere adulation. Colenso had helped to nurse Gray through one of his nervous breakdowns. They came, in the end, to harbour a good deal of bitterness, each against the other—but for neither of

[1] E. Hodder, *Life and Work of the Seventh Earl of Shaftesbury*, 1887, p. 532
[2] See e.g. his letter quoted *supra*, p. 116
[3] C. N. Gray, *op. cit.*, I, p. 55   [4] P. Hinchliff, *loc. cit.*
[5] Rees, *op. cit.*, p. 34
[6] Bishopscourt Archives, Cape Town; Minutes of Episcopal Synod; In the sessions of December 1860/January 1861 Colenso was present and subscribed a number of contitutional resolutions.

them was there ever a complete escape from the earlier affection. Part of the tragedy of the Colenso affair was the personal tragedy of two friends driven apart by opposing ideals of truth and duty, until each had said things of the other which were almost unforgiveable. Worse still, when either of them harked back to the old days of close friendship, the other put it down to hypocrisy or an attempt to gain popular sympathy. And yet when they were both old men Colenso told one of his acquaintances:

If you ever meet Bishop Gray, tell him, I have never through all this trouble, lost my deep personal love and respect for him.

And when the message was delivered to Gray, not long before he died, the bishop of Cape Town was almost unbearably moved. 'I could see by his tears the struggle between personal affection and his strong sense of duty'.[1] Even Tait, who was not sympathetically disposed towards Gray, was obliged to admit that there was something very like tenderness in some of his dealings with Colenso. When the moment came for the metropolitan to pronounce sentence in the heresy trial he very nearly broke down altogether.[2] And Colenso felt just as deeply. When Gray died, he preached a sermon which Stanley described (in the Convocation of Canterbury) as magnanimous. It *was* magnanimous, it was also somehow tragic. The bishop of Natal spoke of Gray as 'my friend and my father' and paid tribute to his achievements on behalf of Christianity in Southern Africa.[3]

But the bishop of Cape Town was no more likely to be swayed by personal friendship, where truth and duty were concerned, than was Colenso himself. He saw the matter quite simply and clearly as a challenge he must meet in order to defend the ancient faith. Nor was he, by temperament or opinion, the man to allow any uncertainties over the Long case to deflect him from his course. He believed implicitly that his office as bishop was one of enormous spiritual importance and authority. It might not be pleasant to have to use that authority, but that was neither here nor there. His brother bishops in England had spoken, but they could not take action

[1] The incident is quoted in M. A. Hooker, *The Place of Bishop Colenso in South African History*, unpublished thesis (University of the Witwatersrand: Ph.D), II, p. 290.   [2] See *infra*, p. 137
[3] See Cox, *op. cit.*, II, p. 638.

The responsibility now lay with Gray and he felt compelled to act.

The metropolitan's court assembled on the due date. This in itself was not only a measure of Gray's inflexible devotion to duty, it was something of a miracle. Almost everyone connected with the case had had considerable difficulty in reaching Cape Town. Bishop Twells of the Orange Free State, travelling by post-cart, was caught in a flooded river and almost drowned. Gray himself got back from a tour of visitation 'nearly knocked up with work and bad weather'.[1] The bishop of St Helena could not come at all because of the expense and difficulty of chartering a special ship to bring him from the island. Two of the accusers, the archdeacons Badnall and Merriman, arrived at the last moment, when anxiety about them had almost become panic.

On 16 November, however, the metropolitan took his seat before the altar in the cathedral—not in the vestry as the citation had originally decreed, for the trial was public and a large crowd had assembled in the nave. The old cathedral in Cape Town was an eighteenth-century building, quaintly classical, with a row of 'Greek' pillars at the entrance. It stood at the top of one of the main thoroughfares of the city, with a long vista towards the sea, and the mountain behind it. A space had been cleared in the chancel for the court to use. Gray was flanked by his assessors, Cotterill of Grahamstown and Twells of the Free State. Cotterill was an out-and-out Evangelical, trembling for those twin pillars of the Faith, the penal substitutionary theory of the Atonement and the verbal inspiration of the Scriptures. 'Circumstances have wonderfully changed him', said Gray,[2] for Cotterill was more and more becoming convinced of the necessity for an unestablished provincial organisation in South Africa and had made himself something of an expert on canon law and constitutional theory. Twells was, for those days, an 'extreme' Anglo-Catholic, sent to South Africa with glowing testimonials from the catholic party in England.[3] He had only recently arrived in South Africa, but his opinions must have been well known already. Gray and

[1] C. N. Gray, *op. cit.*, II, p. 74
[2] Keble College, Oxford; Keble Papers; Gray to Keble 17/12/1863
[3] There is a chalice in Bloemfontein which was presented to Twells by a group of extremely eminent Tractarians, when he first came to his diocese.

Cotterill had already discussed the evidence against Colenso (i.e. his books) and decided how they would deliver judgment. Gray's biographer defends this apparent prejudging of the issue on the grounds that the heretical teaching already existed in print and that the only real issue at stake in the case was 'the possibility of Bishop Colenso withdrawing or retracting his utterances'.[1] Nevertheless, if Colenso had known of this meeting, it would only have confirmed him in his opinion that he was being tried by an obscurantist, a fundamentalist and a crypto-papist and that they had rigged the case against him beforehand.

Colenso was not present in person on that summer morning in the small cathedral. He was represented by his friend, Dr Wilhelm Heinrich Immanuel Bleek, (son of Friedrich Bleek) librarian of the Grey (now the South African Public) Library in Cape Town, and a noted expert on the language and culture of the aboriginal Bushmen. Bleek is variously described in the sources as Unitarian, rationalist, unbeliever, Socinian, Lutheran and atheist, and much play was made of the fact that Colenso chose to be represented by someone who was not 'a member of the Church of England, or of any communion which would recognise its formularies'.[2] The truth of the matter was that Bleek was Colenso's friend. He had worked with Colenso as philologist and anthropologist. He was the son of one of the leading German critics of the more conservative school. Of all the available people he was obviously the man Colenso would have judged best able to present his point of view.

The diocesan registrar having read all the formal documents, the case opened with a moment or two of subdued drama.

Dr Bleek then rose and read a formal protest against the jurisdiction of the Bishop of Cape Town.

The Bishop of Cape Town: The Bishop of Natal tells me he has instructed you to read a certain letter. Are you reading that letter?

Dr Bleek: I am instructed first to protest, and then, if your Lordship assume jurisdiction, to read the letter.

The Bishop of Cape Town: Will you produce the authority of the Bishop of Natal to protest.

[1] C. N. Gray, op. cit., II, p.75n
[2] Ibid., p. 79, quoting Archdeacon Merriman

Dr Bleek then read the following passage of the letter of the Bishop of Natal.

I have instructed Dr Bleek of Cape Town, to appear before your Lordship on my behalf for the following purposes:

(i) First, to protest against your Lordship's jurisdiction.

(ii) Secondly, to read this letter (of which I have sent him a duplicate), as my defence, if your Lordship should assume to exercise jurisdiction.

(iii) Thirdly, if you should assume jurisdiction and deliver a judgment adverse to me, to give you notice of my intention to appeal from such judgment.

The Bishop of Cape Town: It is a letter, as I understand, that you are instructed to read. First read the letter.

Dr Bleek: Then does your Lordship assume jurisdiction?

The Bishop of Cape Town: Will you read the letter if you please? That is your business.[1]

Dr Bleek then read Colenso's letter of 5 October[2] denying that Gray possessed any lawful jurisdiction in the matter and asserting that his own writings contained nothing which constituted 'an offence against the laws of the United Church of England and Ireland'. Bleek refused to argue in support of the protest, maintaining that the bishop's letter was sufficient defence. The accusing clergy then addressed the court.

The dean of Cape Town spoke at great length. For hour after hour, for the whole of the rest of that day and the morning of the next day, while the bishop's 'magpie' wilted in the November warmth, he analysed Colenso's theological system and showed where it differed from the formularies of the Church of England and from the views of the accepted Anglican authorities of the day. Merriman of Grahamstown followed, occupying the afternoon of 18 November and the morning of 19 November. Then the archdeacon of George covered the ground for the third time and 'with greater minuteness'[3] in a speech which lasted until well into 20 November.

There then occurred a very curious incident. In his letter of protest—the letter dated 5 October 1863—Colenso had referred to another letter he had written to Gray in August 1861 replying to certain criticisms of *Romans*. Gray now caused this

---

[1] *Report of the Trial of Bishop Colenso*, pp. 38f
[2] See *supra*, p. 126
[3] C. N. Gray, *op. cit.*, II, p. 87

earlier letter to be read *as part of Colenso's defence*. The letter
was very long and took about an hour and a half to read. Gray,
no doubt, believed that he was giving Colenso a fair hearing
in spite of the bishop of Natal's reluctance to defend himself,
and he could also argue that Colenso had virtually asked for
the letter to be read.[1] But to Colenso it seemed that he was
being compelled to recognise the court by having a 'defence'
thrust on him and that his private correspondence with a
former friend was now being used by that friend in order to
fake a case against him. Some colour is given to this complaint
by the fact that Gray tabled his own letter of 1861 (to which
Colenso's was a reply) 'for the use of the prosecuting clergy'.
These gentlemen then replied to Colenso's 'defence' and the
court was adjourned.

For over three weeks the bishops considered the evidence
before them. On 14 December the court assembled again,
though Bleek refused to attend, to hear the assessors' opinions.
Cotterill of Grahamstown spoke first, reviewing the whole
history of the case and Colenso's teaching and concluded by
saying 'that the offence of promulgating error is aggravated by
the spirit, reckless of all consequences to the faith of the young
and unstable, in which opinions, unsound in themselves, are
pushed forward to conclusions subversive of all faith in Divine
Revelation'.[2] Twells of the Free State concurred saying, on
the vexed question of everlasting punishment, 'Protestants, only
were the small majority [*sic*] among Christians who held the
dogma of everlasting punishment, inasmuch as no doctrine of
purgatory has ever interfered with the uniform teaching of the
whole Catholic Church in all ages, according to the literal
words of the Athanasian Creed'.[3]

The court assembled again two days later, on 16 December,
for the metropolitan to deliver his judgment. He considered
first the question of his own jurisdiction and found that he was

---

[1] 'For further explanation of my meaning in some of the passages objected to
—I beg to refer your Lordship to a letter which I addressed to you on or about
May 1861'—Colenso, in his formal letter of protest, October 1863. The letter
read in court is actually dated 7 August 1861. It appears that Colenso was
mistaken about the date and that this was the letter referred to. Colenso's
biographer raises no question as to the date (Cox, *op. cit.*, 1, p. 312) and Gray
did not see the commentary until June or July 1861 (C. N. Gray, *op. cit.*,
II, p. 21).   [2] C. N. Gray, *op. cit.*, II, p. 90
[3] *Ibid.*, p. 91. Colenso had argued that the Roman doctrine of purgatory did,
in fact, explain away the damnatory clauses of the Athanasian Creed.

entitled to try the case. He then proceeded to lay down the
criteria he proposed to use in his judgment.

> In forming a decision as to the soundness or unsoundness of
> the Bishop's views I shall be guided entirely by the language of
> the Articles and Formularies, including, of course, the whole
> Book of Common Prayer. I do not mean thereby to imply that
> these are the only tests by which the Bishops of this Church
> should try the teaching of its Ministers. I am of the opinion that
> the decisions of those Councils which the Church of England
> regards as Oecumenical are the very highest authorities by which
> they could be guided; and the received faith of the Church of all
> ages, even if not defined by any Council, if it can be ascertained
> —as, for example, on such a question as Inspiration in connec-
> tion with the Holy Scriptures—must also be a guide to them
> which cannot be disregarded. . . .
> In interpreting the Church's standards of faith, I shall endea-
> vour to ascertain their 'true, usual, literal, plain and full mean-
> ing'. Wheresoever it is possible, I shall decide this by the 'literal
> and grammatical sense' of the words. Where the sense of the
> words is not plain, where they are theological words, and have a
> historical meaning, I shall interpret them by a comparison of
> passages; by the history of the controversies which gave rise to
> them, by the analogy of the Faith. I shall always have regard,
> when this is possible, to the *animus imponentis*, the intention of
> the Church in the wording of its documents.[1]

By and large this is precisely what Gray did. He takes the
excerpts quoted in the articles of accusation, tests them to see
whether they are merely incidental, casual passages or whether
they are essential to the argument of the book, and then mea-
sures them against the literal sense of the XXXIX Articles,
using the creeds and the canons of the early ecumenical
councils as a further standard, and considering the teachings
also of patristic theologians and Anglican divines. A great deal
of what he says is, of course, the product of the age to which
he belonged. A modern Anglican bishop might acquit Colenso
on half the charges brought against him. But allowing for this
fact, Gray's judgment is bound to impress one for its fairness,
learning and care. He found Colenso guilty on all the nine
charges:

[1] Bishopscourt Archives, Cape Town; Judgment of the Metropolitan in the
case of Bishop Colenso

I. That he maintained that Our Blessed Lord did not die in man's stead, or bear the punishment or penalty of our sins, and that God is not reconciled to us by the death of His Son;

II. That he maintained that justification is the *consciousness* of being counted righteous, and that all men, even without such consciousness are treated by God as righteous, and counted righteous, and that all men, as members of the great human family, are dead unto sin and risen again unto righteousness; and that he denied that men are justified by faith;

III. That he maintained that all men have the new birth unto righteousness in their very birth-hour, that is to say, are regenerated when born into the world, as members of the great human family; and also that all men are at all times partaking of the body and blood of Christ; and denied that the holy Sacraments are generally necessary to salvation, and that they convey any special grace; and further denied that faith is the means whereby the body and blood of Christ is received and eaten, and that faith is necessary in order that the grace bestowed by God in sacraments may have a wholesome effect and operation;

IV. That he maintained that he could no longer maintain or give utterance to the doctrine of the endlessness of future punishments;

V. That he maintained that the Holy Scriptures *contained* the word of God, but are not the word of God;

VI. That he treated the Holy Scriptures as a merely human book, not inspired by God the Holy Spirit, or inspired only in such a manner as other books may be inspired;

VII. That he denied the authenticity, genuineness, and truth of certain books of Holy Scripture in whole or in part, and that by this denial he called in question the authority and canonicity of these books in whole or in part;

VIII. That he maintained that Our Blessed Lord was ignorant and in error upon the subject of the authorship and age of the different portions of the Pentateuch, and so denied the doctrine that Our Blessed Lord is God and Man in one person;

IX. That he depraved and impugned and otherwise brought into disrepute the Book of Common Prayer, particularly portions of the Ordinal and the Baptismal Services, and in so doing violated the law of the United Church of England and Ireland.[1]

One is bound to ask whether Colenso was really a heretic or not. With what has already been said earlier, it will be sufficient to say here that on the fifth, sixth and eighth charges against him, neither Colenso nor his accusers were (by conventional modern Anglican standards) entirely free from error. On the seventh and ninth charges he was really convicted of 'biblical criticism' rather than heresy, and most undergraduates taking theology would now be expected to share some of his points of view. On the second and third charges, the specifically doctrinal rather than critical charges, the weight of theological opinion would still be decidedly against him. And on the first and fourth charges Colenso was condemned for teaching a decidedly universalist Christianity. In these days then, supposing modern Anglicans had any taste for heresy trials, Colenso would probably be found guilty on half the charges against him. In his own day men thought differently and it was believed to be vitally important to 'stop the mouth of wickedness'. Gray was certainly of this opinion.[2] He believed that he had no alternative but to find Colenso guilty.

Gray proceeded to pass sentence, indicating that he would submit his sentence to review by the archbishop of Canterbury if Colenso desired to appeal. An eye-witness account says that, 'he grew pale and his voice trembled' as he declared 'the said Bishop of Natal to be deposed, from the said office as such Bishop, and to be further prohibited from the exercise of any divine office within any part of the Metropolitical Province of Cape Town'. Colenso was allowed a four-month period of grace within which to recant, in which case the sentence would be null and void.

Bleek was present to hear the actual sentence passed. He protested once more against the illegality of the proceedings and against the sentence. He notified the court of Colenso's intention to appeal and to resist, by process of law, any attempt

---

[1] The wording given here is copied closely, including italics etc., from the actual articles of accusation. Some of the tenses of verbs have been changed, and some recurring formulae omitted, and the order of words altered.

[2] For a consideration of the special reasons why it was thought necessary, 100 years ago, to bring Colenso to trial, see P. Hinchliff, *op. cit.*, pp. 93ff.

to carry out the sentence. Another eye-witness records that
'Bishop Gray, after a brief pause, calmly but with the utmost
impressiveness, stated that any appeal from the judgment of
the Court could only lie to the Archiepiscopate of Canterbury,
and must be served within a certain short period'.[1]

In this matter, as in so many other points of procedure in
the trial, Gray acted on the advice of Sir Robert Phillimore,
the Queen's Advocate.[2] (He also accepted advice from James
Green, a most foolish thing to do under the circumstances.[3])
On Phillimore's advice, the bishops met in synod on the day after
the court rose. They confirmed the sentence and agreed that if
Colenso continued in contumacy he should be formally excommunicated. Here, again, the different presuppositions of
Colenso and Gray were clearly revealed. Colenso regarded this
synod as another, and hurried, attempt to condemn him without even the pretence of a hearing. Gray regarded himself as
reporting to the bishops of the Province, now not as assessors
but as his comprovincials, the sentence passed in the court,
so that action might be taken to put it into effect.

Clearly Colenso thought that the whole thing had been a
travesty of justice. He maintained that the metropolitan had
no right to try him after what the Privy Council had said in
the Long case. His bitterest enemy, Green, had had a hand in
framing the rules of the court. Gray, the judge, had at an
earlier stage been Colenso's accuser to the archbishop of
Canterbury. He had also been at least partly responsible for
choosing the 'prosecuting counsel' and for briefing them. He
had tried to force Colenso to enter a defence and so recognise
the court. The judges had virtually decided on their judgment
before the case was heard. They had met again in another
capacity and, without evidence, defence or opportunity of protest, had retried the case. The ninth article of accusation had
specifically alleged a violation of the law of the Church of
England, but no appeal was allowed to the courts of England.
The only appeal permitted was to the archbishop personally in
a quasi-patriarchal character.

It need hardly be pointed out that all these things had a

---

[1] See A. E. M. Anderson-Morshead, *Pioneer & Founder*, 1905, p. 88.

[2] Phillimore's opinion is to be found in Bishopscourt Archives; Memorandum
E.H.D. III; Summary of facts relating to the Organisation of the Church of the
Province, and is discussed in C. N. Gray, *op. cit.*, II, p. 71.

[3] See Hinchliff, *op. cit.*, p. 28

completely different (and justifiable and honest) meaning for Gray and his fellow-bishops; we are concerned simply with Colenso's reaction to what he called 'the whole farrago of the Bishop of Cape Town's judgment'.[1] He would not even recognise Gray's court to the extent of appealing against its judgment. He had come to believe that the only impartial tribunal he could hope to find was one which was part of the English legal system. He applied direct to the Crown-in-Council (i.e. the Judicial Committee in fact), not in appeal against Gray's judgment, but for an order preventing Gray from interfering with Colenso's exercise of his episcopal office.

Colenso's opinions had changed somewhat since the days when he had declared that the Natal legislature had no right to interfere in the affairs of an unestablished Church in the colony, and also since the days when he had maintained that he and Gray were both the direct subordinates of Canterbury. Part of the explanation of that change of opinion has been traced out already. The next chapter will deal with the rest of the story. For the moment it is enough to note that men like Maurice began to veer back to Colenso's support. Maurice did not change his mind about biblical criticism. Friendly relations were not yet completely restored. But Maurice was clear on two points. Gray had not behaved in a legal fashion; no English bishop or archbishop would have dared to do what he had done.[2] And ecclesiastical courts were, in any case, hateful things. 'Every Churchman', Maurice wrote, 'about to undergo any trial himself, owns how much rather he would be in the hands of lay judges than of Presbyters and Bishops; he believes that he has ten times the chance of a fair hearing and a decision according to the evidence'.[3] This was precisely how Colenso felt.

While the trial was being prepared and acted out in Cape Town, Colenso continued with his Old Testament studies. Further parts of his *Pentateuch and Joshua* came from the press, but with diminishing sales all the time. The initial excitement was over. Interest turned from Colenso's opinions to Colenso's fate. In September he set off on a tour of the continent of Europe. He called on several of the leading German and Dutch

---

[1] Cox, *op. cit.*, I, p. 248   [2] Cox, *op. cit.*, I, p. 330
[3] S.P.G. Archives, London: Macrorie papers: Press cuttings—a letter from Maurice to *The Spectator*, date not preserved

scholars, believed himself to have been well received by them, and was encouraged by this to continue his work.[1]

His own unhappiness at this time must not be under-estimated. His mother-in-law was, his wife said, 'really in a great state of indignation' against him and it had caused a frozen, bitter separation between the two women for a time.[2] Mrs Colenso herself had no doubts, of course, as to the right-ness of her husband's cause, but her brother, the bishop of Labuan, disapproved of Colenso's work. Colenso was cut and snubbed in the streets of London by bishops with whom he had previously been on friendly terms. His letters began to count the score of who was against him and who was for him. An inevitable bitterness crept into his assessment of personalities. And perhaps his greatest moment of triumph came at Harrow, where the boys cheered him loudly in the very presence of his old headmaster and arch-opponent, Dr Wordsworth.[3]

Once Colenso decided to apply to the Crown for redress, a subscription list was opened to help him to pay the legal costs involved. The subscribers included people like Anthony Trollope, Dean Stanley, Sir Joseph Hooker and Sir Charles Lyell. The Lyells became Colenso's closest friends and most faithful supporters in England. It was a matter of real sorrow to the Colensos that they were alienated from friends and rela-tions because of the bishop's teaching. It was some compensa-tion for them that they made new friends, and gained the support of some of the most eminent men in the secular world of learning and literature. Lady Lyell and Mrs Colenso became especially fast friends and their correspondence has fortunately been preserved.[4]

Sir Charles Lyell was by this time an old man. He was some-thing of a snob.[5] But he was of enormous importance to Colenso in establishing himself in this new world of the Athe-naeum, and the scientific and literary circles of London society. Colenso himself became, in a sense, a snob at this period. He was driven to count up his friends and his enemies. His friends could obviously help him more if they were important and influential. He was, after all, not a particularly well-born or

[1] Cox, *op. cit.*, I, pp. 221 & 243
[2] Rees, *op. cit.*, p. 78. The ice seems later to have been broken—*ibid.*, p. 88.
[3] Cox, *op. cit.*, I, pp. 241 & 243 & cf *supra*, p. 30
[4] See Rees, *op. cit.*, *passim*.
[5] See the quotation in Rees, *op. cit.*, p. 87n.

eminent man. His books had caused a scandal and had been a nine-day wonder. He was the central figure in an ecclesiastical *cause célèbre*. But he was bishop of an obscure colonial see. His claim to fame was that he had written a well-known arithmetic textbook, a commentary, and an increasingly less popular essay in biblical criticism. It was important for him to cultivate the support of the well-to-do and the influential.

Bishop Gray felt himself to be battling alone for the truth, overwhelmed by the powers-that-be in Church and State. Everyone of importance was against him, and he lacked even the ephemeral naughty-boy popularity which Colenso possessed. Colenso felt almost exactly the same about his own position. All the forces of the traditionalists were marshalled against him. Without money or support or influence he could not hope to defend his right to preach the truth. It is little wonder that he began to collect tufts. If Trollope and Dickens, Lyell and Huxley, Stanley and Milman would back him, he might yet be able to maintain his position. When Tennyson said a few kind words about the bishop at a dinner party, Mrs Colenso became quite lyrical with excitement. Tennyson said, 'Though all the world should shriek against you, I would receive you with open arms', and Mrs Colenso's comment was, 'Small words from him are worth more to me than the approbation of all the Bishops in conclave. We are such enthusiastic admirers of Tennyson'.[1]

More and more Colenso began to try to make estimates of his own influence and importance.

A gentleman was introduced to me at the Athenaeum two or three days ago, who told me he had just come from Rome, and the book [*Pentateuch and Joshua*] was producing an immense sensation all over the continent.[2]

Of course I am brought into daily connexion with all the great men of science, who are warmly with me.[3]

You will see by the Times of May 25 that I dined *as Bishop of Natal* with the Colonial Ministers on Her Majesty's birthday.[4]

My reception . . . in this thoroughly *evangelical* city [Bath] was remarkable.[5]

[1] Rees, *op. cit.*, p. 88
[2] Cox, *op. cit.*, I, p. 241
[3] *Ibid.*
[4] *Ibid.*, p. 253
[5] *Ibid.*, p. 257

Colenso, in fact, believed at this stage that there was a real danger of his losing his office altogether. He believed that it might prove (for the *Essays and Reviews* judgment had not been delivered) that he was not entitled to hold the views he did as a bishop of the Church of England. He was still half-afraid that he might be a heretic in the eyes of the law. He needed every bit of support he could possibly muster.

CHAPTER 6

The Erastian

STRICTLY speaking an Erastian is one who believes as a matter of theological principle that the State *ought* to control and exercise all jurisdiction in the Church. Erastianism is not just a vague feeling that the Church ought to be established. It is a *belief* that all ecclesiastical authority flows from God through the State.

Colenso's opinion had been moving in this direction for some time. It will be convenient to gather together the various points, most of them already mentioned, which suggest this, and try to indicate the course his thinking had been taking. We know that as an adolescent he was attracted by the freedom which the Establishment seemed to offer. In so far as it is proper to look for consistent thinking in the letters of a sixteen-year-old, this indicates something less than Erastianism proper. To say that the State connection and the parson's freehold is a good thing because it enables one to preach without fear or favour, is a very different thing from maintaining that state control is of the *esse* of the Church.

There is very little evidence from the Forncett period from which one can reconstruct any clear picture of how Colenso's thought on this point developed. But this is the period when he became, in his own estimation at least, a 'Maurician'—believing that there was no single, exclusive 'view of the truth' to which the national Church was committed. Colenso's comments on the Gorham case make it clear that he still saw a tremendous value in the Establishment because it protected the freedom of the individual. This is clearly a Maurician point of view. There must be some means of restraining the majority from coercing the individual in the name of ortho-doxy. So far as the evidence goes one may conclude that when he first went to Natal his opinions had not much changed from the days when he first thought of being ordained in the Estab-lished Church. He was not yet an Erastian in any real sense.

During the first decade of his episcopate several incidents bear upon this question. In the bishop's quarrel with the laity of Durban he maintained that the colonial legislature had no authority to intervene in matters of Church discipline—that the Church in the colony was not established. In order to pacify the laity Colenso made various gestures which might be construed as a willingness to accept a form of establishment in the colonies. But this is still a matter of convenience. It may be a help to have some form of State connection—or it may not. It is certainly not yet a matter of principle.

The position was unchanged when Colenso wrote to Cotterill about Gray's plans for a bishopric in Zululand and when Green delated Colenso for heresy on the Eucharist. In the one case Colenso maintained that it was ridiculous for a metropolitan appointed by royal letters patent to claim jurisdiction over an area which was not British territory. He was willing to go and work in Zululand himself, so he did not believe that the authority of the Crown was necessary for the Church; it was a limitation which might or might not be convenient. In the other case Colenso argued that Gray's authority as metropolitan was incomplete because the letters patent by which he was appointed could only convey to him such jurisdiction as the State desired him to have. Letters patent could not in themselves convey an ecclesiastical authority and had, indeed, reserved certain rights to the archbishop of Canterbury. Again, the term Erastian can only be applied to Colenso, at this stage, in the loose and pejorative sense of which the controversialists were so fond.

What does all this add up to? Colenso clearly believed that there were times when the State connection might be useful —or even necessary, in the sense that it might be the only way in which to achieve some necessary object. But clearly Colenso did not believe that the State connection was necessary to the *existence* of the Church, nor that it was in principle desirable for the Church always to be established. His Natal Church Council was to administer matters of Church discipline. The Council had no coercive powers conferred by the State. It was not the creature of Crown or legislature. Therefore Colenso did not believe the Crown to be the only source of disciplinary authority in the Church. In effect Colenso is concerned to use the State connection where this will enable him to maintain the right, and to evade it, if possible, where it will not. He is concerned with what is lawful and what is right. He does not confuse the two (as some of his English colleagues sometimes seem to do) but he is not the kind of person, as yet at any rate, to defy or to break the law. He has the Englishman's respect for the law.

In the critical year 1863, with his own trial pending and the committee of the Convocation of Canterbury manoeuvring for a synodical condemnation of his Pentateuchal criticism, Colenso was still concerned with legality. He had feared that his views might be illegal in the Church of England. We have seen how the Lushington judgment in the *Essays & Reviews* case had partly reassured him on this point. So long as he was not breaking the law, his position seemed to him to be secure. He is still not confusing legality and right. He believes his books to be morally right because he believes his views to be the truth. But he sees no reason to resign his bishopric on account of his views, since it has been declared lawful to hold some such views within the Church of England. Colenso had faced a real moral problem and had solved it conscientiously. When others, faced with the same problem, wrote to him for advice, he gave them the same counsel. To an unnamed correspondent who was unable conscientiously to recite the Athanasian Creed or 'prayers which involve belief in the story of the Deluge as told in Genesis', Colenso wrote, 'As a subject of the Queen you have a right to be represented in the National Church, just as much as in the National Parliament'.[1]

In other words when the Cape Town trial started Colenso's position was in practice, something like a combination of that of Tait, with his deep concern for what was legal, and that of Arnold, with his desire for a comprehensive national Church. The bishop seems closer to this conventional Broad Church position than to Maurice and Coleridge. Maurice had condemned him. Stanley was his champion. It was inevitable, perhaps, that there should be something of a realignment and that this should be reflected in Colenso's thinking. At all events his attitude to Robert Gray's court is perfectly consistent with the advice he gives to his correspondent. He denies that Gray has any right to try him for his views. He will not recognise a

[1] Natal Archives, Pietermaritzburg; Colenso Collection, 215; letter dated 11/2/1863

court not created by English law. He will resist, in every legal way, any attempt to sentence him. He refused Gray's offer to allow an appeal to the archbishop of Canterbury. He went straight to the Crown and the Privy Council for protection—to the one place where he believed he would obtain the protection necessary to allow him to proclaim the truth.

The *Essays & Reviews* case convinced Colenso of the legitimacy of his position. When Lushington had pronounced against Williams and Wilson in 1862, Colenso believed himself also to fall within the terms of the judgment because of his universalism and his attitude to 'everlasting punishment'.[1] But, on the other hand, he was protected by the same judgment on the crucial point—the verbal inspiration of the Scriptures.[2] We have already seen how the biblical issue came to overshadow all the rest. No doubt Colenso believed that he was justified on the main point at issue. Certainly he was completely convinced that the appeal in the Williams/Wilson case would prove to be in the essayists' favour. And in this he was right.

The case was heard before the Judicial Committee in the latter part of 1863, before the trial of Colenso in Cape Town. The bishop of Natal was elated by the case presented by the essayists. Every point on which he was accused of heresy seemed to him to be covered by their argument and the general impression he received was that the unfavourable part of Lushington's judgment must be upset by the appeal court.[3] When the judgment was delivered early in February 1864, Colenso's hopes were fully justified.

The Judicial Committee had on this occasion consisted of the Lord Chancellor, Westbury, the two archbishops, Bishop Tait, and three law lords, including Lord Kingsdown. The Gorham judgment had already laid down that where the formularies of the Church were not precise, clergymen could not be deprived for holding opinions which others might regard as heretical. Now Lord Westbury, asserting that it was the job of the court to interpret the articles and formularies of the Church of England 'according to the legal rules for the interpretation of statutes and written instruments', maintained that no-one could be in any way punished for expressing an opinion unless it clearly and directly contradicted the

---

[1] See Cox, *op. cit.*, I, pp. 187 & 232
[2] *Ibid.*, p. 238   [3] *Ibid.*, p. 242

written formularies of the Established Church.[1] He held that the Church of England nowhere enunciated a doctrine of the unending nature of future punishment. The essayists were restored to office. Tait concurred. The two archbishops, Longley and Thomson, dissented. By and large public opinion was with the archbishops. Tait became an unpopular figure in Church circles. Convocation condemned the book. But Stanley became dean of Westminster, and Colenso felt that his own stand for truth had been vindicated.

Unfortunately there were others, comprising by this time a large body of Anglican clergymen, who felt that this judgment proved that the Judicial Committee could not be regarded as a proper ecclesiastical court. The Gorham case was the first time that it had functioned in this capacity. Even then the Tractarians, in particular, had protested against such a usurpation of spiritual authority by a secular court. After the *Essays & Reviews* judgment this feeling became even more bitter.

On 11 September 1863 Gray wrote to Wilberforce, describing the course of the Williams/Wilson case thus:

> Here are 10,000 clergymen calling upon their Bishops to put down a heresy, the Bishops in Synod condemning it. A lay judge [Lushington] tries whether it is heresy; says he is told all the Bishops declare it such, but cannot be governed by their opinion, however respectable; declares certain parts of the teaching, which the Church calls heresy, *not* to be heresy, other portions to be heretical; decides that the heretics shall be suspended for one year, and then being still heretics shall resume the cure of men's souls, and the office of ambassadors of Christ. Against this the heretics appeal to another Civil Court. Archbishops and Bishops are upon it. The lay Judges, against the view of the Bishops of the Church, decide that these heretics shall not be condemned, so they resume at once their office.[2]

A leader in the *Guardian*, 6 July 1864, said that it was perfectly possible that no-one would feel themselves bound in conscience by the judgment of a lay lord chancellor in a matter of theology, and that the opinion of Queen Victoria herself

[1] Compare and contrast this with the principles enunciated by Gray in the Colenso trial, *supra*, p. 135.
[2] C. N. Gray, *op. cit.*, I, pp. 532f. Gray is actually writing before judgment was delivered. Presumably he, like Colenso, saw pretty clearly how things were likely to go; cf C. N. Gray, II, p. 113.

would not add much weight to the opinion of laymen, however eminent in the law. This proved to be an accurate
prophecy. Later in the century when the famous prosecutions
for ritualism took place, so many priests declared themselves
unable conscientiously to obey a secular tribunal that the whole
question of clerical discipline had to be reconsidered—but
without much notable success. When the 1927/28 Prayer Book
was being drawn up, nearly three-quarters of a century after
the *Essays & Reviews* case, one of the chief considerations in
the minds of many bishops was the hope that the new book
might make discipline an easier matter.

But in 1864 Colenso was delighted by Westbury's judgment.
He wrote to Shepstone about six weeks after the judgment.

> I need not say that it sweeps away at a stroke the whole farrago
> of the Bishop of Capetown's judgment. On the very point of
> 'endless punishment' on which the three Cape Bishops were so
> positive, the three English Bishops are agreed in the very oppo-
> site direction. And on every single point of the nine (on which
> they have condemned me) which has been under discussion in
> the English courts, either in the Gorham judgment, or Lushing-
> ton's, or this last of the Privy Council, *I* am justified and they
> are condemned.[1]

It was, therefore, with something like calm confidence that
Colenso waited for his own petition to be considered by the
Privy Council. He was not without his doubts and hesitations.
He was uncertain whether it would be possible for him to
return permanently to Natal. He maintained that it was Gray's
unfair, biased and vindicative spirit which made it necessary
for him to continue in office and to persist in fighting for his
rights. If the Privy Council placed him, in any sense at all,
in Gray's hands, he would not return to Africa except to pack
what remained of his belongings. But in the main concern,
the Pentateuchal study, he believed himself already justified
by the courts, and the more he read, the more convinced he
became that to retract would be to deny truth and honesty. In
the meantime he proceeded with his Old Testament studies.
He realised that the proceedings before the Privy Council
would make it virtually impossible for him to leave England
before the end of the year (1864). One gets the impression

---

[1] Cox, *op. cit.*, I, p. 249

that he was too distracted to get on with the direct work of writing *Pentateuch and Joshua*, but he read more deeply in the works of the German critics and he completed a translation of one of Kuenen's Old Testament works.[1]

In the first half of 1864 Colenso produced a *Letter to the Laity*, a pastoral addressed to his diocese. It is significant in two respects. In the first place its very title indicates how things were developing in his own diocese. The bulk of the clergy (if one can speak of 'bulk' when the total number involved was ten or twelve) were irrevocably against him. All but two or three had signed the petition asking Gray to remove him. His one hope was that the laity would come out strongly in his support. Shepstone was invaluable to him, acting as his agent, enlisting the sympathy of influential laymen in the colony, continuing in constant communication with the bishop. As secretary for native affairs he was ideally placed to prevent Green and Gray from gaining control of the mission reserves which had been granted to Colenso.

The substance of the *Letter to the Laity* itself is chiefly a statement of the legal rights which Colenso believed himself to possess, and an expression of his conviction that the Privy Council would support him. The *Guardian* of 11 May 1864 characterised the pastoral thus:

> The burden of the letter from the beginning to the end is simply, 'Great is the committee of the Privy Council', the supreme and ultimate authority on the principles of the Christian Faith! There is a flourish about the 'blood of the Reformers', introduced with happy contempt of logic and history. But there is no arithmetic, and Dr Colenso, when not arithmetical, is nothing. If the laity of Natal are induced by this pamphlet to alter their views, they must be easy of persuasion indeed.

Colenso's letter contains a hint that he is becoming an Erastian in the stricter sense. He was being pushed into a new position. A large number of people declared that for laymen to be the ultimate judges in matters of theology was nonsensical and contrary to proper Church order. Gray asserted that the archbishops must repudiate the *Essays & Reviews* judgment or allow the Church to appear apostate.[2] Pusey and others

---

[1] Cox, *op. cit.*, I, pp. 252 & 257
[2] He wrote to Keble saying this and subsequently to enthuse about the archbishops' pastoral—C. N. Gray, *op. cit.*, II, pp. 128 & 132

organised a petition signed by about 10,000 clergymen. And the archbishops of England, in pastoral letters, asserted that the opinion of the Privy Council was not the same as the opinion of the chief pastors of the Church. But none of this impressed Colenso. He believed that a high proportion of the signatories of the petition were Irish, curates, deacons, or non-graduates, not 'the genuine, intelligent, English clergy'. More-over the archbishops' action merely demonstrated how in-effective episcopal authority was and how absolute the control of the Privy Council. And Colenso was beginning to adopt, in appearance if not in reality, the view that all ecclesiastical jurisdiction and authority must derive from the Crown. The *Letter to the Laity* implies that this is more than a mere con-venience or an acceptance of the legal position in practice. The suggestion is that the Crown *ought* to be the ultimate authority. If this was the bishop's opinion, then he *was* becoming an Erastian. He was probably not conscious of any change of opinion. Perhaps he was influenced by the expatriate senti-ments of the Natal laity and was appealing to what was for them a most important part of religion. At all events from this point on it is the State connection rather than the biblical or the theological question which comes to the fore. In a great part this was due, not to Colenso, but to the Judicial Com-mittee itself.

On 11 May 1864 Colenso 'heard' that his case was about to go before the Privy Council, probably early in June, but 'in its most general form'. This Colenso interpreted to mean that the Judical Committee would deal only with the question of jurisdiction. The theological issues would not be discussed. The Judicial Committee would not even be sitting as the final court of appeal in ecclesiastical causes. In other words he was led to suppose that his case would be of the same type as the Long, rather than the Gorham or Williams/Wilson cases. His 'heresy' would not interest the court. It would be con-cerned with Gray's authority and the source from which it was derived. Events were driving Colenso into an Erastian position.

Colenso's petition was, in fact, first considered by the Judicial Committee on 27 June 1864. Colenso himself was present at the proceedings. Gray was not, for he had gone to Natal on the day (16 April 1864) Colenso's sentence was due

to take effect. James Green had the supreme honour of reading the sentence of deposition on 31 April in the cathedral in
Pietermaritzburg, and the sentence was ordered to be read in
all other churches in the diocese at the same time. A meeting
of the clergy and representatives of the laity on 19 May
formally declared the see vacant, leaving the appointment of a
successor in Gray's hands.[1] Gray for the moment appointed
Green to act as vicar-general. The Judicial Committee met,
then, at a time when Gray was already putting his judgment
into effect. For Colenso this was a frustrating time, not least
because the lord chancellor merely ordered the petition to
stand over for six months, declining even to inhibit Gray from
carrying out his sentence.[2] There was a technical legal point
at issue here. To inhibit the execution of the sentence while
the Privy Council decision was pending would have been to
recognise Gray's jurisdiction and have turned Colenso's *petition* into an appeal. The bishop of Natal would have to wait in
patience till the end of the year.

This is one of the most curious periods in Colenso's life.
The men he regarded as his arch-enemies were loose in his
diocese, organising it so as to suit themselves, trying to convert his supporters. Even the famous William Ngidi, who was
supposed to have been responsible for starting Colenso's Old
Testament criticism, was visited by Gray and was said to have
renounced Colenso.[3] And Colenso was prepared to sit back
and let this happen. It is difficult to reconcile his apparent
apathy and inaction at this period with the vigorous, not to
say impetuous, way in which he conducted his affairs in the
first decade of his episcopate. The truth of the matter was
probably that Colenso was still not certain whether it would
ever be possible for him to return to Natal even if he were
upheld by the courts. At this stage his support in the colony
was very slender. When one reads the letters and other material
for this period in the biographies of both Gray and Colenso,
one gets two principal impressions—first, that the Natal laity,
Protestant and Erastian though they may have been, were no
more favourably inclined towards Colenso's critical studies

[1] See Cox, *op. cit.*, I, pp. 172ff; C. N. Gray, *op. cit.*, II, pp. 142ff and Lewis
& Edwards, *Historical Records*, p. 170. Two of the clergy were absent from this
meeting.
[2] See C.N. Gray, *op. cit.*, II, pp. 152f
[3] C. N. Gray, *op. cit.*, II, pp. 141f

than the Tractarian clergy; and secondly, that Colenso himself doubted whether he would ever do more than make a token return to his diocese, to establish the principle that he was the legal bishop, and then to retire. Even after the case had been heard, Colenso wrote to Shepstone indicating that he might like to be appointed inspector of native education or given some other secular job which would enable him to continue to work for the African people of Natal.[1] He was obliged to wait in England till the case was settled. He was uncertain of his future as *bishop*. There were very few in the colony on whom he could rely for positive and active support. He was virtually compelled to sit back, for the moment, and give his opponents a free hand. From this time forward one of the bishop's chief problems was that he had so few agents and lieutenants on whom he could rely to act on his behalf. Even when he was at his most popular he was hamstrung by the lack of able and efficient supporters. What had to be done, must be done by himself.

The case was finally settled at the end of the year. Gray and Colenso had each set forth his own view of the proceedings to date. Colenso in his *Remarks on the Proceedings of the Bishop of Capetown* issued the challenge, 'Either you will leave it to the Queen, or reject the Queen's supremacy'. Gray asserted publicly on several occasions that he could not and would not recognise the Privy Council's right to thrust a heretic back into South Africa.

The hearing began on 14 December. Dr Lushington, the Dean of Arches, and Lord Romilly, the Master of the Rolls, were both members of the Judicial Committee on this occasion.[2] Gray was not present but was represented, 'under protest', by Robert Phillimore, the Queen's Advocate, and Sir Hugh Cairns. His brother, Edward Gray, and the bishop of Oxford had arranged matters for him, rather against his will.[3] He feared that any appearance at all would commit him to recognising the court and contradict his public assertions. And it appears that his counsel, though they protested against the jurisdiction of the court, did in some sense recognise that the

---

[1] Cox, *op. cit.*, I, p. 259
[2] No bishops were members because in this case the Judicial Committee was not acting as an ecclesiastical court.
[3] See C. N. Gray, *op. cit.*, II, pp. 179ff.

Crown might be the proper court of appeal from the Church in South Africa.[1] The argument was continued on 19 December, and lasted two more days, and then there was a further long wait of three months before the judgment was delivered on 20 March 1855.

The judgment was concerned, as Colenso had been warned, with jurisdiction and not with theology. It was this fact which led Tait to say that Colenso would probably have been found guilty if he had been tried for *heresy* in the English courts.[2] The judgment[3] was founded on the points which had already been established in the 'Eton College' case and the case of the Reverend W. Long. The lord chancellor began by saying that both bishops were 'ecclesiastical persons' and at the same time 'creatures of English Law'. The case was to be determined in accordance with that law, the Royal Supremacy, and the terms of the letters patent. He reviewed the contents of the letters patent, noting that they appeared to give Gray a metropolitan's jurisdiction over Colenso, but pointing out that this jurisdiction was defective on two grounds. First, the see of Cape Town was technically vacant at the time when Colenso was consecrated since Gray did not receive his second letters patent until a week after the consecration. Secondly, the same point as was made in the Long case, the Crown could not by a prerogative act confer coercive jurisdiction on a bishop in a colony where there was already a separate legislature. Lord Westbury considered the various occasions on which coercive jurisdiction had been granted to newly created bishops and found that in each case this had been done, not by prerogative act of the Crown alone, but by act of Parliament or of a colonial legislature. The letters patent had, therefore, pretended to confer on Gray an authority which they were quite unable to convey.

A distinction was made, as in the Long case, between 'coercive legal jurisdiction' and 'pastoral or spiritual authority incidental to the office of Bishop', but it was held that 'suspension or privation of office' was a matter of coercive jurisdiction and must proceed from the Crown unless it could be

---

[1] '. . . this Sir Hugh Cairns has allowed in plain words, for which I fancy Bishop Gray will not thank him'; Colenso to Shepstone, Cox, *op. cit.*, I, p. 259.
[2] See *supra*, p. 101.
[3] III Moore P.C.N.S. 115 and see also Bishopscourt Archives; 'Judgment of Privy Council in re Colenso'.

shown that Gray had obtained jurisdiction over Colenso by contract or consent. Colenso's oath of canonical obedience was the only possible ground for such a contention and 'even if the parties intended to enter into any such agreement (of which, however, we find no trace), it was not legally competent to the Bishop of Natal to give, or the Bishop of Cape Town to accept or exercise, any such jurisdiction'. The Cape Town trial was therefore null and void in law. Legally Colenso was still bishop of Natal.

For Colenso, of course, this seemed the final vindication. The *Essays & Reviews* judgment had justified his theology: the new judgment guaranteed his immunity from persecution. He was morally justified in teaching what he taught and remaining a bishop of the Church of England—provided one accepted that the only authority in the Church derived from the Crown. The bishop wrote Shepstone a long letter, setting out the position as he now believed it to be. It is an important letter because it outlines the policy which Colenso proposed to adopt, and it is therefore worth quoting at length.

Doubtless before this the news of the 'decision' will have reached Natal, and you will agree with me, I think, in considering that we have gained a complete victory. The Tractarians (Dr Pusey, etc.) try to make out that they have got as much out of it as I; that, if Bishop Gray has lost his power, I have lost mine; that the Church of South Africa is free, etc. These gratulations are, in reality, only pretences to hide their discomfiture. As they do not mean to give up their posts and incomes within the good old Church of England, it was, of course, necessary to make out that the decision was just what they wanted. But every day shows more and more clearly the importance of it to *our* cause, and the devastation which it brings to theirs. The whole edifice which they have been so carefully piling up for years has toppled all at once to the ground. Of course, the Long judgement prepared us to find that we had no 'coercive jurisdiction' by *patent* over our clergy, but only that which their *contracts* under their licences have given us. But, as I have not the least wish to exercise any such jurisdiction . . ., this part of the decision, however destructive it may be to Bishop Gray's notions of authority, is perfectly acceptable to me. It is not, indeed, certain that it does apply to Natal, for the question would still have to be decided, if any case of discipline arose, whether Natal had *representative institutions* when it had merely a *nominee* Legislative Council.

However, I am never likely to raise the question, and so we will consider all coercive jurisdiction by patent-right gone. But what then? The patent is perfectly valid, as ever, to give title, position, protection, independence, and (which is of most importance perhaps) to constitute me a lay-corporation for holding lands in trust for the English Church, and transmitting them to my successors. . . . Thus there can be no Bishop of the Church of England in the colony but myself; and no one can hold land for the English Church but myself. If any like to join the Church of South Africa, of course, they may do so, as they might have done all along.

But Bishop Gray has no power whatever to interfere in any of the affairs of the *Church of England* in Natal,—not even, I suspect, as holding lands in trust for it, for a very curious case arises out of the recent decision. . . . By his *old* patent the Bishop of Cape-town was a *lay-corporation*, and, as such, had lands granted to him in Natal in trust for the English Church. What became of these lands when *that* corporation was *destroyed* by the cancelling of his former patent? With whom was the trust vested during the fifteen days when there was no Bishop of Capetown, and no patent constituting the office? Lawyers tell me that by English law the property in that case would return to the *donor*, and be held by him in trust for the object in question. But who was the donor? Not the Queen in England, but the Queen in Natal, represented by the Governor and Executive Council, and the Queen had no power, by a stroke of her pen in the new patent, to re-grant those lands in trust to the new Bishop of Capetown. He should have applied to the Colonial Government. If so, the cathedral and other lands supposed to be held by Bishop Gray in Natal on trust, are really held by the Government, and would, I suppose, on application be re-granted to me, in accordance with the decision of the Privy Council.

The imputation of unworthy motives to 'Dr Pusey, etc.' is, no doubt, nothing more than an indication of the bitterness which the controversy had aroused. The language might easily be matched by equally vindictive remarks on the part of the bishop's opponents. But Colenso is quite right in his account of the reaction which the judgment provoked in some circles. Once Gray had recovered from the first shock of the decision of the Judicial Committee, he perceived that it enabled him to create an independent, unestablished province in South Africa, with a synodical government, its own courts, and a workable system of Church discipline which would be based, so far as the civil courts were concerned, on the constitution of a voluntary association. The way was open for the emergence of the Province of South Africa. The Privy Council had declared that the Church of England as by law established did not and could not exist in South Africa. The judgment in the Long case had maintained that a contract could be created by means of a 'synod'. The majority of Churchmen in South Africa were prepared to follow the same procedure on a provincial level. Bishop Cotterill of Grahamstown came to the fore as the architect of the provincial constitution.

But that is another story. It is the reaction of people in England rather than South Africa with which we are concerned here.[1] The Colenso case was one of a series of incidents which brought to a head the crisis in Church and State relations. The comments of the leading ecclesiastical figures of the time demonstrate how contentious and critical the issue was.

Pusey wrote in the *Churchman*, expressing the views which Colenso had mentioned to Shepstone. 'It is no loss to us that it is discovered that the Queen had no power to give the temporal powers which the former legal advisers of the Crown thought she could. It is the Crown deciding against itself. It is no concern of ours which of the two sets of lawyers was right. The present advisers of her Majesty have limited her powers, and we may thank God for the limitation, and pardon gladly the gratuitous insolence of the Erastianism of the preamble for the results which, with no goodwill of Erastians, must result from it. The Church of South Africa, then, is free. . . .'[2] By 15 May 1865 Gray had received a private letter in this vein from Pusey and another from John Keble, so far had Tractarian thought on the value of the Establishment moved since the day of the *National Apostasy* sermon.[3] A certain Prebendary J. W. Joyce, in *The Sword and the Keys*, expressed the views of most Tractarians. He is scathing in his comments on the decisions of the English courts in ecclesiastical matters and he insists, with a wealth of quotation from canon law, that no layman has any business at all to comment on matters of faith and doctrine.

[1] For an examination of the consequences of the Colenso case in the constitutional development of the South African province; see P. Hinchliff, *op. cit.*, pp. 82ff.   [2] C. N. Gray, *op. cit.*, II, pp. 196f
[3] C. N. Gray, *op. cit.*, II, p. 202

Questions were asked in Parliament, whether the Crown would continue to issue 'illegal' patents. The upper house of the Convocation of Canterbury passed an address to the South African bishops, thanking them for their noble stand against heresy. The motion was introduced by Bishop Wilberforce, without much warning and when some of the most prominent members had already left, and it was itself to become something of a bone of contention. In the lower house the same motion was sponsored by Denison and vigorously challenged by Stanley. But by this time even Longley had written to Gray,[1] saying that he believed that the South African bishops might now take steps to provide a new bishop for Natal. When Convocation had passed the address, Longley intimated that to communicate it to Gray would be 'a duty he should discharge with very great satisfaction'.

The hard core of Evangelical opinion in England was as much opposed to Colenso as was Cotterill in South Africa. Shaftesbury had, after all, joined Pusey in a somewhat unexpected alliance aimed at having the authors of *Essays & Reviews* condemned by the courts. He had described Colenso's *Pentateuch and Joshua* as 'this puerile and ignorant attack on the sacred and unassailable Word of God'.[2] But after the judgment of the courts in the *Essays & Reviews* and in Colenso's case, Evangelicals were less willing than Tractarians to condemn 'Erastianism' and by the end of the decade (when 'ritualism' was the major issue) Evangelicals tended to stand aloof from the conflict between conservative and liberal theologians.[3]

Support for Colenso was, of course, forthcoming from various leaders of liberal and Broad Church sympathies. We have already seen how Maurice began to veer back to Colenso's side after the trial in Cape Town.[4] In 1865 he published in *Macmillan's Magazine* 'A Letter to a Colonial Clergyman' in which he defended Colenso's right to remain in office and insisted that the secular courts were an important means of maintaining liberty in the Church. He would not defend, even now, Colenso's Old Testament studies. But others were more wholehearted in their support; Dean Stanley was perhaps Colenso's greatest champion.

[1] For reference to various letters received by Gray from sympathisers in England, see C. N. Gray, *op. cit.*, II, pp. 196ff.
[2] E. Hodder, *Life & Work of the 7th Earl of Shaftesbury*, 1887, p. 591
[3] *Ibid.*, p. 639   [4] *Supra*, p. 139

Colenso's methods had never appealed to Stanley.[1] The Regius Professor of Ecclesiastical History professed that Colenso's 'Old Testament arithmetic is entirely beyond me. But I bow, as always, so here, to the greatest living authority on his own subject'.[2] To Colenso, himself, he wrote, 'To fix the public attention on the mere defects of structure and detail [in the Old Testament] is, to my mind, to lead off the public mind on a false scent and to a false issue'; and, on another occasion, he urges Colenso not to be a 'martyr by mistake'.[3] Yet when the controversy came to the point of trial and excommunication, Stanley had no doubt that he must defend Colenso. He believed, like Maurice, in the great value of an 'impartial' and secular court in deciding ecclesiastical causes. He had spoken of the Privy Council judgment in the *Essays & Reviews* case as having a 'healing effect'.[4] Nor was he merely content to defend Colenso's right to preach a doctrine of which he personally disapproved. He broached the theological issue itself before Convocation in June 1865, pointing out that St Gregory of Nyssa on eternal punishment, William Law and St Anselm on the Atonement, held views very like those of Colenso.[5] It may be that a professor of Church history ought to have been a little more careful in his account of some of the authorities he cited, but no-one can fail to be stirred by his willingness to court unpopularity in order to defend a man whom he believed to be unjustly treated.

Other apostles of liberty came to the defence of the bishop of Natal. One of the quaintest documents of the period is a letter to Colenso from Garibaldi in which the Italian claims the bishop as his colleague, working in a different field for the emancipation of mankind.[6]

The English liberal, W. E. Gladstone, was less certain of Colenso. By this time Gladstone had come to believe that a separation between Church law and State law was a desirable thing.[7] But in the Colenso case the statesman's High Church

[1] *Supra*, p. 103
[2] R. E. Prothero and G. G. Bradley, *Life & Correspondence of Arthur Penrhyn Stanley*, 1893, 2 vols, II, p. 101
[3] Prothero & Bradley, *op. cit.*, p. 104
[4] *Ibid.*, p. 334
[5] *Ibid.*, p. 192 & cf C. N. Gray, *op. cit.*, II, p. 214
[6] Campbell Library, Durban; Colenso folios, M. 78; letter dated 21/4/1864.
[7] D. C. Lathbury, *Letters on Church & Religion of W. E. Gladstone*, 2 vols. 1910, I, p. 131

principles were also involved. And yet he seems to have believed, unlike Gray and Pusey, that the Privy Council decision was wrong, 'bad law', and that the Church in the colonies *was* part of the Established Church. Miss Burdett-Coutts wrote to him in 1866 about her endowment of the diocese of Cape Town.[1] Gladstone (who often seems to have found it difficult to express himself succinctly) is rendered almost unintelligible by the conflicting sentiments in his mind.[2] One thing alone emerges fairly clearly: Gladstone does not sympathise with Colenso.[3]

Bishop Tait's reaction to the Colenso case is more difficult to assess. He was pained by Colenso's teaching, finding his Old Testament criticism too negative and destructive, and he always seems to have believed that Colenso's teaching on the Person of Christ was quite definitely heretical. But, on the other hand, he was almost as uncertain of Gray, believing him to be a bigot and as extreme in one direction as Colenso was in another. He was careful always to treat Colenso with great personal friendliness, when some of the other bishops were cutting him dead. He regarded the decision of the Judicial Committee as settling the issue. It was the law as far as the Church of England was concerned, and that was that. Since he might himself have to sit as a member of the Privy Council, acting as the final court of appeal in ecclesiastical causes, and since he had none of the Tractarians' conscientious objections to such a court, he refused to comment publicly on Colenso's theology and protested vigorously against any attempt on the part of the bishops or of Convocation to pronounce any quasi-judicial sentence in the matter. This gave an appearance of inconsistency to some of his actions, since he maintained, for instance, that the bishops had a perfect right, by virtue of their spiritual office, to warn and to guard against the dangerous tendencies of Colenso's writing—so long as spiritual authority and judicial power were not confused. In fact his behaviour was entirely consistent throughout. He believed in the Royal Supremacy. He believed that the Church of England was and ought to be subject to English law. He was kind and he was

[1] See *supra*, p. 23
[2] St Deiniol's Library, Harwarden, possesses a copy of Colenso's *Natal Sermons* in which Gladstone has scribbled a number of rude comments.
[3] Lathbury, *op. cit.*, pp. 143ff

a gentleman. However much he disapproved of Colenso's theology his disapproval was conditioned always by these other considerations.[1]

Thirlwall, bishop of St David's, was even more sympathetic to Colenso, less inclined to take his stand simply on the desirability of the State connection and more disposed to defend the actual opinions of the bishop of Natal. In a famous charge to his diocese he attacked the whole of Gray's claim to exercise jurisdiction over Colenso.[2] The Cape Town trial he condemned as a mockery. He reiterated the opinions he had already expressed at the bishops' meetings of 1862 and in Convocation. He maintained that it was open to a clergyman of the Church of England to approach the study of the Bible critically. 'If the inquiry is to be free, it is impossible consistently to prescribe its results.' He asserts that Colenso is right in maintaining that the Bible is not the Word of God. If the two terms 'Bible' and 'Word of God' are simply to be regarded as interchangeable then 'the Bible itself would be degraded to a dead and barren letter, and would not be a living spring of Divine Truth'. He will not accept that either the Articles or any passage of Scripture require one to believe that the whole of the Pentateuch was written by Moses any more than that the Psalms are all written by David. But, like Stanley, Thirlwall is principally concerned that the link between colonial dioceses and the 'Mother' Church should be maintained and that the rule of English law should restrain colonial metropolitans.

And so one might continue to sample nineteenth-century opinions for and against the Erastian idea; but there is one other person whose reaction to the Privy Council judgment is worth recording, particularly since, in fairness to Bishop Gray, it may help to show that the South African metropolitan was not simply an arbitrary, bigotted despot, forcing his policy on the Church in South Africa in defiance of justice, common sense and honesty.

Lord Selborne (Roundell Palmer) was attorney-general in England in the critical period of late 1864 and early 1865. He was not an admirer of Lord Westbury, the lord chancellor.

---

[1] See R. T. Davidson & W. Benham, *Life of Archibald Campbell Tait*, 2 vols, 1891, I, pp. 332-97 & II, pp. 305 & 317.
[2] J. J. S. Perowne, *Remains of Connop Thirlwall, Charges*, II, pp. 59ff

He was a great Churchman and sympathetically disposed towards Gray whom he advised on several occasions. He had appeared for Gray before the Judicial Committee in the Long case. He was, nevertheless, one of the principal law officers of the Crown. His opinion is that of a lawyer, not merely of an opponent of Colenso's. Indeed he says:

I had known Colenso, in the days when I used to examine at Harrow. I was once his guest for nearly a week, when he was mathematical master under Christopher Wordsworth. He was a man of fine presence, a famous Cambridge mathematician, with considerable force of character. These, as far as I know, were his only qualifications for the office of Bishop; though it may be added, to his praise, that, when he filled it, he was zealous for justice to the native races of South Africa.[1]

Lord Selborne recalled that Colenso's petition was referred to Sir Robert Phillimore and himself, as law officers of the Crown, for their opinion. Their belief was that it was 'very difficult to understand how the Queen in Council could interfere summarily in such a case'.[2] Nevertheless it was 'for the Judicial Committee, and not for the law officers of the Crown, to decide that it could not be entertained . . .'. Thirty years later Selborne still believed that Westbury's judgment had been wrong *in law*, and that the Privy Council ought not to have assumed jurisdiction. If there were need for some way by which Colenso could seek for legal redress he could have applied, as Long had done, to the civil courts of the Cape Colony.[3]

Meanwhile Colenso remained in England. In many ways he was now at the height of his influence and popularity. A portrait painted at about this time by Sidley shows him better groomed and dressed, more the prelate and man of affairs, than at any other time.[4] There is a certain sameness about Victorian faces, at least on the surface. There is always the same long, rather wavy hair, the same full side-whiskers, the same cravat or stock. At first sight a picture of Colenso, or Gray, or Keble, or Tait, or even the young Newman (before he began to look like somebody's grandmother) might be interchangeable with any of the others. But once one gets behind

[1] Lord Selborne, *Memorials, Family & Personal*, 2 vols, 1896, II, p. 482
[2] *Ibid.*, p. 484   [3] *Ibid.*, p. 485
[4] The portrait is reproduced in Rees, *op. cit.*, p. 161.

the conventional trimmings and the gold-rimmed spectacles, Colenso's face does possess certain particular characteristics. It is a long face; long nose starting from between heavy eyebrows, and long upper lip over a wide mouth which seems only just not to be smiling. It is, one would say, a kindly face, good-looking in a strong, self-contained manner. There is a touch of pride in the way the head is held; the chin and the eyes reveal the courage and determination that were so characteristic of the man. And perhaps the strength of Colenso's personality has been somewhat dimmed by the painter. Mrs Colenso complained that the artist had changed his picture because Ruskin had said that 'he had made him look more like a military commander than one who had *thought* long and deeply. . . .'[1] A photograph taken at about the same time[2] shows a decidedly less handsome Colenso. His mouth is wider, more firmly set. His hair is less carefully groomed, and there is a slight frown gathering between the eyebrows. But the face is, perhaps, a little stronger—it *is* more the face of a military commander, a man in the thick of a great battle.

The bishop remained in England until August 1865, nearly six months after the Privy Council decision had been made public. The uncertain life in hired lodgings dragged on. Colenso was once more in financial difficulties, both personal and official. The S.P.G. had already removed him from the list of vice-presidents and now directed that its grants were to be administered by a committee in Natal and that Colenso was to have no control over any missionaries sent out by the Society.[3] Tait protested against both these decisions; Longley approved of them. The Society also cut down its grants to the 'orthodox' party in Natal, and Gray was convinced that this was because Colenso had friends and relations in the inner circles of the S.P.G.[4] So both bishops felt themselves to have been blatantly ill-treated by the Society.

They were both also losing income from another source. The Colonial Bishoprics Fund had stopped paying Colenso his salary on the grounds that he had been declared deposed by a court of the Church. But then, after the Privy Council

[1] Rees, *op. cit.*, p. 116
[2] The frontispiece to Cox, *op. cit.*, I
[3] Society's Minute Books, 20/2/1863 & 13/5/1866
[4] Keble College, Oxford; Keble papers, Gray to Keble, 17/9/1864

decision, Gray's income was stopped also. Colenso believed that the whole thing was a merely spiteful trick on the part of the committee, an attempt to delay his return to Natal by keeping him short of money.[1] There seems to be no reason to accept this point of view. Not only had Gray also been deprived of his income, but other colonial bishops with letters patent of about the same date were sent a letter asking them why they should not be treated in the same way.[2]

Colenso filed a bill in Chancery in order to compel the committee of the Fund to pay him his salary.[3] There eventually developed from this an action known as *The Bishop of Natal against Gladstone & Others*[4] which was not finally decided until November 1866, by which time Colenso was back in Natal. 'As I anticipated,' he wrote to Theophilus Shepstone in July 1865, 'the attempt to crush me by stopping my income has resulted in a miserable failure'.[5] A subscription list was opened to defray his expenses and soon amounted to about £3000.[6] This may have seemed to Colenso a considerable sum of money, as indeed it was, but £3000 is not enough to pay for a string of costly law-suits, to keep a bishop and his family and to run a diocese. Money was henceforward to prove to be one of Colenso's principal problems.

At all events, by June 1865 the bishop was making preparations to return to his diocese. He had been away from Ekukanyeni for three years. In all that time he had kept in touch with Shepstone and others of the laity, with some of the Africans on his mission station and with those one or two clergymen in South Africa who would still recognise him. But he had not really been able to administer the diocese 'in exile'. His resources were too slender, his contacts too few. To decide to return meant virtually to decide to begin all over again, and in far less propitious circumstances than those of twelve years earlier. It was, perhaps, one of the most courageous decisions of Colenso's life. The family packed up all their belongings once more. For the third time in their lives the

---

[1] Cox, *op. cit.*, I, pp. 265f
[2] A copy of the letter, a printed document, is in the Bishopscourt Archives, Cape Town.
[3] Cox, *op. cit.*, p. 266
[4] Mr Gladstone was one of the treasurers of the Colonial Bishoprics Fund.
[5] Cox, *loc. cit.*
[6] See Rees, *Colenso Letters from Natal*, p. 86 & Cox, *op. cit.*, I, p. 266

Colensos were setting out for a life which could not be planned in advance. Mrs Colenso wrote to Mrs Lyell[1]: 'We are in a delightful state of uncertainty about the time of our vessel's sailing.' 'I am haunted by a fear that something important will be left undone. John is so taken up with the Israelites that our Exodus devolves upon me in all its details'.[2]

Colenso was indeed busy up to the last moment. The fifth part of *Pentateuch and Joshua*, the most constructive of his critical studies, was brought out of cold storage and completed before the bishop left England. It was to be 'a token of farewell at once to my friends and my enemies'.[3] The preface makes the proud claim, 'this volume contains *the most important part of my work*'.[4] It also contained a good deal which had nothing to do with Old Testament scholarship at all—an attack on Bishop Gray and on Bishop Harold Browne, and an expression of thanks to the bishop of Limerick and Sir Charles Lyell.

> I now return to the duties which have been so long interrupted —of late, by circumstances not under my own control. In the midst of those duties, I shall find frequent opportunity for acting on the principles which I have here enunciated, and shall rejoice in breathing myself, and helping others to breathe, the fresh, free air, which the recent decisions have made it now possible to breathe within the bounds of the National Church. I shall also, as I hope and fully purpose, find time to pursue these enquiries, and, perhaps, hereafter return to publish them. But all these things are in the hand of God. Should I never return, I bid my friends in England farewell, to meet them again, I trust, on another shore. But if I should return, a few years hence, it is my firm belief that as we are now ashamed of those trials for witchcraft and sorcery . . . which disgraced the Christianity of our forefathers in the Middle Ages . . . so I shall find in that day my fellow-Countrymen and fellow-Churchmen ashamed of that religious fear and frenzy which has raged so furiously in these our times. . . .[5]

It was obviously *Pentateuch and Joshua* that kept Colenso in England for the last six months. Since he does not seem to have worked at it much while he was waiting for the Privy

---

[1] Mrs Lyell was sister to Lady Lyell, and married to Sir Charles' brother.
[2] Rees, *op. cit.*, p. 88   [3] *Pentateuch aud Joshua*, Pt. V, p. v
[4] *Ibid.*, p. xliv   [5] *Ibid.*, p. xlvi

Council hearing to begin, it is probable that he then felt he had better finish it before facing the challenge of renewed work in Natal. He was immersed in the book almost to the last moment. The preface is dated 3 June 1865. The volume appeared on sale in July. The bishop was at work on other projects, more critical studies and a scheme for a new translation of the Bible with a commentary. Various scholars from different countries were to collaborate and Colenso was to be general editor. An hour before he was due to leave Kensington to catch his ship, Colenso was writing to Sir Charles Lyell that this 'important proposition' might bring him back earlier than he 'had at all thought of'.[1] H.B. Wilson, of *Essays & Reviews* fame, and Colenso's Dutch friend, Kuenen, had already been approached. But nothing came of the scheme.

The bishop was still pressing the Colonial Bishoprics Fund; his solicitors were trying to speed up the Chancery case, but it was no nearer a hearing by the middle of August. In a kind of frenzy to do all the things he wanted to do before returning to Africa, the bishop was agitating for the clergy to be allowed to subscribe the Articles in a general sense only, to hold secular jobs and be Members of Parliament, and generally to be allowed freedom from the bonds of dogma within the 'National Church'. He was also working for the establishment of a scientific society to investigate 'the origin and history of all religions'. At last a definite date for the sailing was fixed. The raising of the gangplank put an end to this feverish activity. On 15 August 1865 Colenso left England and for nearly three months he was perforce cut off from the bustle of controversy. He was too active a man to cease from work altogether, of course. In the dimly lit cabin, during the most frightful weather, the bishop went on with his reading and writing. But at least there was a rest from the strain of the past few months.

The Colensos arrived in Durban on 4 November 1865.[2] The bishop had especially asked Shepstone to meet him, but he could not be there. But the harbour had been dressed with flags. Some of the Bishop's friends came aboard to greet him: 'We've come through the water to you, as you've come through fire and water to us'. There was a great, silent crowd of sightseers on the shore. The Colenso family stepped ashore, puzzled

---

[1] Cox, *op. cit.*, I, p. 270
[2] The voyage was a rough one, see Rees, *op. cit.*, pp. 92ff.

and a little apprehensive, perhaps. And then there was a great burst of cheering to honour the landing of the bishop himself.[1] For Colenso it was a great and moving moment. He had come back to his diocese, as its only lawful bishop. And yet his own view of his office had changed in the stress of controversy. Twelve years earlier he had landed at the same port. Then, fired with the missionary ideals and the fervour of Maurice, he had proclaimed, 'I come among you as an ambassador of Christ.' Circumstances now compelled him to alter the emphasis, to claim an authority derived from the Crown as well as from Christ. In a letter to the colonial press the bishop quite deliberately wrote:

> In the system of the Church of England the Queen *does ordain* —not directly, but virtually,—the *clergy of all orders*, bishops, priests and deacons. What is done by *ecclesiastics* in this matter is done by them ministerially by virtue of *power committed to them by the Queen*, I mean, as representing the State—the people.[2]

The stress of controversy had made Colenso an Erastian— perhaps in a modified form, but nevertheless an Erastian by conviction.

[1] See Rees, *loc. cit.*, & Cox, *op. cit.*, II, p. 4.
[2] Quoted in A.T. Wirgman, *James Green*, I, p. 202.

CHAPTER 7

The Father of the People

THE Colenso family settled in again in their home at Bishopstowe,[1] six dusty miles from Pietermaritzburg. Those six miles
were important. They cut the family off from the immediate
rumpus of the controversy, for a trip into the town and back
really meant the loss of a whole day, but at the same time
prevented the bishop from intervening as effectively as he
might have done. Green reigned in Pietermaritzburg, visiting
assiduously, putting his side of the case. The bishop came in
on Sundays and whenever he had urgent business to attend
to. Mrs Colenso, who was inclined to be snobbish about
colonial society, always maintained that it was a great relief to
her that they should be out of touch with life in the capital.

> Everybody here has something queer about them, or else they
> are mere colonials, born and bred in the place without an idea.
> There are some superior people, but they are scattered about
> over the colony and very glad to receive and entertain the Bishop
> when he is out on his travels.[2]

And so the Colenso children also were isolated from colonial
society such as it was. The two boys, in their teens, were
tutored by their father until he managed to find a clergyman
who would act as dean of Pietermaritzburg and tutor to the
boys—an oddly revealing piece of pluralism, showing how very
much Colenso's 'Church' was to become a personal, almost
private concern. The girls suffered more from the isolation.
Frances, indeed, was sent to England for a while to 'visit', to
see what really civilised society was like. Harriette busied herself with good works in the little Colenso settlement, teaching
in a school for Africans, supervising work in the fields, attending an occasional ball at Government House, until she grew
to mature spinsterhood, inheriting all and more of her father's
social conscience. Agnes, very shy, very tall for her age, shared
her sister's life and work but, since social occasions were an

[1] This account of the Colensos' life at Bishopstowe is based upon Mrs
Colenso's letters in W. Rees, *Colenso Letters from Natal.*
[2] Rees, *op. cit.*, p. 217

agony for her, she lacked even that little contact with the outside world. The bishop worked on at his Old Testament
criticism in a study darkened by exotic creepers. Here he
wrote his sermons, page after page of them, desperately trying
to retain, by the vigour of his preaching, the great crowds of
people who came to his services. Here, too, he kept his oddly
uninformative diaries, which show him as the farmer, ordering
bags of mealies for planting and a new ploughshare, keeping
careful accounts of his petty-cash, noting what the weather
was like, and preserving the details of his extensive travels.[1]
Mrs Colenso presided over all this varied activity, riding her
horse about the farm, entertaining her husband's more influential supporters, collecting ferns for Mrs Lyell's botanical
work, mending, making—and 'making do'—dresses for herself
and her girls and for the Africans on the settlement.

It is difficult to establish just what the private financial
circumstances of the family were. The bishop's work continually suffered from lack of funds. Probably the family was
fairly poor too. Mrs Colenso was very glad that she did not
have to move in Natal society and dress in accordance with
her husband's station. She hoped he might be given some
well-paid job, either in the colony, or elsewhere. One gets the
impression that it was a struggle to make ends meet. Yet the
Colensos were good parents and sent their sons to be educated
in England in 1868, Robert to Oxford and Francis to his
father's old college at Cambridge. Mrs Colenso had hoped
that one of them might have become a clergyman under his
father. This did not happen—but at least they were spared
the narrowness of colonial education and were given wider
opportunities than were open to most sons of Natal contemporaries. Robert nearly became a 'colonist', but in the end it
was decided that he had better be educated instead!

It will be clear that the Colensos did not really regard themselves as *settlers* in Natal. Mrs Colenso loved Bishopstowe and
the climate.

This place is a perfect paradise. I wish you could see what I see
now by turning my head to the right—our Table Mountain[2] with

[1] The diaries are in the Natal Archives, Pietermaritzburg; Colenso Collection, 119 (1).

[2] There are a large number of flat-topped hills and mountains in South Africa
and many of them have inevitably been named after the famous Table Mountain at Cape Town.

the sloping lands between, and the shrubs and trees of our garden for the foreground—there is a dove cooing in the orchard, and though our birds do not sing like thrushes and blackbirds, they utter sounds soft or shrill which make the air full of feeling if not of music; a little sugar bird is continually busy with the honeysuckles on our verandah and the coral plants and others in the bed in front; there are two Cape Jessamins, quite *bushes*, full of their luscious flowers; the moon flower (datura) is full of bud.[1]

But, though she loved the countryside, it is fairly clear that Mrs Colenso would have preferred to live in England among her 'own sort'. The bishop, too, was uncertain still how long he would remain in Africa. He hankered a little for the comparative peace of a proposed new chair of Biblical Study at Cambridge.[2] He seems to have hinted to Stanley that an English canonry might be the best niche for him to retire to.[3] And as he grew older he came more and more to feel that he had fought long and hard enough for the principle of a colonial Church firmly tied to the Establishment at home, and that it was time for a younger man to take up the struggle. Mrs Colenso felt herself cut off from her friends, her family, and the intelligent, well-bred circles in which they had moved in London. The bishop felt himself similarly cut off from the liberal theological world. His academic work was a sort of retreat, a small, peaceful corner into which the furore of colonial controversy could not penetrate so long as he was immersed in his Hebrew.[4] But there was so little time left once the demands of controversy had been met.[5] And once he was caught up in the controversy there was no withdrawing. Almost from the moment he had become a bishop, Colenso had been involved in one argument after another. Once he came back to Natal he had to stay there, simply because to leave again would have been to acknowledge defeat.

The schism had affected the whole colony. Colenso and Green were the chief protagonists. Gray was for the most part in the background, emerging from time to time to take part in some phase of the struggle. Eventually a new 'orthodox'

[1] Rees, *op. cit.*, p. 96
[2] Cox, *op. cit.*, II, pp. 447f & Rees, *op. cit.*, p. 86; and see also Campbell Library; Colenso folios, A 27; Colenso to Dr W. Bleek, 5/4/1864.
[3] Campbell Library, Durban; Colenso folios, F. 35
[4] Rees, *op. cit.*, p. 120   [5] See Cox, *op. cit.*, II, p. 19.

bishop came to the colony, but even then it was Green who was Colenso's most bitter opponent.[1] It is quite impossible to reconstruct here the details of the quarrel step by step. Both sides distorted the facts. Each is concerned to exaggerate the number of its own supporters and to suggest that its opponents are riff-raff, not 'Church people', merely women, or in some way or another not to be counted as worthy of note. To place side by side the account of an event from Colenso's biography with the account of the same event in Green's biography makes one feel that somehow or other one is dealing with two quite unrelated episodes. And it would require a painstaking Ph.D. thesis to disentangle, detail by detail, the exact course of the controversy, the numbers engaged on both sides, and the real opinions of the people most concerned.

For one thing there were so many issues involved. Some people supported Colenso because of his liberal theology, but these were a mere handful.[2] Again and again the bishop pointed out that he required no-one to accept his teaching.[3] He required them merely to accept the law.[4] And large numbers of Evangelicals, fundamentalists, and Church-and-State men, together with colonial laity who wished to preserve every possible link with Queen and 'home', the conventional C. of E. churchmen in the civil service and the army, the men who liked a 'no nonsense' religion, and the few who really were troubled by what seemed to contemporary Englishmen to be grounds for unbelief—all these followed Colenso. But they did not follow consistently. They wavered back and forth. An Evangelical might follow Colenso because he fought against the supposed tyranny and Romanising tendencies of the bishop of Cape Town, and then hesitate when he heard the bishop 'attack the Bible'. Someone else might like Bishop Colenso's Low Church ways and yet feel a little nervous about heresy and excommunication. Amongst the clergy, Lloyd first refused to receive Colenso because of his unorthodox views, and then later joined him because he was upheld by the law. A priest

---

[1] It is typical of the curious way in which the story of the schism has been unconsciously distorted that a recent article on Colenso does not even mention Green—see P. O. G. White, 'The Colenso Controversy', *Theology*, LXV, No. 508, pp. 402ff.   [2] Rees, *op. cit.*, p. 91

[3] See e.g. Cox, *op. cit.*, p. 146—'I saw no reason for rejecting him because his views were very narrow' [i.e. Evangelical].

[4] Rees, *op. cit.*, p. 133

called Newnham impartially attacked Colenso for his Old Testament criticism and the orthodox bishop for his failure to obey the law of England. Dr Callaway tried to remain aloof from the hysteria of those who attacked Colenso, but was eventually forced into the other camp because of Colenso's theology. And if this was true of the clergy, it was even more so in the case of the laity. It would seem, so far as it is possible to judge at all, that the laity began to rally to Colenso from the moment he appealed to the Crown. After the judgment of the Judicial Committee was known and when the bishop returned to Natal, he was very popular. But even then his support was divided. In Durban there was still a very strong Protestant and Erastian laity—yet the churchwardens protested against Colenso's attempts to enter St Paul's. Here the bishop was supported because he was 'Church of England'. In Maritzburg the laity were divided between 'bishop's party' and 'dean's party' and the former was certainly in the majority at first. Probably the division in the capital was largely along personal lines, with an element of churchmanship thrown in. In the country districts the laity were probably chiefly on the side of the orthodox, at least so far as the simpler folk were concerned. In 1866 Bishop Gray estimated that about 300 of the laity would actively support, and about 100 repudiate a new bishop for Natal.[1] He was probably more optimistic than the facts warranted. Colenso, when he first returned to Natal, made an almost identical, but inverted, estimate: 'more than 300 have signed for me, and only 150 against me . . .'.[2] The overall impression one gains from the letters and papers of the time is that the laity were, on the whole and at first, inclined to support Colenso. Most of the clergy—all except three—were on the other side.[3]

The bishop had to fight for every foot of ground. He was met by protests from the parson and churchwardens in Durban. In the cathedral at Pietermaritzburg a tense and dramatic clash occurred. On Friday 10 November 1865, in Colenso's first week at Bishopstowe, the churchwardens came out from Pietermaritzburg with a formal protest against any possible attempt on the bishop's part to minister in the cathedral. On

---

[1] C. N. Gray, *op. cit.*, II, p. 302   [2] Cox, *op. cit.*, II, p. 5
[3] Both sides imported clergy after the struggle began. These figures refer to the original clergy.

the Sunday Colenso drove into the see city determined to officiate somehow, somewhere. Theophilus Shepstone's son (also called Theophilus) procured an interdict to oblige the dean to allow the bishop entry to the cathedral. The dean had spent the whole night locked in the church, half disposed to defy the bishop and the courts. A vast crowd, black and white, gathered in the dusty street outside the gate. At almost 11 o'clock, Colenso drove up. The churchwardens emerged from the door of the cathedral and read their protest. Colenso, armed with his interdict, forced them to open the gates. Followed by the crowds, the bishop crossed the twenty yards to the cathedral doors. The doors were opened and the people poured in, filling the narrow nave to capacity. Those who had come to see the sights crowded to the front, some standing up on the pews or jostling their way to the chancel steps. The stocky figure of the dean, his hair and sidewhiskers beginning to go grey, could be seen kneeling before the high altar in his cassock. Then the bishop, in gaiters and apron, carrying his top hat and his robes, walked into the cathedral. Half way up the church he was met by the churchwardens who again read the protest. In the silence which followed the bishop solemnly proclaimed his purpose, 'I am come to discharge the duties committed to me by the Queen'. Then the registrar, at the dean's command, read Bishop Gray's sentence of deposition, and the dean's voice rang out dramatically from the sanctuary, 'It is written, "That which ye shall bind on earth shall be bound in heaven". This sentence therefore is binding in the sight of Almighty God. Depart! Go away from the House of God!'

The dean then knelt down again with his back to the people while Colenso robed himself in rochet and chimere at the top of the chancel steps (the vestry was locked) and the churchwardens read the judge's order to explain why nothing could be done to exclude the bishop by force. Colenso proceeded to read morning prayer, pitching the chants and hymns himself, and preaching a sermon in which his distinctive theological opinions were in no way disguised or glossed over. It was a gorgeous scandal for the gossips; the beginning of a terrible tragedy for those on either side who were deeply religious.[1]

For some time an uneasy compromise was agreed upon.

---

[1] For the details of this episode see A. T. Wirgman, *James Green*, I, pp. 203f; & Cox, *op. cit.*, II, pp. 6ff.

Dean and bishop agreed to have their services in the cathedral at different times on Sundays. On 13 December 1865 Gray formally promulgated the sentence of excommunication passed upon Colenso by the synod of bishops two years earlier. Gray wrote a letter to Colenso urging him to agree to appeal to a court of bishops, either English or drawn from the wider Anglican world, but the letter was doomed to fail in its purpose from the first. Gray would not allow an appeal to anybody 'except the Bishops of the Church'.[1] Colenso would not recognise any court not constituted by the authority of the Crown, though he offered to allow the orthodoxy of his theology to be judged by the law of England.[2]

It will be remembered that the bishop's teaching had never been judged on its merits, the Privy Council concerning itself merely with the matter of jurisdiction. People like Tait and Gladstone had long believed that the course now proposed by Colenso ought to have been followed in the first instance. For Gray and Wilberforce, and many others, this would have been impossible. It would have involved them in a deliberate and conscientious acceptance of the right of a secular tribunal to judge matters of faith.

Gray also sent a private letter to Colenso, making a last desperate appeal. But the letter was not very tactfully worded for the purpose and perhaps it is not surprising that Colenso remained unmoved.[3] His suggestion that the whole matter be re-opened in the Court of Arches, Gray described as a 'monstrous proposal'.[4] Accordingly in January 1866 the sentence was published. Green read it from before the altar in the cathedral during a celebration of the Eucharist.[5] Even after this event—which Colenso regarded as deliberate incitement to break the law and disobey the Queen—the two parties continued to share the cathedral. For the moment they were chiefly concerned with petty squabbles over the registers, the organ and the bells. Colenso's preaching drew great crowds to *his* services and within a short while the first volume of these *Natal Sermons* was ready for publication.

[1] C. N. Gray, *op. cit.*, II, pp. 240ff   [2] Cox, *op. cit.*, II, p. 14
[3] C. N. Gray, *op. cit.*, pp. 242ff
[4] Keble College, Oxford; Keble Papers, Gray to John Keble, 5/2/1865
[5] Conflicting dates for this event are given by Colenso (14 January, Cox, *op. cit.*, II, p. 14) & Green (7 January, Wirgman, *op. cit.*, I, p. 208). In this case Green is certainly correct!

The series eventually comprised four volumes. They created comparatively little stir in England. They were noticed by the ecclesiastical press, particular points caused some comment, but on the whole people 'at home' were no longer much concerned with the thoughts of the notorious bishop of Natal. In a way it is a pity that they are not better known, for they are the mature exposition of all Colenso's theology, as it had been gradually formulated since his days at Forncett, and they are applied to practical considerations for the benefit of Colenso's congregation. The sermons are not a system of theology, of course, for Colenso was implacably opposed to any rigid formulation of dogma. But the ideas are no longer newly inspired. They have been in the bishop's mind for some time. He has reflected upon them, followed up their implications, and begun to fit them into a single pattern. Almost every episode of Colenso's life and every phase of his thought finds some place in the sermons.

One may find in these sermons the conclusion of Colenso's thinking about the fatherhood of God, which Maurice's *Kingdom of Christ* first put into his mind. Dogma and theology are relatively unimportant—the good and moral life is what matters. The purpose of Christ's Incarnation was to 'show us the Father', His 'sympathizing love for His own dear children, the faithful and true in heart, the meek and pure and loving, those who are hungering and thirsting after righteousness, those who are striving by God's help to be perfect, even as their Father in heaven is perfect'.[1] To follow this pattern is to eat and drink the flesh and blood of Christ, and so the theme of Colenso's early Eucharistic sermons finds its place in the whole scheme. But the Church has tangled this simple truth of the Father's love in a net of dogma and hierarchy. The second coming, the devil, hell and punishment are dismissed as superstitions and delusions, the product of human misunderstanding of God, due partly to borrowings from other religions. Christ's pattern is before us; to follow that pattern is to be free for ever from the threat of death. But the example of Christ can only be followed if we are infused by love, the love which has made us children of God by faith. The bishop is then able to weld his interpretation of the Pauline doctrine of justification by faith into the whole scheme, thus incorpor-

[1] *Natal Sermons*, I, p. 81

ating the ideas he had set out in his *Romans*, ten years earlier. He reiterates his contention (set out already in the commentary) that baptism is the symbol of the belief that infants are from their birth-hour the children of God.

Christians are, says Colenso, to look in the Bible for the pattern of God's love. 'Nothing is more plain in the New Testament than that the sum and substance of it, as of the Old, is not a system of religious worship, not a summary of many things to be believed or done, so that "whosoever shall not believe or do them, without doubt he shall perish everlastingly", but a revelation of God and of our relation to Him, as that of children to a loving Father'.[1] Even his biblical criticism is fitted into the whole pattern. The Book of Ezra, the ten commandments, and particularly the Books of Chronicles can all be shown to be unhistorical and unreliable. (The Chronicler, in particular, Colenso pursues with something of the fervour of a private vendetta.) But when the critic has done his work, the Bible can be seen to be the more clearly the word of God, because man can now be liberated from subservience to the letter and free to follow the spirit of God. When one compares the two Old Testament versions of the decalogue, for instance, one is bound to realise that they cannot both be the work of Moses. What authority is there, then, to impose the Sabbath upon Jew or Christian? Man is delivered from the horrors of the Scottish Sabbath.[2] The Church of Scotland, says Colenso, compensated for all the gnats it was forced to strain away, by swallowing a variety of camels. The Church of England, he now believed, was, for all its shortcomings, the best kind of Church. He regarded the Church as a human association. He would have nothing to do with the idea of an infallible Church or an infallible Bible. The Church of England 'rejected all arbitrary and artificial restrictions' and 'refused to limit the terms of communion to those who had a reputation for orthodoxy'.[3] In this sense it was, for Colenso, the ideal Church.

But there *was* one part of *Natal Sermons* which attracted some attention, his attack on *Hymns, Ancient & Modern*.[4] The backwash of this part of the controversy reached the national press. Letters to *The Times* and the *Pall Mall Gazette*, and articles in the *Spectator*, all helped to make Colenso's name

---

[1] *Natal Sermons*, II, p. 275
[2] *Natal Sermons*, I, pp. 230ff
[3] Cox, *op. cit.*, II, p. 70
[4] *Ibid.*, II, pp. 144ff

familiar again as a famous free thinker. Since his principal criticism of the hymn book is that some of the hymns are prayers addressed to Christ, his remarks raised again the whole question of whether the bishop believed our Lord to be divine. It is a question which is even now difficult to answer. Colenso argued that Christ teaches us to pray to the Father—not to the Virgin, the Saints or to Himself, and that Christian practice has always been to pray *to* the Father *through* the Son. But when he says that this is not simply the normal but also the only possible form for prayer to take, he appears to be denying Christ's right to be worshipped and, therefore, his divinity. It is not clear from Colenso's words how far he is prepared to press this. *Natal Sermons* contain many passages which are patient of a perfectly orthodox interpretation, where Christ is spoken of as Son of Man and Son of God, Saviour, etc. But these passages can equally be taken to mean that Christ is perfect man and in that sense God's Son, endued with his Spirit. And Colenso's language about the Spirit again suggests that he is thinking of a vague outpouring of power, not a Person of the Trinity.

The bishop became at one time involved with the Reverend C. Voysey, a clergyman of the Church of England who was deprived for his heretical teaching on the Trinity and the Person of Christ. Voysey maintained that the worship of Christ was idolatry, that the idea of an Incarnation was a degenerate and pagan concept, and that there had been no Atonement because there had been no fall of man. Voysey founded the Theistic Association and invited Colenso to become president. In his reply Colenso makes it plain that he is not entirely in agreement with Voysey,[1] though he seems prepared to agree that the doctrine of the Trinity is not necessary to salvation— but then it is likely that Colenso would have said that about any doctrine. Acceptance of dogma was not in his view part of the process of salvation at all. Christianity meant 'receiving Christ's doctrine concerning the Father, as His Father and our Father, His God and our God, and trying to live in the spirit of Christ'.[2] But he was not prepared to call himself a theist—he was a 'Christian theist'.

It has recently been suggested that Mrs Colenso was a

[1] Cox, *op. cit.*, II, pp. 244ff, 250ff, 260ff
[2] *Ibid.*, p. 246

'better' theologian than her husband and influenced him a good deal.[1] This is a difficult point to assess. It is clear that Mrs Colenso did not hold an 'orthodox' view of Christ's divinity,[2] but whether she objected to worship of Christ's *human nature* as idolatrous, or whether she had ceased to believe in Him as God, is never quite clear. Perhaps the most revealing statement of all is Mrs Colenso's near-pantheistic assertion that God cannot really be 'jealous' of worship paid to another, because 'Surely no creature, the most perfect, is another; as far as it is perfect, God is in it'.[3] But even this conflicts with the bishop's own arguments that prayer ought not to be addressed to Christ.

It is probable that Colenso, by the time he returned to Natal, had really ceased to subscribe to the Nicene and Chalcedonian definitions. He believed in an exemplarist Christ who had come into the world to reveal the Father and man's proper relationship to Him. He was more concerned with Christianity as a way of life than with particular dogmas. He had, perhaps, ceased to believe in the Son and the Spirit as distinct Persons. For Colenso Christ was probably the Son of God only in the sense that He was also the son of man in perfection. God was in Christ, less as an incarnation, than as an indwelling power, love made manifest. He probably did not think of Christ as God Himself.

Nevertheless this is all only 'probable'. It is never quite fair to take sermons and analyse them as though they were carefully balanced theological treatises. One single passage from Colenso's sermons will serve to illustrate how great was his devotion to our Lord and at the same time may show how difficult it is to be absolutely certain just how far Colenso could be said to regard Christ as divine.

The faith of Christ, the faith which cares for the weak, which reclaims the fallen, which makes us see in every human creature our Father's child, which teaches us that we ought to lay down our lives for the brethren, which sets before us the Cross, the sacred emblem of love and suffering, as the glory of humanity —how can the Author of that faith, of this pure doctrine, be any other than the Lord and Saviour of men, the dear Son of man

[1] Rees, *op. cit.*, p. 30 & cf Cox, *op. cit.*, p. 21
[2] Rees, *op. cit.*, pp. 130, 135, 182, 252 & cf p. 68
[3] *Ibid.*, p. 156

and Son of God, in whom 'the Father was dwelling' by the
Eternal Word, to whom He 'gave not the Spirit by measure'?
Yes! Christianity is a fact,—a fact of the present as well as the
past. No criticism of documents, no discovery of glosses, no sifting
of history, can ever disprove it or rob it of any of its glories, as
the Light,—the Great Light,—which has 'come down from above,
from the Father of Lights' to lighten our race.[1]

To the accusation that Colenso denied the divinity of Christ,
we should probably be obliged to return the verdict, 'Not
proven'. He came perilously close to it, but that he ever
actually reached such a position remains in doubt. Nevertheless
it is quite clear that a good many of his contemporaries believed
that Colenso had really ceased to be a Christian. H. P. Liddon's
Bampton Lectures of 1867, *The Divinity of Our Lord*, was meant
to be the orthodox answer to modern doubt, infidelity and
liberalism. Its success was limited, yet it shows very clearly
how the more conservative and 'catholic' would react to
Colenso's teaching.

In Liddon's final lecture—'Some consequences of the Doctrine of Our Lord's Divinity'—he twice alludes to Colenso's
Pentateuchal criticism. Liddon is concerned with the whole
question of limitations on Christ's knowledge, and the only
limitation he will allow is our Lord's ignorance of the day of
the Last Judgment—'Of that day and that hour knoweth no
man, no not the angels which are in heaven, neither the Son,
but the Father' (Mark 13:32).[2] To suppose that our Lord was
in any other way subject to ignorance not only denies that He
is infallible God, but also suggests that He was capable of moral
error, since He could quote a 'pious fraud' as if it were a
genuine book.[3] Liddon believes Colenso to be in error on both
these points and to have formally allied himself with the classical heresies like Arianism. Liddon also devotes an appendix to
Colenso's attack on *Hymns, Ancient & Modern*.[4] He argues
that one *Christe eleison* would be proof that Christ was worshipped in the early Church or in the Church of the Reformation. He shows how large a part of the *Book of Common Prayer*
is, in fact, devoted to the worship of Christ. And he maintains
that if Christ is God this is both proper and to be expected.

---

[1] *Natal Sermons*, II, p. 323
[2] H.P. Liddon, *The Divinity of Our Lord*, 1878 ed., p. 458
[3] *Ibid.*, pp. 454ff & 469ff   [4] *Ibid.*, p. 520

He stops the loophole of the argument that it is idolatrous to worship Christ's *humanity*, by saying that humanity and divinity are not separable in that sort of way. In fact Liddon is convinced that Colenso could not attack the worship of Christ if he was orthodox in terms of the Nicene and Chalcedonian formulae.

> . . . if, as a consequence of the Hypostatic Union, our Lord's Manhood rightly and necessarily shares in the adoration offered to Deity, this is because His Divine Person is ultimately and in reality, the object adored. 'O God the Son, Redeemer of the world, have mercy upon us miserable sinners'. 'O Lamb of God that takest away the sins of the world, have mercy upon us'. In either case it is Christ's Eternal Person which claims our adoration; that Person with which His Manhood is now for ever joined, as an attribute of It. And Christ's Person is adored, for precisely the same reason as that which leads us to adore the Father; nor could such adoration be offered to any created personality whatever, without repudiating altogether the first, the most sacred, prerogative of Deity.[1]

However liturgically correct it may be to say that Christian prayer ought to be addressed to the Father, through the Son, yet to maintain outright that *no* prayer ought to be addressed to the Son is bound to raise suspicions of heresy. To deny what is proper to the godhead, must also be to seem to deny the godhead itself.

It was an unfortunate moment for Colenso to 'write himself down as an heretic' once more. 1866 and 1867 were the years in which Gray took the necessary steps to provide an orthodox bishop for Natal and there can be no doubt that Colenso's doubtful statements on the subject of Christ's divinity alienated support in England and made Gray's task somewhat easier. Not that it was by any means an easy achievement even then; it was a long and wearisome process, full of every kind of difficulty and disappointment. As a consequence of the meeting of clergy and laity in Natal in 1864[2] the Convocation of Canterbury was asked three questions. Gray asked if Colenso could still be considered as in communion with the Church of England. Green asked whether the appointment of a new bishop would sever Natal from the Church 'at home', and how a new bishop could be appointed if it were possible.

[1] Liddon, *op. cit.*, pp. 531ff   [2] *Supra*, p. 151

Bishop Wilberforce undertook to pilot the questions through Convocation on 28 June 1866. Thirlwall and Tait led the opposition in the upper house and were able to prevent any explicit statement that the bishops regarded Colenso as excommunicate. The house declared itself in communion with Gray and his comprovincials but made no specific reference to Colenso's status at all. It also declared that the acceptance of a new bishop would not 'impair the connection or alter the relations between Natal and England'. 'A formal instrument declaratory of the doctrine and discipline of the Church of England should be prepared' and be signed by all the clergy and the new bishop. If such a document could be agreed on there was no reason why a new bishop should not be consecrated either by the archbishop in England or by the South African bishops.[1] The lower house approved the resolution, though Stanley strained every nerve to defend Colenso.

On 25 October 1866 the elective assembly was held in Pietermaritzburg. The public gallery was packed with Colenso's supporters. The orthodox party occupied the floor. Of all the original clergy of the diocese only one refused to have anything to do with the proceedings at all. The clergy who participated included several imported into the diocese since Colenso's departure and were, therefore, almost certain to approve the election of a new bishop. Mr Lloyd, Mr Newnham and Dr Callaway, while disapproving of Colenso, refused to take part in the election, though Callaway announced that he would accept the candidate who should be elected. Others of the clergy thought the election inexpedient and, after a full day of debate, the house divided equally on the matter. It required the dean's casting vote to carry the resolution to proceed to election—to the delight, of course, of the bishop's supporters in the audience. Callaway, Lloyd and Newnham withdrew while the election took place. Several others abstained. Seven votes were cast for the single candidate, William Butler of Wantage,[2] a leading Tractarian and one of those responsible for the revival of religious communities in the Church of England. Newnham and Callaway then returned and joined

---

[1] See C. N. Gray, *op. cit.*, II, pp. 264ff
[2] Butler seems to have been suggested by Liddon as the best man for the job—Keble College, Oxford; Liddon papers; Liddon to Butler, 7/10/1865; Pusey to Liddon, 9/10/1865.

in a debate about various other matters connected with the appointment of the new bishop. Thirty-one laymen were present, from Pietermaritzburg and the country districts. The laity of Durban refused to attend. Twenty-eight of the house of the laity assented to the election.[1]

Colenso's comment on the proceedings was, 'It seems to me hardly conceivable that Mr Butler of Wantage will accept the proposed bishopric, when he hears the facts about the election, and that he would only be Bishop of a small sect, and would be refused admission into any of the churches belonging to the Church of England, not by me, but by the people and their elected churchwardens'.[2] He is scathing in his remarks on the narrowness of the majority amongst the clergy and the small number of the laity who were present.

Butler was indeed hesitant. Longley and Wilberforce both advised him to withhold his assent until he was sure that he would be accepted by a majority in Natal. There was considerable doubt about this. Gray assured, and seems to have convinced, the archbishop that Butler would be accepted. But his estimate of the number of laity supporting Colenso is probably unreliable.[3] Callaway and Newnham were trying to organise a centre party, repudiating both Colenso and Butler. They had little success but their efforts made the whole situation even more unsettled than before.[4] Bishop Gray and his advisers were undecided as to the proper title and status of the new bishop, if he should come. And while things were in this tense and uncertain state Archbishop Longley called the first Lambeth Conference, largely as a result of the Natal schism.

In the meantime the actual quarrel in Natal had grown worse. Colenso could no longer tolerate the Box and Cox arrangement by which he shared the cathedral with Green. Not only was Green planning the election of a rival bishop, but there had also been a tragi-comic episode involving Bishop Twells of the Free State, known as the most 'advanced' Tractarian in the country. Green had invited Twells to take a confirmation in the cathedral. Colenso's supporters chose to counter this by washing the floor of the building on that particular day, a

[1] A full report of the proceedings was published under the title *The Election of a Bishop*, reprinted from *The Natal Mercury*, 1866.
[2] Cox, *op. cit.*, II, p. 61
[3] *Supra*, p. 171
[4] Cox, *op. cit.*, II, p. 67

process which involved flooding the cathedral with several inches of water. Onlookers were presented with the edifying sight of one of Colenso's churchwardens 'accidentally touching' Green's party with a wet broom.

The overtones of comedy in this incident are misleading; it was to have serious repercussions. Twells became identified with the Green party and three years later was involved in a homosexual scandal which ended in the bishop's passing through Durban and escaping from the country disguised as a sailor. Green and his followers seem to have refused to accept Twells's flight either as confession of guilt or as automatically leaving his see vacant. Gray and Green, whose relations became in any case very strained in later years, quarrelled violently about the matter and the year before he died Gray wrote to Twells's successor that Green was really the biggest source of trouble to the South African Church.[1] And Colenso, of course, was able to point out that his trial in Cape Town had only been made possible by the presence of a bishop of scandalous morals.[2]

The immediate issue, the possession of the cathedral, was settled by the Natal Supreme Court at about the same time as the Chancery Court in England finally decided Colenso's suit against the Colonial Bishopric's Fund. In both cases Colenso was successful. Lord Romilly, the Master of the Rolls, based his judgment in the Chancery case[3] on the decision of the Judicial Committee of 1865. He maintained that the letters patent not only created ecclesiastical persons, but corporations capable of holding endowments. Colenso was therefore entitled to his income from the Fund. The Master of the Rolls added that, because in 1856 Natal was a crown colony and a dependency of the Cape (i.e. it had no independent legislature though the Cape Colony had one), it was possible that Colenso's letters patent might possess some validity. The series of judgments had thus come a full circle from the time of the 'Eton College' case. Romilly had virtually declared that though the

---

[1] Bloemfontein Chapter Library; Diocesan Archives; Unbound papers, 1850–1871, B, 13 & cf S.P.G. Archives, London; Macrorie papers; Bishop Macrorie's correspondence, 8; document from the Synod of Bishops in reply to resolutions passed by the diocesan synod of Maritzburg.

[2] Cox, *op. cit.*, II, p. 221

[3] 3. Eq. 1. and see also Bishopscourt Archives, Cape Town, folio 5; Bishop of Natal *v.* Gladstone and others.

Church of England as by law established could not exist in the colonies, in some sense it did exist where property was concerned. The judgment seems to have been something of an embarrassment to the law officers of the Crown.[1]

Colenso also gained possession of the cathedral, the deanery and of other Church property, including that which had originally been vested in Bishop Gray before the diocese was divided.[2] The Natal court decided for Colenso on all these points. Green held on as long as he could. The courts had declared him to be in perpetual contempt and an 'outlaw', and he was eventually evicted from the deanery in 1868. An attempt to persuade the Legislative Council to pass an act transferring Church property from Colenso to the orthodox party also failed. On the other hand when Colenso, attempting to act on Romilly's *obiter dicta*, tried the recalcitrant clergy *in foro domestico* as a letters patent bishop, the Natal court refused to allow that he possessed any coercive jurisdiction. Some of the clergy, like Lloyd, were now prepared to support Colenso on the grounds that he was the 'Queen's bishop', manifestly upheld by the law. By 1868 Colenso and Lloyd were completely reconciled.[3]

This was probably the high point of Colenso's popularity in Natal. He possessed the property and the endowments. A large proportion of the laity and several of the clergy were willing to support him because of his attitude to the Crown and the support given to him by the courts. The orthodox party retained two mission stations, Callaway's in the south and Robertson's in Zululand, and the support of the S.P.G. Colenso's teaching on the divinity of Christ had alienated many, but this had been countered to some extent by a sort of by-product of the Colonial Bishoprics Fund case. Baroness Burdett-Coutts, who had originally endowed the diocese of Cape Town, wrote to the archbishop of Canterbury, to Gladstone and to Colenso, pointing out that she had had no intention of endowing a Church independent of the Established Church in England.[4] The courts maintained that if letters

[1] See S. C. Carpenter, *Church & People*, p. 446n
[2] Bishopscourt Archives, Cape Town; Pleas in Reserved Bill of Legislative Council of Natal; and papers in same
[3] See e.g. Campbell Library, Durban; Colenso folios, N. 28
[4] Bishopscourt Archives, Cape Town; Bill of Complaint in Chancery; Campbell Library, Durban; Colenso folios, N. 38; D. C. Lathbury, *op. cit.* p. 145; Cox, *op. cit.*, II, pp. 36, 38 & 233

patent could create corporations capable of holding endowments, Gray was as much protected as Colenso. Nevertheless popular opinion regarded the baroness's attitude as a point in Colenso's favour.

While all this was going on the Lambeth Conference came into being. Its history is too well known to require more than a brief outline here. Some of the Canadian bishops, distressed by the scandal of the Natal schism, asked the archbishop of Canterbury to provide some opportunity for the matter to be considered by the whole Anglican Communion. Longley seems to have felt that a gathering of bishops from all over the world would be desirable on other grounds as well. But liberal circles in England, and those who believed in the importance of the Royal Supremacy, objected vigorously. The mild and amiable archbishop stood surprisingly firm against the opposition who feared that the Conference would become the means of stifling the sort of freedom of which Colenso had become the symbol, or would create a final authority for the Church of England other than the Crown. Dean Stanley, for instance, refused to allow Westminster Abbey to be used for a special Conference service 'because he feared that the influence of the Conference would be used in favour of the Bishop of Capetown, and of some modification of the constitution and government of the Church'.[1] Longley nevertheless issued his invitations and the Conference assembled in September 1867. The archbishop had made it clear that the Conference was not a legislative body but a consultative one—for brotherly counsel and encouragement. Out of 144 bishops invited, only 76 came. (Colenso, of course, received no invitation.) None of the bishops of the province of York would come at all. Other bishops only did so on condition that Colenso was not discussed. Bishop Gray and Bishop Selwyn of New Zealand were anxious to use the opportunity to create a system of graduated synods to control the whole Anglican communion. Others were no less determined to maintain the *status quo*. The result was bound to be a stalemate. To call a meeting to settle the Natal 'scandal' and then prevent any discussion of Colenso was a sure way of frustrating any real achievement.

In fact discussion of Colenso could not be kept out of the

---

[1] Prothero & Bradley, *Life & Correspondence of Dean Stanley*, II, p. 197

debates. Selwyn moved a resolution that the whole Church was injured by the Natal schism. The bishop of Vermont, senior bishop in America, called for the excommunication of Colenso. Longley attempted to still the consequent uproar by forbidding the Conference to pass judgment on either Gray or Colenso, but suggested that a committee should be appointed to try and find a solution to the situation in Natal. Gray made a fairly moderate speech and was thanked by Colenso's brother-in-law, the bishop of Labuan, for being so gentle with the heretic. But then the bishop of Labuan did not really approve of Colenso. The bishop of Salisbury, on the other hand, accused Gray of weakening. Fifty-five bishops drew up a private statement recognising Gray's sentence on Colenso as spiritually valid. One of the bishops proposed a resolution thanking Longley for not inviting Colenso to the Conference, but this attempt to evade the archbishop's ruling was eventually withdrawn. Then, at the last minute, Gray moved a further motion asking the Conference to approve the answer of the Convocation of Canterbury to the questions concerning the appointment of a new bishop for Natal. He forced Longley to allow the motion to be put, threatening to resign if it was ruled out of order. The resolution was finally carried by forty-three votes to three.

Colenso thus became, by accident and very much against his will, the cause of a most important step in the creation of the modern Anglican Communion. But the real work of the Conference, the decisions which became so important in the work of building up the present system of independent provinces in communion with one another, was done by committees which never reported to a full session of the Conference. The bishops issued a pastoral letter which Colenso described as a 'feeble, unmeaning document' and the actual resolutions passed by the Conference (except Gray's final motion) were so vague that Colenso was able to say that he could accept them himself, in the letter if not in the spirit.[1]

The attempts to find an orthodox bishop for Natal were no nearer success. The archbishop of Canterbury advised Butler to withdraw and this he did, in spite of Gray's pleas, very soon

[1] Cox, *op. cit.*, II, pp. 187f. For the proceedings of the conference see R.T. Davidson, *The Lambeth Conferences of 1867, 1878 and 1888*, 1896, pp. 9ff.

after the end of the Conference.[1] The choice of a new candidate then fell to Gray and it was some time before he was able to find someone who was both suitable and willing, the Reverend W. K. Macrorie. In December 1867 the South African bishops agreed to invite him to accept the bishopric, but over a year elapsed before the consecration took place. The Colonial Secretary, the duke of Buckingham, was partly responsible for the delay. Early in 1868 he sent out instructions to the Natal government directing all officials 'that any participation in, or countenancy by them of [the consecration of Macrorie], will be viewed with grave displeasure by Her Majesty's government'.[2] The duke seems later to have modified his attitude, requiring the new bishop to confine his ministrations to members of the 'South African Church' and to take his title from some place other than Natal or any town within the colony. It was finally decided that Macrorie should be 'bishop of Maritzburg'—the name being an abbreviation of Pietermaritzburg and thus not strictly the name of a place at all! Buckingham at one stage practically invited the archbishop of Canterbury to apply for a licence from the Crown to perform the consecration. Tait, on the other hand, threatened everyone concerned with prosecution under the *praemunire* Acts. And then Dean Green dug in his heels and insisted that the consecration take place in South Africa so that there should be no shadow of a suggestion that Macrorie was bishop by royal authority.[3] The ensuing disagreement between Gray and Green, together with the consequences of the Twells affair, completely ruptured the old alliance between the two men. Gray complained that Green was jealous of Macrorie, and certainly the new bishop found Green consistently unhelpful and difficult in the first few months after his arrival.[4] The consecration finally took place, since Bucking-

---

[1] C. N. Gray, *op. cit.*, pp. 362ff. It would seem that Butler was not very anxious to go to Natal. Green published extracts of a letter from Butler which gave a different impression, but the original appeared in full in the *Guardian*— 'Nothing can be fairer than his letter . . .' wrote Colenso: Natal Archives, Pietermaritzburg; Colenso Collection; Correspondence, 136; Colenso to Sanderson 30/7/1867.

[2] The dispatch is printed in Rees, *op. cit.*, p. 157

[3] For Gray's negotiations with Buckingham see Rees, *op. cit.*, pp. 166ff and cf C. N. Gray, *op. cit.*, II, pp. 383ff, 415ff, 425ff, 434ff.

[4] S.P.G. Archives, London; Macrorie papers; Bishop Macrorie's correspondence, 8

ham again hesitated and changed his mind, in Cape Town in January 1869.

Macrorie's arrival gave new strength to the orthodox party. Pietermaritzburg society was as divided as ever, but Macrorie was invited to official receptions just as Colenso was. When Sir Garnet Wolseley was in Natal he is said to have invited both bishops to dinner, but to have refused to attend either of their cathedrals. Colenso regarded any recognition of Macrorie as treasonable. Macrorie said that his Christian principles forbade him to acknowledge Colenso when they met in the streets. Certainly both bishops said some very bitter things. But from the time of Macrorie's arrival both Colenso's letters and those of his wife suggest that the tide had begun to turn. Colenso begins to speak more often of retiring. It is true that he had twice been nearly killed in accidents in the latter part of 1867 and had been very ill. Colonial medicine was not very highly regarded by Mrs Colenso and it would seem that at one time she nearly despaired of her husband's life. But quite apart from this fact, there are so many occasions on which both Colensos are anxious to point out that things are not so bad as they appear, that they still have a good deal of support, that one is left with the impression that they have begun to fear for the future. They seem to protest too much.[1]

In 1870 the Provincial Synod of the Church of the Province of South Africa met for the first time in Cape Town. It was Gray's great moment of triumph. The Colensos were much amused by some of the reports they heard of the synod.[2] Colenso called a meeting of his own Church Council, including as many important laymen as possible, to act as a sort of counter-blast. But it was already tragically clear that his little Church of England in Natal was an isolated community, doomed to grow smaller and more cut off from the main stream of Anglican life. Colenso's home at Bishopstowe, remote, placid, out of touch, was becoming a symbol of his ecclesiastical position. Of the meeting of the Church Council Mrs Colenso wrote that it had 'gone off and *very*! well, . . . There was great unanimity, and a warm interest in the affairs of their Church, the Church of England as it exists here under their Bishop'.[3]

[1] See Rees, *op. cit.*, pp. 177, 199f, 210, 226, 239, etc.
[2] Cox, *op. cit.*, II, pp. 226ff and Rees, *op. cit.*, pp. 210ff
[3] Rees, *op. cit.*, p. 222. On the meeting of the Council itself see Cox, *op. cit.*, II, pp. 227ff.

But she spoils the effect rather by going on to attempt to explain away the fact that a German missionary whom Colenso could not employ had joined Macrorie and taken his African congregation with him.

The principal item on the agenda of the Council was an address delivered by Colenso which lasted one and a half hours and which was virtually a survey of the principles and position of the Church of England in Natal. To this the members of the Council, 24 laymen and 6 clergymen, replied '. . . we shall continue as heretofore to support you as Bishop of Natal, head and ruler of the Church of England in this colony, under Her Most Gracious Majesty Queen Victoria as "supreme head"'.[1] But in the course of his address the bishop was compelled to touch upon the gloomy financial situation of his Church. He had gained most of the Church property in Natal. He had neither the men nor the money to use it properly. The S.P.G. supported the orthodox bishop. Colenso was reduced to trying to play off the Colonial and Church Society against the S.P.G.[2] —a stratagem which failed. He was also, and most pathetically, obliged to appeal to Gray to continue to pay him the £100 per annum which he had promised Colenso out of his own pocket when he had first offered him the see of Natal. When Gray refused, Colenso threatened to sue him in the courts for breach of promise. To Gray Colenso wrote explaining how he had made real financial sacrifices in leaving an English living to come to Natal. Gray had promised the money without condition. And, completely ignoring the fact that Gray regarded him as an obstinate heretic and would be glad to see him go back to England, Colenso pleads, 'Yet at least you might pay it to my sons who are guiltless of what in your eyes must seem to be their father's fault'.[3] In his account of the matter to other people, Colenso put a braver face on things, 'It was settled between us as a matter of *business* not of *friendship*, and I received the sum regularly up to January 1, 1864'.[4] The very difference between the two accounts, the very fact that Colenso was driven to *plead* with Gray, indicates how bad things had become. He had his income from the Colonial Bishoprics

[1] Cox, *op. cit.*, II, p. 233

[2] Natal Archives, Pietermaritzburg; Colenso Collection, 136; Colenso to Goodliffe, 5/10/65

[3] Natal Archives, Pietermaritzburg; Colenso Collection, 136; draft of a letter to Gray   [4] Cox, *op. cit.*, II, p. 156

Fund, he had £300 from the Natal Legislative Council,[1] the laity gave quite well to support the bishop and the clergy but there was something of a slump in the colony. There was not enough to keep his family, pay the clergy, and maintain the missions.

The difficulty of finding clergymen to staff his churches was also a perpetual problem for Colenso. Throughout the period from 1865 till his death there were never more than six or seven in his diocese, compared with two or three times that number under Macrorie. Again and again clergyman licensed by Colenso had to depart suddenly in unsavoury or acrimonious circumstances.[2] Colenso was tied to Pietermaritzburg, forced to preach twice each Sunday, because there was no-one else whom he could trust to take charge of the cathedral which was the centre of his staunchest support.[3]

The case of the second Robert Gray illustrates how badly the bishop was placed. Gray, the namesake of the bishop of Cape Town, came from St Helena. The orthodox party said he was not altogether a desirable person. The Colensos refused to believe this. Gray was welcomed with enthusiasm. He was tutor to the Colenso boys and was rapidly promoted from canon to archdeacon to dean. His wife was 'a sweet little thing, with a glorious voice' and such a nice companion for the elder Colenso girls! Best of all the bishop would be able to leave the cathedral in his care. But Gray did not last for long. Colenso's biographer says he left because of 'monetary misfortunes (caused by the failure of a bank) which lay beyond his control'.[4] Mrs Colenso's letters of the period (1869–70) tell a different story—a story of the dean's growing unpopularity with the Colensos and with the congregation. His sermons were boring. He gradually ceased to be the bright and hopeful sign of better times. Mrs Colenso eventually is quite as severe as the orthodox originally were. And one of Colenso's own unpublished letters fills in part of the missing story. Gray resigned because the cathedral congregation found him lazy as well as too much inclined to contract debts he could not pay.[5]

[1] *Ibid.*, p. 183

[2] M. A. Hooker in an unpublished thesis, *The Place of Bishop Colenso in South African History*, devotes a whole chapter to Colenso's clergy (Witwatersrand University, Ph.D. thesis).

[3] See Rees, *op. cit.*, p. 110

[4] Cox, *op. cit.*, II, p. 235

[5] Natal Archives, Pietermaritzburg; Colenso Collection, Correspondence, 136; Colenso to Sanderson, 5/5/1870

He eventually got into a brawl with a native policeman who struck him with a knobkerrie.[1]

Under these circumstances Colenso was almost entirely unable to undertake any real missionary work.[2] When he returned from England in 1861, Ekukanyeni was only a shadow of its former self.[3] Such work as was being done was in the hands of the faithful William Ngidi and his brother. The congregation of Africans numbered about thirty. There was St Mary's church in Pietermaritzburg with another small congregation. And there was one other mission station at Umlazi. On his return Colenso tried to get Ekukanyeni and St Mary's going again. He tried to get money from the government for the work. There were endless delays. His daughters helped him run a school. There were small services at which the Ngidis preached. But even after grants began to come again there was very little real achievement and certainly nothing to compare with the former grandiose plans of the bishop's early days.

Colenso was trustee for certain 'native reserves' set up by the government as part of an attempt to settle and civilise the African. The Umlazi mission, mentioned above, was one of these. The mission had been established in 1862 but after Colenso returned the priest there had to leave because he would not accept the bishop's authority. The work was left in the hands of a lay catechist. At the other reserves of which he was trustee, except one which was worked for a time, there was hardly any activity. Colenso simply had not the resources to tackle the work. The colonial administration later charged him with neglecting his duties as trustee and he appears to have been most haphazard in keeping his accounts. A handful of baptisms took place on the various stations. A small African 'Sobantu Church' grew up which existed in parallel with the Church of England in Natal. *Sobantu* was the African name for Colenso. It means 'The Father of the People' and was apparently first bestowed on the bishop by Theophilus Shepstone in an attempt to explain the function and nature of a bishop. The 'Church of England' missionary work was inherited by Colenso's daughters and kept alive by them after the bishop's death. At the turn of the century there were some thirty small

---

[1] *Ibid.*, 4/2/1871   [2] Rees, *op. cit.*, p. 127

[3] This survey of Colenso's later missionary work is largely based on the final chapter of an unpublished thesis—B. B. Burnett, *The Missionary Work of the first Anglican Bishop of Natal* (University of S. Africa, M.A.).

congregations of the Sobantu Church, each about thirty or forty strong.

It has sometimes been said that in his later years Colenso modified his theological opinions, at least in so far as his missionary work was concerned. If this means that he is supposed to have kept 'biblical criticism' out of his missions, it is not true. Colenso was certainly still working on *Pentateuch & Joshua*. Part VI appeared in 1871, Part VII and a popular edition in 1879. *Lectures on the Pentateuch & the Moabite Stone* (originally sermons preached in Natal) came out in 1873. A good many of the bishop's sermons were on critical subjects. A governor of the colony returning to England reported that 'his sermons (so far as they had heard) ran almost entirely on the criticisms of the Pentateuch, which, though disposed to agree with the general conclusions, seemed to them as unsuited to the congregation as the sermons on the same topic from the other side'.[1]

This, of course, refers to Colenso's sermons to white congregations, but there is no reason to suppose that he made any effort to remain fundamentalist for the benefit of his black ones. Very soon after his return Colenso reported that he found Ngidi and the other Africans on the mission 'perfectly prepared for what I have to tell them'.[2] Mrs Colenso's account of the same episode makes it plain that Colenso discussed a great many of his liberal and critical ideas with Ngidi.[3] Later we have accounts of Ngidi preaching simple little critical sermons on the history of the decalogue, and of his desire to see 'Sobantu's gospel' taken to the Zulu people.[4] It would, in any case, be entirely out of character with what we know of Colenso to suppose that after committing himself in the *Commentary on Romans* to an ideal of the gospel to be preached to the heathen, he should then lack the courage to put it into practice. The idea of Colenso acting the fundamentalist for the African is too comic to be taken seriously. No doubt he did not regale them with sermons on the Moabite stone, but he is quite likely to have told them that the Sabbath was a post-Exilic invention and need not be taken seriously.

[1] Campbell Library, Durban; Colenso folios, F. 35; letter of A. P. Stanley 28/11/72

[2] Cox, *op. cit.*, II, p. 9   [3] Rees, *op. cit.*, p. 94

[4] *Ibid.*, pp. 103 & 107f and cf pp. 111 & 127

The last ten years of Colenso's life, when in every other respect he seems to be lonely, ineffective, down-at-heel, are redeemed by a kind of glory when, a 'Maurician' such as Maurice would have been glad to recognise, he fought for the African people of Natal. The old courage of Colenso carried him through a long struggle which cost him the support of Theophilus Shepstone, his most influential lay adherent.

Shepstone was, as Secretary for Native Affairs, the real ruler of the Africans in the colony. He was a cold, withdrawn man, an autocrat because he believed that he understood the African and could rule them justly and in the best possible way. He was conservative, refusing to change the patterns of African life. Like Colenso he believed that polygamy must not be swept away: it was too much part and parcel of the traditional way of life.[1] For twenty years the two men were close friends and allies, and then an African chief, Langalibalele, was arrested for refusing to disarm his tribe in 1873. He was tried in a curious court, which claimed to proceed in accordance with 'native custom'. The African assessors gave their verdict on the first day, evidence was heard on the second, and the accused was permitted counsel on the third. Two years earlier an Oxford mathematician, searching for a real absurdity that would amuse children, had written, 'He's in prison now, being punished: and the trial doesn't even begin till next Wednesday: and, of course, the crime comes last of all'.[2] Colenso, the Cambridge mathematician, might be forgiven for thinking Langalibalele's trial the same kind of fantasy. The Lord Chancellor, describing the case in the House of Lords, drew loud laughter from his audience.[3] Shepstone defended himself, not by arguing that the trial was just, but by saying that his reputation 'as a statesman, and as the humane ruler of these natives' would be vindicated in the end.[4] In the face of the most violent public hostility, Colenso strained every nerve to see that Langalibalele was fairly treated. He returned to England in 1874 to lobby on the chief's behalf. He called on Tait, by then archbishop of Canterbury, and spoke to him of the 'shameful treatment' of Africans in Natal, saying he

---

[1] See J. R. Sullivan, *The Native Policy of Sir Theophilus Shepstone*, 1928, pp. 24ff and also C. J. Uys, *In the Era of Shepstone*, 1933, pp. 412 and 430.

[2] Lewis Carroll, *Through the Looking Glass*

[3] Rees, *op. cit.*, p. 265   [4] Uys, *op. cit.*, p. 104

thought he had convinced Lord Carnarvon but that he was being cut off from 'all his present friends among the colonists'.[1] Stanley invited him to preach at Westminster Abbey but with unexpected tact, and to Stanley's secret relief, Colenso declined.[2]

The effect of the Langalibalele affair on English politics was marked.[3] The Gladstone administration fell. Carnarvon became Colonial Secretary. The Aborigines Protection Society was revived and joined Colenso in his campaign. It was almost like the old days of 'Exeter Hall' and the abolition of slavery. But in Natal Colenso was hated. Bishop Macrorie rejoiced to find that *he* was now to be treated by the government as 'the Lord Bishop'.[4] Green and others might feel as Colenso did, but they hesitated to speak out.[5] The bishop became the most unpopular man in Natal, where only a few years before he had been the most *popular*.[6]

But Colenso's courage never faltered.[7] As a consequence of the Langalibalele affair he clashed directly with the Shepstone family, demanding a commission of inquiry into certain actions of Shepstone's brother John and entering into direct personal rivalry with Shepstone himself—for the bishop planned to become official 'protector' of the Africans.[8] The climax came in the very last years of his life when Colenso, in alliance with F. W. Chesson, secretary of the Aboriginees Protection Society, campaigned for better treatment for Cetshwayo the defeated Zulu king.[9] In 1881 Colenso received some recognition for he was made a member of the Natal Native Affairs Commission which had replaced Shepstone's sole personal rule. This appointment had the unexpected effect of putting Colenso on slightly more friendly terms with Green, who was also a

---

[1] R. T. Davidson, *Life of Archibald Campbell Tait*, II, pp. 305f
[2] Prothero & Bradley, *op. cit.*, II, pp. 290ff
[3] C. J. Uys, *op. cit.*, pp. 91ff
[4] S.P.G. Archives, London; Macrorie papers; Letters to F. Pott, letter dated 17/1/1875
[5] See Cox, *op. cit.*, II, p. 381
[6] *Ibid.*, p. 626
[7] An account of all these various episodes, from Colenso's point of view, is given in Cox, *op. cit.*, II, pp. 313ff and Rees, *op. cit.*, pp. 258ff, 290ff and 325ff. See also *Langalibalele and the Amahlubi Tribe* by the Bishop of Natal, published by H.M. Stationery Office and tabled in the House of Commons, 1874.
[8] Public Record Office: C.O. 178/116 for Colenso's proposals. I am indebted to Dr C. Goodfellow of Rhodes University for a transcript of Colenso's memorandum.
[9] Campbell Library, Durban; Colenso folios, Z; letters to Chesson; and also 'Colenso's Commentary on Frere's Zulu Policy', a collection of pamphlets

member of the commission, though neither man gave way in
the least on any matter of ecclesiastical principle.[1]

Colenso summoned his Church Council for the last time in
the year before he died. It was already obvious that the bishop
could not live much longer. Photographs of this period show
Colenso as a tall, thin old man, his clothes hanging on him as
though they have survived from earlier days. His hair has
become white and receded a little from his high forehead,
though it is still thick and healthy looking. The bishop peers
out through small gold-rimmed spectacles, a little like a mole
caught in the sunlight. His long upper lip is shut in a firm
strong line, but a smile lurks at the corners of his mouth. It is
a strong, kindly face. The lines are lines of strength and suffering rather than of age, but still it is quite clear that at 69,
Colenso is an old man. He is beginning to look a little bit like
the caricature drawn by 'Ape' ten years earlier.[2] Quite plainly
neither the bishop nor his Council expected him to go on much
longer. The bishop said, 'My body and soul are crying out for
rest, before I go hence'.[3] The Council, consisting of seven clergymen and eighteen laymen (of whom Shepstone, significantly,
was not one), began to take the necessary steps to provide a
successor for Colenso.[4] There was little hope of obtaining a
new letters patent bishop, but it might be possible to *elect* a
new bishop who would accept the 'Rules of the Church Council
of the Diocese of Natal'. After Colenso's death the Council
several times attempted to persuade the archbishop of Canterbury to consecrate a bishop of its own choice, and failed.
Shepstone emerged again as the leading figure in the Council.
The number of clergy dwindled away until in 1901 there were
only two. Archbishop Benson made an attempt to heal the
schism, sending his own chaplain, A. H. Baynes, to act as bishop
of both groups in Natal. This scheme broke down altogether.
The Church Council ceased to exist early in this century and
most of the Colensoite parishes accepted the ministrations of
Baynes's successor. In 1910 the Natal legislature passed an Act
to allow the bishop to become trustee of the property vested
in Colenso. The Misses Colenso, who were struggling to main-

[1] See Rees, *op. cit.*, pp. 363ff   [2] Reproduced in Rees, *op. cit.*, p. 305
[3] Cox, *op. cit.*, II, p. 594
[4] *Address delivered by the Rt. Rev. J. W. Colenso, D.D., at the 7th Session of
the Church Council of the Diocese of Natal, together with the Rules to be observed
in the Diocese of Natal*, 1883

tain their father's mission at Ekukanyeni, were given a pension but were compelled to leave the station. Gradually the Colenso churches became associated with the Church of the Province of South Africa, the last of them only a few years ago.[1]

Colenso died on 20 June 1883. His family were taken by surprise. He had not been very well, feverish, and not sleeping at night, and then he suddenly became very weak and tired. 'I should be so glad of a little rest',[2] he said. But almost up to the very last, while his body got rapidly weaker and weaker, his mind was hard at work planning what could be done for the African people whose champion he had become. Quietly, gently, without any deathbed scene or famous last words, he looked at his family for the last time, closed his eyes, and died.[3] He was not quite seventy. 'He died', his daughter said, 'for the cause in which he has fought so long, the cause of justice, truth and mercy, for truly it was the overwork in that cause, and the sorrow of seeing it still trampled underfoot, that wore away his strength and took him from us'.[4]

Theophilus Shepstone, cold and unmoved, commented that Colenso's death might help to settle the political situation.[5] Colenso was still unpopular with the colonists. Nevertheless there were large numbers left to mourn him. One of his clergy described the funeral:

> At the entrance to the town we all put on our surplices and stoles, and headed the procession up the streets. There were only six of the Bishop's clergy present. Then came the Artillery with the body, and then a carriage with Dr and Miss Colenso inside, and after that all the other people, in carriages and on foot. The streets were packed with people, all in mourning. Such a sight I have never seen: there are grander spectacles in England, no doubt, but I have never before seen all the people of a city moved to tears as on this occasion.[6]

Colenso was buried before the altar in his cathedral. His African people asked, 'Is there any other man that will care for us natives as the Bishop has?' Three months later Bishopstowe was destroyed by fire, as though the symbol of Colenso's life could not survive that life itself.

[1] For an account of the history of the Church of England in Natal after Colenso's death, see P. Hinchliff, *The Anglican Church in South Africa*, p. 106ff.
[2] Cox, *op. cit.*, II, p. 631
[3] Rees, *op. cit.*, p. 373
[4] Cox, *op. cit.*, II, p. 631
[5] M. A. Hooker, *op. cit.*, II, p. 291
[6] Cox, *op. cit.*, II, p. 635

Index